FIVE FAT HENS

FIVE FAT HENS

A Guide for Keeping Chickens and Enjoying Delicious Meals

TIM HALKET

Skyhorse Publishing

Skyhorse Publishing books may be purchased in bulk at special discounts for sales, promotion, corporate gifts, fund-raising, or educational purposes. Special editions can also be created to specifications. For details, contact the Special Sales Department, Skyhorse Publishing, 307 West 36th Street, 11th Floor, New York, NY 10018 or info@skyhorsepublishing.com.

Skyhorse® and Skyhorse Publishing® are registered trademarks of Skyhorse Publishing, Inc.®, a Delaware corporation.

Visit our website at www.skyhorsepublishing.com.

10 9 8 7 6 5 4 3 2 1

Library of Congress Cataloging-in-Publication Data is available on file.

Cover design by Erin Seaward-Hiatt
Cover photo credit Thinkstock
Interior design by Sara Driver

Print ISBN: 978-1-62914-542-6

Printed in China

CONTENTS

INTRODUCTION

I was born at home, just in time for lunch—the doctor lured me out with a cold roast chicken sandwich. Dad had just popped downstairs to make up a few rounds—one for the doctor, another for the midwife, and one for himself. Mum was busy. There was a pretty standard way of making sandwiches in my family as I grew up; two pieces of buttered sliced-white bread, a little carefully carved chicken, a generous smearing of Heinz salad cream, and some salad for those who wanted it. Nothing fancy; a thick slice or two of tomato, the same of cucumber, and a couple of leaves of "English" lettuce—it's the lettuce of our childhood. If there wasn't any chicken, it might have been cold roast beef or a slice of cheese. Cheddar or cheddar—take your pick.

Just as those sandwiches have a comforting familiarity about them, so too does the food in this book. I expect some of the recipes will be new to you—Burmese Chicken Curry or *Duelos y Quebrantos*—but then again, I feel it's just as important to know how to make an egg and cress sandwich properly and that everyone has the know-how to poach an egg with confidence. The recipes you are unfamiliar with won't take hours of preparation in the kitchen and no fancy gadgets or specialist equipment is needed. What I can confidently predict is that many of them will become firm favorites to be cooked again and again. I probably cook more new dishes in a week than most people (it's my job), yet when I'm tired of novelty or it's the end of the week or I've got to conjure dinner from the contents of the store cupboard alone, it is this type of cooking—and sometimes these actual recipes—that I fall back on. I hope that some of these recipes will become your family's favorites too.

Everything in this book is real food, no weird impossible to get ingredients or esoteric items for your shopping list. Sure, there are some unusual spices but they are all available from the supermarket (that is one thing that they are exceptionally good at). It is important to shop carefully, to know what you're buying, and ideally where it's been grown or produced. And, I'm afraid, this is especially so when buying chicken. I could write pages about the cruelty and suffering inflicted on battery hens but everyone nowadays, I think, understands this issue (even if they choose to ignore it). I would implore you to eat less chicken—but to spend more when you do. Welfare issues aside, you will notice the difference on your plate. A proper organic chicken will be a revelation in taste and a textural delight if you've spent the last few years eating battery-farmed pap. Try one once and you won't go back.

I have started to shop very differently since we moved to Suffolk. I have always gone to good butchers, but I now go to the bakers for our bread and buy what vegetables I can from the local farm shop, or in the summer I'll walk up to Stumpy's allotment and see what vegetables he is selling on his little roadside table, leaving a few pence in his honesty box in return. Perhaps it's because my children are young and rapidly growing that I'm more aware of the quality of food that I'm buying and feeding them. I can't be alone in feeling this way—have you noticed how virtually all baby food is organic? When do parents stop wanting to feed their children the best they possibly can, and think "oh, good—now that little Harry's on solids he can eat the same crap we eat?"

Another thing that I'd urge you to change is the way that you serve food; nowadays almost everybody puts food on the plate in the kitchen like they do in restaurants. I like to place big bowls and plates of food on a table. What could be nicer than passing round steaming bowls of vegetables or plates the size of trays generously laden with hearty salads? I seldom bother plating food in the kitchen anymore. You may get a smaller "*wow*" when you take the food to the table, but that's a small price to pay for being a good host. And when feeding the family the same applies—even if it's sausages, peas, and mash for supper, I'll still put the mash and peas in bowls so that people can help themselves.

I've written this book in monthly sections for two reasons. Firstly, I have included snippets from a diary I kept over the course of a year as I wrote the bulk of this book. It turned out to be an eventful one; we moved to Suffolk, raised some chicks in an incubator, and then had a broody hen to contend with. I hope that those stories and some of the monthly introductions show how rewarding and what fun sharing your garden with a few hens can be. Secondly, and importantly, all food is seasonal. This doesn't just ring true for the "locally grown vegetable" brigade, but intuitively we all eat seasonally. I would no more want to eat a warming coq au vin in the heat of summer than I would a vibrant salad Niçoise in the depths of winter.

It was a couple of years ago, on a whim, that I decided to get some hens. And hens lay eggs—and everybody wants them. Friends come round with empty egg boxes. Not for themselves, of course, no, no. If we've got a few extra then I'm happy to give them away. In fact, I have only once had to buy half a dozen eggs in the past two years now—what a disappointment they were. I'm delighted to say that my enthusiasm for keeping hens seems to be rubbing off. Various friends have also started to keep a few hens in their garden. They enjoy having the chickens pecking about in their run, and who wouldn't want such fabulous eggs at breakfast time. At the smallest possible end of the scale, if you have the time and space to keep a couple of rabbits, then you have the time and space for a couple of hens.

I let them lead as natural a life as possible. They have a run under one of the big apple trees in a corner of the garden. Sadly the run is too small to support grass. They quickly ate all the grass when they moved in. Thinking it was due to the poor quality of the moss-ridden grass, I laid some turf. I gave it plenty of time to set while they were elsewhere in temporary accommodation but they still wrecked it within a couple of months. But, still, they thrive on their diet of kitchen scraps and leftovers, prunings from the vegetable patch, lettuces and herbs that have bolted, a few handfuls of grass clippings when I cut the lawn, and some whole grain feed. In the winter months I let them out into the garden; the children won't be running barefoot and so what if the hens scratch a little earth out from the borders. I suppose they get through about half a big bag of mixed grain each 27.5 lbs (12.5 kg) over the course of a year. Total running cost—less than eight dollars (or five quid) per hen per annum—they pay their rent with about 250 eggs each. It's easy math!

I don't use a heated or lit henhouse. Electricity has not been kind to the chicken. Their commercially raised cousins have suffered with the invention of electric incubators and brooders—even such simple things as heating and the light bulb have taken their toll. Electricity allowed us to create the battery-hen and all the cruelties that go along with it. Chickens used to have a simple seasonal cycle of reproduction and growth; this has been interrupted and mastered with electrical gadgets. Nobody nowadays would think of chicken as a seasonal food, as they would their game-bird relatives or oysters or spring lamb. Eggs are now available year round and at a consistently low price. It may surprise you to learn (it did me) that hens will often stop laying over winter if left to their own devices. However, if you keep them commercially, they can be easily fooled into thinking it is forever summer simply by automatically switching on their dormitory lights at three in the morning. The battery hens' laying thus continues apace because the inside of that enormous, horrible, artificially lit shed is all the world they will ever know.

I want a better life than that for my lovely hens.

So, the purpose of this book is to provide you with some new recipes to try out—hopefully you'll enjoy them enough to want to cook them again. That sounds a little self-evident, I know, but too many cookbooks of late have been about everything under the sun *except* cooking food you might want to eat again and again. I sincerely hope you will keep this book—food splattered and grease stained—in the kitchen and not on a coffee table. Hopefully it will encourage you to cook a few new meals, and maybe even to get five fat hens for your own back garden.

BEFORE WE BEGIN   *Roasted—No!*—it's *roast*, just plain *roast*. Have you ever in your whole life said "Hmm, I rather fancy some *roasted* beef for Sunday lunch" or, "Darling, these *roasted* potatoes really are delicious"? No, I thought not. *Roasted* has been assimilated into food writing through inappropriate use by restaurateurs/chefs as a way to obscure the absurdity of the things they were "roasting," for example, "oven-roasted tournedos of monkfish."

• Please remember there are alternatives to using extra virgin olive oil on everything.

• In 1879 Fannie Farmer graduated from the Boston Cooking School. She then became a teacher there before publishing her book *The Boston Cooking-School Cook Book* in 1896. Her recipe writing was as joyful and imaginative as the title. The big thing about Fannie was her obsession with turning each recipe into an instruction manual. She was an obsessive measurer and timer, a real stickler for the process. It was food writing reduced to the level of school chemistry experiments. Apparatus, Method, and Conclusion became Ingredients, Method, and Serving Suggestion. The sad thing is that virtually all food writers have followed this model ever since. I get thoroughly depressed when I see exact lists of ingredients (even down to salt and pepper), and never more so than when that is followed by numbered steps to walk you through a recipe. Okay, I agree baking is different. But overall, a little vagueness will help you learn to be intuitive in the kitchen. Cooking is a craft not a science. And yet, she gets the last laugh—with over 4 million copies sold. And it's still in print. Grrr.

• Ovens vary—so cooking times and temperatures will, at best, only ever be approximated.

• Please read the whole recipe through to the end before you start.

• Why do we buy books by Michelin-starred chefs and then try and recreate their restaurant food in our own kitchens? Who are we kidding? If you or I could cook like that, then *we* would also be three-star chefs! Accordingly, I try very hard to repress the urge to present food as professional kitchens do. Have you ever stopped and wondered why you're busting a gut in the kitchen when friends and family are seated round the dining table missing the company of the host. Meanwhile you're packing *garlic scented crushed potatoes* into a little pastry ring in the middle of a plate. I say, just cook your guests some good food, put it on the table in big bowls or generously cover a big plate, and sit down to enjoy their company. Let them help themselves and pass it on.

• I seldom ever try cooking something for the first time if friends are coming round (obviously, there are exceptions— bollito misto for two, would be insane). Here's a top tip which will get you out of anything: if you are, for any reason, facing a culinary disaster of great magnitude, if you're quivering in the kitchen, if you wish the ground would swallow you up whole to avoid presenting the food you have just cooked to your family or friends, simply tell them you followed a Jamie Oliver recipe. Everyone will understand.

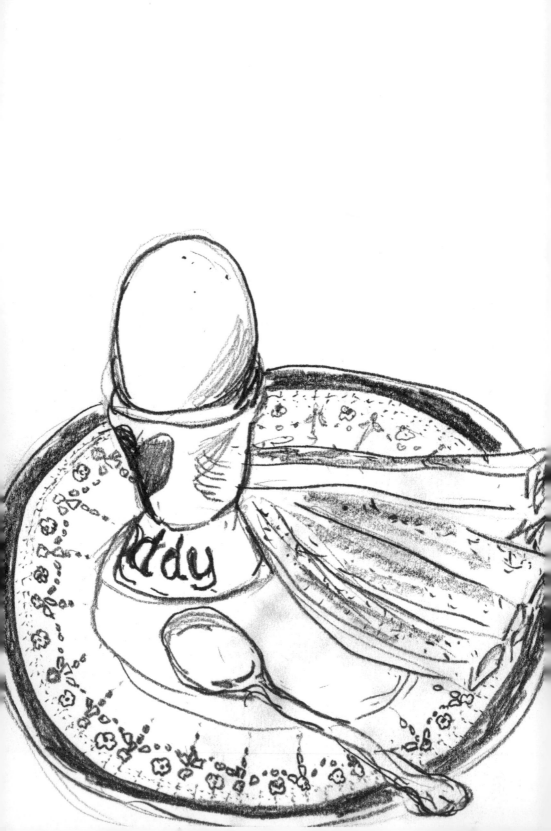

Boiled Egg and Soldiers
Chicken Soup with Dumplings
Latkes
Duelos y Quebrantos
Persian Chicken Supper

JANUARY

Poached Chicken with Six Vegetables
Legless Chicken with Greens
Stuffed Chicken Legs
Wedgie Fries
Piri-Piri Chicken
Queen of Puddings
Spotted Dick and Custard

I decided to start the year by hatching some eggs. Previously I'd always bought growing hens (called pullets) from a breeder—it's the easiest way to get a few chickens. You can buy them sexed and almost ready to lay their first eggs. But it is a strangely unsatisfying arrangement. For some time now it had been something I wanted to try, and the children would certainly enjoy seeing them grow. If I was careful choosing the breed, then the law of averages would deliver a few good laying hens and a few surplus tasty cockerels for the pot. My biggest problem would then be how to eat them? Coq au vin is *such* a cliché . . .

It's necessary to choose the right breed if you want to do this; some breeds will lay a lot of eggs but are too scrawny to eat; some breeds gain weight quickly but the hens are poor layers. Some breeds, like Light Sussex, are both good layers and very tasty table birds.

Traditionally, someone like me, with a few birds in my back garden, would wait until one of the hens got broody and then slip a few fertilized eggs under her. I've neither a cockerel nor likely to get a broody bird—the three breeds I already have are not known for their broodiness. I needed to get hold of an incubator.

I persuaded a nearby farmer to lend me his spare one (for thirty quid, or about fifty dollars). It would hold forty eggs. After a hunt through various smallholder magazines and websites, I finally found someone who was happy to sell me a few fertilized eggs. It couldn't have been simpler. Get the incubator ready, put the eggs in for twenty-one days, and, when they've hatched, move them into a brooder (it really needs to be no more than a light bulb hung over a draft-free secure run). Supply them with chick crumbs and plenty of fresh water, and then just sit back and watch them grow.

Back in the kitchen, January is a lean month. If you're eating seasonally—buying fresh local food—then this will surely be a trying time. The gluttonous excesses of December have passed, and, from the depths of January's long nights, it seems impossible that there will ever be another summertime. The only solution is to lock the doors, put another log on the fire, and cook up something that you know will warm you. There is something so very right about eating hearty wholesome home-cooked food when the weather is depressing you like this.

Comfort food. I don't know anyone (at least anyone who lives in Britain) who would call a tomato salad comfort food. Lovely though it is, it's still a summer dish and absolutely not what I want to eat as the snow is falling all around. But comfort food is more than what your mother used to make, or school lunches, or even teatimes at granny's kitchen table. It sounds almost asinine to say it but comfort food must be comforting—you must be comforted whilst both preparing and eating it—and that point, about preparing it, often gets overlooked. To eat well, you don't need to be a domestic goddess—you can feast on a very reasonable steak and kidney pudding from Marks & Spencer—but why miss out on the joys of going to the butcher, grating the suet, making the pastry, browning the meat, slicing the onions, assembling the dish, and then topping the steamer up with more boiling water as and when needed. When you steam the pudding slowly over a few hours, you'll gently get a good fug-up in your kitchen, and that's all part of the anticipation.

I know I'm preaching to the converted here (after all, you're reading a cookbook) but surely all that shopping, chopping, cooking, and serving—in fact everything you do from the moment you first pick up the food to putting the prepared plateful in front of your loved ones—is all part of the joy of good food.

I'm saddened by the number of people I know that have no interest in the craft of cooking. They like to eat, many like to eat very well indeed, but they miss out on time spent just pottering (and there really is no better word for it) in the kitchen. Cooking can be every bit as pleasurable as eating.

So don't just settle for casseroles and apple pies; be a little more adventurous. January is my favorite time for cooking a big pot of osso bucco and Milanese risotto (that's the plain one with all the saffron). If you crave some heat, then feel the burn from my piri-piri chicken, or go traditional with a poached chicken and indulge in a really big helping of six locally-grown winter vegetables, each of them at their best, just pulled from the ground. The Persian chicken supper will do the job when you're too full of British stodge and carbs and want a meal that is interesting, light, and yet satisfyingly filling. And don't forget to try the other big dishes from Italy, France, and Spain—it gets cold there too.

JANUARY'S DIARY

WEDNESDAY 1 JANUARY
Omelettes for lunch. Angelica and Anastasia laying well, lots of eggs to hand. 4 BIG eggs, so 2 big omelettes.

THURSDAY 2 JANUARY
Found a shell-less egg on the droppings board.

SUNDAY 5 JANUARY
Another shell-less egg. Suspect Princess Amidala is the culprit. Must get some oyster shell for them.

SUNDAY 19 JANUARY
It's time to get started on the incubation. I phoned round a few places and eventually found an incubator.

THURSDAY 23 JANUARY
No eggs at all today—first time in months.

FRIDAY 24 JANUARY
Five eggs today!

SATURDAY 25 JANUARY
Brought a copy of *Farmers Weekly*, hoping to find useful stuff in the classifieds. Wasn't disappointed.

SUNDAY 26 JANUARY
Cleaned out chicken coop—amazed by new bale of sawdust. Packed so tightly that scraping out a couple of handfuls with my fingernails was enough to fill a bucket. I suspect just one bale will last the best part of a year. Pet shops must have a good margin in repackaging this stuff for the hamsters.

MONDAY 27 JANUARY
Good haul of old and interesting cookbooks from Oxfam.

TUESDAY 28 JANUARY
Children playing up today. Tried to research commercial breeds —didn't get anywhere with it. Decided to hatch Light Sussex, Minorca and maybe some other eggs too.

THURSDAY 30 JANUARY
First real snow around 2:00 p.m. Hens very confused: started eating snowflakes off each other's backs.

FRIDAY 31 JANUARY
Chickens hate snow! Had to clear an area near the back door for them; they didn't budge from it all day. Spent their time hopping from one foot to the other. News pictures at breakfast-time of people having to sleep in their cars on the M11. Awful!

BOILED EGG AND SOLDIERS

In the beginning, our hens kept us waiting for months until one of them laid the first egg. Annie and I fantasized endlessly about how to eat them. We decided to boil the first two for breakfast—it's the only way to enjoy the shell and the contents on your plate at the same time (if you've specifically chosen your hens for their eggs' shell color, then that will be especially important to you).

Those two first eggs were amazing. Until you have eaten the eggs from hens which have been allowed to roam around spending their days eating all the grass they want, you simply will not have tasted good eggs. The whites are properly firm and flavorsome, a joy to eat just on their own. The yolks possess a depth of color that defies belief, way beyond yellow, almost to a garish day-glow orange. And the texture is thick; not a hint of insipid runniness anywhere.

Boiled eggs may not strike you as a seasonal food but, if you're keeping your hens as naturally as possible, to have a hen that is laying through winter is indeed a godsend (doubly so if you have to buy some extra eggs—yuk!). So putting a home-grown proper plain boiled egg on your breakfast table in January is indeed a great luxury.

Despite popular belief, there simply is no foolproof way of boiling an egg. It's just not as easy as people think it is. I now put the eggs into warm water (either from the hot tap or kettle) and time them for two minutes once they're boiling. Other people are happy to add eggs to boiling water and cook them for three. It depends on your cooker and how quickly it will boil the water. Egg size is another important factor. Either way, those times are about right for an average size egg (supermarket large). Some hens will lay bigger eggs, others smaller, but each hen will always lay the same size, shape, and color of egg, all through its life. I can tell at a glance which of my birds has laid which egg. So, I need to add to or reduce the cooking times by half a minute, maybe more, depending on which hen's eggs I'm cooking.

I've tried out the method where a pan of water is brought to the boil, removed from the heat, and then the eggs are added (see Delia). This is no better or worse than the usual way—it just takes a lot longer to make breakfast. Also, putting vinegar in the water, adding salt, a matchstick, or even pricking the eggs to stop them from cracking are all utterly useless. Don't waste your time. I've realized, quite by accident, that one of my hens (Princess Amidala) lays eggs that will crack each and every time without fail in boiling water, whilst none of the others ever do. Another excellent reason for knowing where your food comes from!

Soldiers need no special introduction or instruction; just use white or whole wheat bread, as takes your fancy. Granary-style bread just doesn't work for me—all those whole grains ruining the unctuous gooiness of the egg. Toast the bread, butter it, and slice it into thin strips.

INGREDIENTS
- One or two eggs per person
- A slice of freshly made hot-buttered toast cut into soldiers

Boil the eggs for two or three minutes (see above) then put them into an eggcup. There really is no sensible way to eat boiled eggs without using an eggcup—every home should have some; so please go and buy some nice ones if you are without.

Now take the tops off in your favorite way: Bang the top with an egg spoon and then carefully peel them; chop the tops straight off with one deft blow from a sharp knife (Samurai-style); or get yourself one of those fancy French *tranche-coque* contraptions. These are sort-of round scissors which fit over the top of the egg and when you squeeze the handle, lots of little teeth shoot inwards, breaking the shell cleanly and allowing you to remove the top with a quick twist. I got mine in France as a child. I don't recall seeing them for sale in Britain—but then I've never been looking for them. I never use mine; it's far too much effort to clean up afterwards.

If you're having two eggs—and I do recommend that you do—remember to take the tops off both. If you don't, the second one will continue to cook and the yolk will become slightly too well set.

Make the soldiers while the eggs cook. Sometimes I sharpen everything up a bit by adding the merest scraping of Marmite to the toast. It's an amazingly good combination.

Some people would not consider eating an egg without salt and pepper, others need a knob of butter. I don't bother with any of those, but if you do want to add a pinch of salt, I suggest that you use some plain ordinary fine table salt rather than those lovely big flakes from Maldon. Too much crunch.

You are now ready to dip the soldiers into the egg. Expect a little yolk to surge up and spill over the side. Watching the dribble run before catching it with your finger is all part of the fun.

VARIATIONS   When asparagus is in season, providing its plentiful glut in May and June, try dipping some tiny, lightly steamed tips into the egg instead. It makes a wonderful lunch or starter at dinnertime. If you pour a little melted butter on the tips before serving, the effect in the mouth is deliciously similar to hollandaise sauce.

CHICKEN SOUP WITH DUMPLINGS

I really couldn't decide whether or not to include a recipe for chicken soup. It seems that it's been done to death recently. I'd guesstimate every other cookbook must have a version. Maybe, though, I've just been noticing it more than usual.

I won't condescend to any Jewish readers out there by telling them how to make kosher dumplings. They surely don't need me to do that. Similarly, I'm not going to come over all "this soup is Jewish penicillin" or "just as my mother used to make when I was a sickly boy." I know next to nothing about kosher food, and—when I was ill—I was given Heinz tomato soup and a slice of Mother's Pride.

I offer you a recipe for simple chicken soup. It is very loose and entirely open to change in any way that you fancy. It is a fairly intuitive and simple thing to cook—what took time was trying to find the right little nuances. Vegetables, herbs, and spices; I tried many, most were dismissed. Basil is not good, nor is oregano. Leek tops will turn the broth an unpleasant shade of green and taste quite wrong. Avoid tomatoes. I can see that some people may appreciate the aniseed kick from a whole star anise or two, but I'm not particularly fond of it—too pungent for this. A small pinch of saffron is pleasant, occasionally—mainly for the color.

Someone suggested that I add a slug of gin just before serving. Initially, I added rather too much; I made a G&S: Gin and Soup. I tried adding dry vermouth, one of my favorite two bottles that I keep at an arm's length from the stove just to cook with (the other being Madeira). The gin was better. Juniper is widely reckoned to be a principal flavoring in gin. I had a look at the bottles, which I normally have in the house, to see what is in gin. The Plymouth gin bottle was of no use to me. It went on about monasteries and Dartmoor spring water but had no list of ingredients. The people who wrote the label for Bombay Sapphire were much more helpful. They informed me of the way in which the flavors of the botanicals are imparted into the spirit and that they are (in the order as listed): almonds, lemon peel, liquorice, juniper berries, orris, angelica, coriander, cassa bark, cubeb berries, and grains of paradise. Not that I would know a cubeb tree if I was sitting underneath one—if it is a tree at all, that is, it might only be a bush. I have settled for adding two or three juniper berries (crushed with the side of a large kitchen knife) to the stock. It works very nicely. I've reverted to using the gin for the odd post-children's-bath-time pre-dinner dry martini. Cocktail hour is definitely due for a comeback.

There are cookbooks out there, huge bestsellers too, that start their chicken soup recipe along the lines of "first take two small or one large boiling fowl." I looked for some at the supermarket. They didn't have any boiling fowl of any size at all. I don't generally buy chickens from my butcher. It's a rash generalization, but butchers, it seems, stock pretty average birds. I think it's because there is no room for their craft. They just buy them in, put them in the counter, and they stay there "till you buy them." They don't slaughter them, hang them, pluck, draw, or butcher them. They just whack them with the chopper. I think butchers find chickens a bit boring. My local supermarket used to stock French free range organic chickens from the area near Le Mans. They now sell hugely expensive but brilliant chickens from Sheepdrove Farm. These are the tastiest chickens I have found that you can simply buy.

Old boilers have pretty much disappeared from the butcher's shop. My butcher can get them if I order them, but they're an expensive chicken. They'll take a week, maybe two, on order. If you are able to wring the necks of your own chickens, then once they're too old to lay any more, this is a good thing to do with them. A proper boiling fowl is an old egg layer that has retired—full of flavor, but tough as old boots. That they are so expensive is particularly galling, considering they are almost worthless at the farm (factory?) gate and would otherwise become pet food or nuggets.

It's more likely that you will want to make chicken soup with the carcass after you've roasted a whole bird. This works out fine but I suggest that you do add some fresh chicken to the pot. It will help tremendously with the flavor. I normally throw in a drumstick or two or some wings. The "hand" and "forearm" (an understandable anatomy analogy) are often available quite inexpensively. I chop them in two and use the forearm (the bit with two long bones in) to make buffalo wings. The tips then get bagged up and frozen until I'm making soup or want extra-potent gravy.

I like to add either some dumplings or some very small pasta to the soup. Often I add both. If you're doing the dumpling thing—and there are lots of sorts to choose from—I suggest you try egg and flour dumplings. They are much easier to make than many other sorts and you will probably have the ingredients in your pantry already. I tried making dumplings with butter and ordinary self-rising flour once. I can't lie; they were awful. Matzo dumplings, called knaidlach, are fairly traditional. They are made with matzo meal and schmaltz, which is just chicken fat. You *can* use butter instead, but it's not kosher. Unless you live in a city and have a kosher butcher nearby, you'll have to make the schmaltz yourself. Ask your butcher to save you a whole heap of chicken skins (I'll be amazed if he charges you for them), then just heat them very gently in a deep-sided roasting tray in the oven until all the fat has run out. Strain it, chill it, and you have schmaltz.

This basic recipe will give you a clear, well-flavored, simple chicken soup. Add vegetables, shreds of chicken meat, rice, pasta, or little dumplings as you like.

INGREDIENTS FOR THE SOUP
ENOUGH TO FILL FOUR SMALL BOWLS OR TWO BIG SOUP PLATES
- A whole chicken carcass (I'm assuming it was an average-sized chicken)
- Some fresh chicken bits
- One onion, skin left on (not the red variety)
- One or two sticks of celery
- One or two carrots
- One bay leaf
- One sprig of thyme
- A few parsley stalks

- A few black peppercorns
- Two or three "leaned on" juniper berries

The first thing to do is *not* add any leftover gravy! This will make the soup intolerably cloudy; in a perfect world it should be "gin" clear (although mine seldom is). Chop the vegetables into very large pieces. Halve, maybe quarter, the onion. Leave the skin on as this helps to turn the stock a nice caramel color and I suspect adds some flavor too. Cut the tops off the carrot or carrots and then split them in half lengthwise. Take a stick or two of celery from the outside of the plant (the innermost sticks are tenderest so use those in sauces and salads). Cut the celery in half to make two shorter pieces. I don't want to be too specific about whether it should be just one or two carrots, etc. It depends on how big they are—use your own judgment on this one.

To prepare the juniper berries, place them on the chopping board and, turning your largest knife on its side, put the heel of your hand on the flat bit of the blade with the berries underneath it. Press down to crack the berries open. If you're a bit scared of accidentally losing a digit or two, you can simply whack them with a rolling pin. Alternatively, put the berries on a kitchen work surface and drop a big heavy chopping board on them.

Now place everything in a large pot, quite probably the largest one you've got. Add lots of cold water, the carcass and vegetables should be comfortably covered, but not with so much water that it's all floating around like baby's poo in a paddling pool. Don't add salt—the carcass will have been salted when it was roasted and so won't need it. Bring it all very gently to a boil. Various scummy bits will float to the surface; remove them with a spoon. A small ladle works well but a tablespoon will do the job at a pinch. Leave the lid off the pot.

Don't let the stock reach a rapid boil—it will go cloudy. Similarly, don't start prodding at the carcass to try and get it to break up—the same thing happens—cloudiness! A very gentle simmer is all that's needed.

If you've put in some drumsticks, you can remove them after forty to fifty minutes or so and carefully take the meat off the bone. Keep the meat to one side and return the leg bones to the pot. When it has cooled a bit, hand shred the leg meat into little pieces to be reheated in the soup just before serving.

It will be ready between two and three hours later. You must taste it and decide. Drain it through a fine sieve, then again through a piece of muslin if you have some—run the muslin under a cold tap and wring it out before using it. I use the children's old baby muslins. Either leave the little pools of chicken fat on the top or remove them with a spoon. If you make it the day before and keep it in the fridge overnight (though wait for it to cool down before refrigerating it) it is a doddle to remove the fat. It rises to the top of the soup and sets solid, like a biscuit.

Taste the soup before serving; it may need some salt—but probably not.

ADDITIONS   Once you have made and strained it, you may want to add some vegetables to the finished soup. I only ever add carrots or celery. Cut them into suitably small pieces and then simmer them in the finished soup until tender. Peel the celery to remove the awful stringy bits that run down the ridges of the stalk.

Pasta can be pretty good, too. But do keep it small. Vermicelli is the most traditional. I tend to keep just spaghetti, linguine, and spaghet-tini, (like regular spaghetti but smaller in diameter) in the house and so use them instead. Simply break up a few pieces in your hand and toss them in the soup. Be very sparing with it, though—you are not cooking a bowl of pasta. It will take however long it says on the packet to cook. My daughter thinks the little alphabet shapes are hilarious and who am I to disappoint her?

DUMPLING   I seldom, if ever, pass up the opportunity of a dumpling. My favorites for this soup are made with just one egg, a very generous pinch of salt, and one very heaped tablespoon of plain flour. They're very much like spaetzle—the Bavarian noodle.

Beat the egg with a whisk and add the salt. It will need a lot more than you think possible, at least a quarter of a teaspoon. Now whisk in the flour. Keep going until it's lump free. It will look like a *very* stiff batter mix. Use an egg spoon to drop little blobs into the simmering soup. They will sink straight to the bottom but rise from the depths when they are nearly done. Let them float on the surface for a minute or so, no more, and then serve the soup without delay. They look a complete mess, but taste fabulous.

LATKES Anyone out there remember the way Master Chef used to be? Loyd Grossman presiding over three contestants, all knocking up their best dinner party menus. Annie and I used to make bets each week on which there would be more of: fruit coulis or rosti potatoes. Of course, there was always more fruit coulis (it might appear in any of the courses) than the rosti, but it was the extraordinary effort Loyd required to get that particular word out that was so entertaining: "… and he'll be serving that on a rrowscchteepotaydoughcayyke."

Rosti have gone. Thank heavens for fleeting foodie fashions. I haven't cooked one, been offered one, or even seen one on a restaurant menu for many, many years. I was reminded of them (and Loyd's extraordinary vowel torture) when I was making some latkes the other day. If you grate a potato and fry it, it becomes a rosti. Mix in some beaten egg and a little flour and it's a latke. Latke is, apparently, Yiddish for pancake. Latkes are really very good and they deserve to be more widely eaten. They are a fabulous light meal on their own. I'd choose one over hash browns to go with a Sunday mid-morning fry-up every time. Traditionally they are served with applesauce. Lindsey Bareham (in *Wolf in the Kitchen,* Penguin, 2000) suggests eating them with applesauce and bacon; a seemingly odd combination—certainly not at all kosher—but, oh, so very right.

INGREDIENTS

THIS QUANTITY WILL MAKE TWO BIG LATKES OR FOUR
LITTLE ONES
- One big potato, the size that would typically make a decent
    jacket potato
- One egg
- One tablespoon plain flour

Heat a big frying pan. As that's warming up, break the egg into
a large bowl and whisk with a really big pinch of salt. Tip the
flour (there's no need to sift modern flour—there are no lumps or
weevils) over the top of the eggs and whisk that in until the batter
is smooth. It will be quite thick but it must be smooth. Peel and
grate the potatoes—use the coarsest side of your cheese grater.
Mix the gratings into the batter.

Add a quarter of an inch of sunflower oil to the frying pan.
When this is properly hot, place two (or four) spoonfuls of the
batter/potato mix into the oil. Flatten them down a bit with the
back of the spoon. Don't try and move them until you're pretty sure
the undersides are cooked (the edges will be noticeably crisp). Turn
them over and cook the other side. The only tricky thing about
cooking these is not frying them too quickly. The finished latkes
should be crisp and golden; any dark brown bits will taste burnt.

Serve with cold applesauce and hot crisp bacon. Eat without
delay.

DUELOS Y QUEBRANTOS

Just as the Tortilla Espanola
is the Spanish egg 'n' chips
(American fries), so this dish
is their version of sausage, bacon, and eggs.

Whilst reading through an old recipe book to see what the
Spanish do with their eggs, I happened upon this recipe. Appa-
rently this dish was one of Don Quixote's favorite treats on a
Saturday night. I can't vouch for the accuracy of that information.

The name (quite literally) translates to "wounds and suffering." I suppose this could be to do with the way the paprika

from the sausage bleeds into the egg or perhaps just the way the omelet ends up looking: frankly, it's a bloody mess. Whatever the reason, it doesn't detract from what quickly became a favorite of mine, and the name: wounds and suffering—it's just so utterly Spanish. Only the nation that invented the Inquisition could come up with such a name for a plate of food.

The original version of this suggested using some ham instead of the pancetta which I'm recommending. I've since tried both and I think the pancetta works brilliantly. Yes, I know pancetta is from Italy not Spain, but I'll do as I please. Use a serrano-type ham if you feel the need for greater authenticity.

Quality of ingredients should always be of concern—never more so than here. If you can, use the best pancetta and chorizo (pronounced chur-ree-tho) you can find, probably from a deli. Whilst most supermarkets now sell chorizo, it's unlikely to be as good, and whilst you can use streaky bacon or those pre-cut bacon lardons from Denmark, in all honesty, I can't really recommend them.

In the autumn, I go to the butcher and buy everything I need to make my own chorizo and dry-cure my own bacon in a pancetta style. I will have been eating that bacon since Christmas, but the chorizo will just about be ready by now. So, with a couple of eggs from my girls, it's an entirely homemade meal.

Whatever the source, the food is just eggs, sausage, and bacon. It's important to have the best ingredients.

INGREDIENTS
MAKES ENOUGH FOR ONE
- A small handful of pancetta crouton-sized cubes
- A small handful of diced chorizo cubes
- Two eggs

Do try and resist the temptation to go over the top with the quantity of meats. They are there as an additional flavor to the eggs, not the other way around.

In a small frying pan gently fry the pancetta (or ham) and the chorizo. I start with the pancetta a little ahead of adding the chorizo because I like the pancetta to be really crisp. Cook this lot very, very slowly to render out all the fats within the meats. If you're in the mood to add a pinch of dried chilli flakes or a similar sized pinch of paprika picante, now's the time to do so. Turn up the heat under the pan. Lightly beat the two eggs and then add a little seasoning (the pancetta will be quite salty, so steady-on with the salt). Using a slotted spoon, remove the meat from the pan and keep to one side. Add the beaten eggs to the pan. If there isn't enough fat left behind by the meat, add a drop of olive oil. Cook as per a normal omelet (page 110), reintroducing the meats just as the egg is starting to set.

When the eggs are done to your liking, turn out onto a plate and scoff with some of your favorite bread and a glass of chilled sherry (or a cold beer).

PERSIAN CHICKEN SUPPER

Is it a stew or a soup? I dunno. It is, however, quite sufficient to make a fabulous evening meal all on its own. It's interesting and exotic enough to warrant serving to friends for a bit of supper in the kitchen, but probably not quite right for a posh-frock dinner-party.

What you get is a big bowl of well-flavored chicken broth, with bits of chicken and meatballs swimming in it. I always serve it with a separate bowl of plain basmati rice. Simply spoon a little rice into the broth as you're eating, and when you've eaten that load of rice, spoon in some more.

The exotic bit comes from the musty scent of dried limes. These are, quite literally, whole limes that have been dried. They aren't widely available apart from specialist supermarkets and corner shops. The good news is that you can make them at home. And this is partly why this recipe is in the winter months of this book: you'll probably need to have the central heating on to make the dried limes. On their home ground they're left out to dry in the sun, but on top of a hot radiator or in the airing cupboard does the job just as well. I guess the back of the Aga would also work. Whilst I normally buy them pre-dried (oddly, they are about half the price of fresh limes), I experimented with putting some on the top shelf in my airing cupboard. Nothing happened way up there, so I put them directly onto the lagging on top of the hot water tank. They then took just four weeks before they became absolutely rock-solid, just as they should be. They will shrink to about two thirds of their original size, become pale brown in color, and sound quite hollow if tapped. If you cut one open, you'll see it has become almost black inside. These home-dried ones tend to be larger than the dried ones you can buy, so use only one instead of two or three of those smaller ones.

The meatballs aren't an essential addition. They do make the soup more substantial though—more of a stew.

INGREDIENTS FOR THE SOUP
SERVES FOUR
- One whole chicken, about 1.5 kg or 3.3 lb, maybe some extra bony bits
- One large onion
- Three dried limes (or one home-dried one)
- ¼ teaspoon turmeric
- One quantity of meatballs, see below

If you're using meatballs, have them prepared in advance and keep them in the fridge. Rinse the chicken under a cold tap. Flush out the cavity. Remove any excess fatty bits from inside the bum flap. Joint the chicken into legs, breasts, wings, and backbone. This makes it much easier to fish the pieces out as and when they are ready. Place the chicken into a roomy pan (probably the largest you've got). Pour over plenty of water. Pierce each lime a few times with the tip of a very sharp knife or stab them with the tines of a carving fork and add them to the water. Sprinkle in the turmeric—too much of this and the soup will not only be a hideous lurid yellow, but it will taste a bit soapy. Bring the water up to a steady *gentle* simmer. Keep skimming any fat and flotsam off the top. Remove the breast pieces after about half an hour, the legs after one hour. Keep them to one side. By now, expect the water to have reduced to about two thirds of its original volume. Don't worry if you need to add a little more water along the way.

One hour after you started, the stock is ready. Pour it through a sieve into a clean saucepan (likely to be your second largest!). Bring it up to a simmer and skim the scummy bits once again.

Drop the meatballs into the simmering stock; they will take about fifteen to twenty minutes, depending on their size. In the meantime put some rice on. Then strip the meat from the breast and leg portions, discarding the skin and bones. Tear this meat down to bite-size pieces. As the meatballs approach their full cooking time, slip the chicken pieces back into the stock to just warm through.

Ladle the broth into deep, wide soup plates. Divide the chicken meat and meatballs evenly between these plates. Give each person a small bowl of plain rice on the side.

INGREDIENTS FOR THE MEATBALLS
ENOUGH FOR FOUR PEOPLE
- 225 g/½ lb best minced beef
- A third of the volume of the beef in semolina
- One small onion, either very finely chopped or grated

Place all three ingredients and generous quantities of salt and pepper into a roomy bowl and mix together. They will eventually form a doughy ball. Take this out and knead it on a work surface. This kneading in addition to the salt negates the need for a binding egg. They will be heavy little meatballs, not at all like the Italian types you may be more used to. Physics teachers would call them "dense."

Pinch little pieces off this lump and roll them around in the palm of your hand to form little meatballs—about the size of small marbles. As you do these place them directly onto a plate. When finished, cover them with plastic wrap and refrigerate for at least an hour, up to half a day, until needed. I wouldn't make them the day before—the acidity of the onions may blacken the meat slightly.

POACHED CHICKEN WITH SIX VEGETABLES

I cooked this just the other night for dinner for Annie and me. She looked at it and said "ooooh—my kind of food." By which, I think, she meant it was simple, tasty, high in veggie count, and (coincidentally) almost fat free.

The vegetables can all be prepared in advance and left in a bowl of cold water until needed. The chicken stock should be pretty light, just simmer a backbone or two for half an hour and call it done.

See my comments on poaching whole breasts before starting to cook this.

INGREDIENTS FOR TWO
- Two chicken breasts (preferably still on the bone)
- 900ml/ 3½ cups of pale, light chicken stock
- One big carrot
- One big parsnip
- One big turnip
- Half a small rutabaga
- Two or three sticks of celery, not the big outside ones
- Four dark green leaves from a Savoy cabbage

Start by bringing the chicken stock up to a rolling simmer. Whilst that is happening, prepare the vegetables. Everything except the cabbage needs to be peeled and chopped into roughly 1.8 cm/¾-inch cubes. I tend to discard the round edges of the rutabaga to get a better cube shape. The carrots and turnip are generally halved or quartered, depending on their girth, then cut to length.

The chicken will take twenty minutes to poach, then needs five minutes resting. Timing is fairly important for this dish since some vegetables will cook quicker than others. Place the chicken breasts in the simmering stock. After five minutes, add the rutabaga.

After a further ten minutes, add the carrot, turnip, and parsnip. Only when you take the chicken out, after its full twenty minutes cooking time, should you add the cabbage and celery. Keep cooking the vegetables for a further five minutes.

After letting the breasts rest for five minutes, remove the skin and cut the breasts, whole, off the bone. Then cut this, on the angle, into thin slices.

Spoon the veg and some stock into deep, wide soup plates; arrange the chicken over the top.

Don't bother with any fancy herb garnishes—just eat it as it is. You'll need a knife and fork, and a soup spoon to finish off.

VARIATIONS   Something this soupy deserves is dumplings. To omit them is just one more wasted opportunity in life when you could have been eating dumplings. I have a bit of a soft spot for dumplings in the winter (sadly Annie doesn't). After trying to cook them in the same pot as the stew, I have come to the realization that on this occasion they are better poached on their own. It's not a problem with, say, a steak and kidney but for this dish they can turn the broth a bit cloudy. Use a separate pan of simmering water with a lid on—better still, cook them in a steamer. Sometimes I like to add a little cooked diced bacon and very finely chopped onion, grated lemon zest, and finely chopped thyme and parsley. Salt and pepper, of course. Mix these flavorings with one tablespoon of suet (buy it in a lump from your butcher and coarsely grate it) with two tablespoons of self-rising flour. Combine with just enough cold water to form a firm paste. Shape into little walnut-sized dumplings and poach or steam separately for fifteen to twenty minutes.

Alternatively, combine the bacon, onion, lemon zest, and herbs with some fresh breadcrumbs and bind with an egg. These are classic forcemeat balls. They should be fried, not poached, then drained on kitchen paper and added directly to the bowl.

LEGLESS CHICKEN WITH GREENS

Next time when you're standing in the meat aisle pondering over which particular packet of skinless, boneless chicken breasts takes your fancy, just have a look at the price and then look at the price for a whole chicken. Chances are, the chicken is about the same—you're just paying more for someone else to chop it up—crazy eh?

I like to buy whole chickens and then butcher them myself: it is just good common-sense housekeeping. One chicken can be stretched to three main meals; this alone helps to justify the cost of buying a proper chicken in the first place. If I've got a particularly large chicken to deal with, I might even be able to squeeze some croquettes out of it for a decent lunch or very light supper. The chickens that I frequently buy in the supermarket are imported from France so whereas a British chicken might have huge bulging breasts and short stubby legs, these little *poulet* (like the best French actresses) are all leg and no breast. I normally choose a smallish one, about 1.2–1.4 kg/ 2.5–3 pounds.

The trio of recipes I tend to go for most often are: on the first night something done with the breasts, second night, risotto, and third night, something with the legs. So, if you start with roast chicken breast on the Sunday, it'll be Wednesday night before you need to even think about defrosting a pizza! Of course, the stock for the risotto can sit in the fridge for two days and as long as you've made a mental note of the "use by" date on the chicken (and don't exceed it), you can cook the legs later in the week. Whatever the timing of this concatenation of meals, it's a frugal way to get the most from the chicken without any wastage.

Because you're going to be using the legs for another time, they need to be removed before roasting the rest of the bird (see the basics on how to joint a chicken). It's at this point that you need to decide what sort of risotto you feel like cooking tomorrow. If you're going to cook a pale-colored risotto, such as the pea risotto (page 222), you need to remove the breasts (still on the breast bone) from the rest of the carcass. If you're doing the mushroom one, then the finished effect will be darker so roast the whole legless chicken. This will result in the stock being correspondingly darker.

INGREDIENTS
MAKES DINNER FOR TWO
- One suitably dismembered chicken
- Butter
- One small onion
- One carrot
- One stick of celery
- Two cloves garlic
- Small bunch tarragon
- Glass dry white wine or dry vermouth (Noilly Prat in my house)

You'll also need:
- Some roast potatoes
- Your favorite leafy green veg; Savoy cabbage, spring greens, cavalo nero, etc.

Roughly chop the onion, carrot, celery, and just bruise the garlic by leaning heavily on it with the flat side of a large knife. Strew these around the bottom of your favorite roasting pan. Smother the skin on the chicken breast with a decent sized knob of butter and add plenty of salt and pepper. This will stick nicely into the butter. Place the chicken on its bed of vegetables and then into the oven, preheated to 200°C/400°F/gas 6. After 15 minutes, take it out and baste with the melted butter in the pan. Shake it all around a bit to stop either chicken or veg from sticking to the pan. Turn the oven down to 170°C/340°F/gas 3–4 and put it back in the oven for about another 20 to 30 minutes until you're happy that it's done. The cooking time will be a little less than for a whole chicken because you needn't worry about cooking the legs through. The breasts always cook quicker.

Remove the chicken to a warm corner to rest and let the juices sort themselves out. I cannot overstress the importance of this: It is infinitely preferable to have *warm* moist juicy chicken than *hot* tight dry chicken.

Now the gravy. Well, it's not really gravy—just an amalgamation of the bits in the bottom of the pan. You should have in front of you a roasting pan with some very well cooked vegetables that are starting to burn at the edges and some juices from the chicken and veg with a fair bit of melted butter floating on the top. If you think there's too much butter, drain a little off but do leave some in the pan—it all adds to the taste. Put the pan on top of the cooker and turn the heat up to its highest; allow it to reach a fierce bubble. Now pour in the wine or dry vermouth (I prefer vermouth) and let it reduce a little. Scratch and scrape at the dish to dislodge all the crusty bits and sort of push the vegetables into a mush with the back of a spoon. Place a fine sieve over a small saucepan and pour the gravy through it into the pan. Gently squeeze the veg into the bottom of the sieve to extract as much of the flavors from the veg as possible. Finely chop the tarragon leaves and add directly into the gravy. Keep it warm over the lowest heat.

This amputee chicken is now, in no way, photogenic so abandon any thought of carving the bird at the table. Simply remove each breast in its entirety from the chicken and serve one whole one per person. I've been cooking this, unchanged, for years so I find it impossible to resist the temptation to stack it all up in the manner in which so much restaurant food was presented in the nineties. Place some potatoes (see below) in the middle of the plate, greens on top of those, and the chicken balancing precariously on top of it all. Surround this mad looking tower with the gravy.

After you've eaten—and maybe even done the washing up—strip any meat that is left (such as the wings, and that bit under the wishbone) from the carcass. Use all the available bones to make a quick stock by simmering them for an hour or so with a little onion, a carrot, and a celery stick (I have to admit that sometimes I just recycle the gravy veg—it works well—but only for a very dark stock). A bay leaf and a few parsley stalks are also good, if you have them. Strain through a fine sieve into a suitable jug or bowl and, once cool, (possibly after leaving it out covered overnight) keep it in the fridge for a day or two.

GREENS I tend to buy whatever looks good on the day and takes my fancy; it's often a plain-Jane Savoy cabbage in my shopping basket. About half a large one between two people will do (although, with a little forethought, I'll cook a whole one, along with some extra potatoes, and make bubble and squeak for lunch the next day). I cut it really finely, almost shredded, and always steam it just for a few minutes. Another green veg that works well is cavalo nero. This needs cooking in exactly the same way. To prepare it, hold the stalk with one hand and then pull the leaf off the stalk by sliding your thumb and forefinger down the length of the stalk. Put the stalks in your compost bucket (or chop them up and give them to your hens) and cut the cabbage into long strips. Steamed purple sprouting broccoli or green beans of most varieties work pretty well too.

I personally think the trick here is to let the quality of the chicken shine through with good gravy and not much else, just one sort of greenery and some excellent roast potatoes.

EXCELLENT ROAST POTATOES Like anyone else, I'm a fan of potatoes that have been roasted in gobs and gobs of goose fat or beef dripping. But I find they're a bit heavy to be partnered with a chicken. So I just use vegetable oil, sparingly, to sort of dry roast them. I think the convection oven favors this process over ordinary ovens, but I can still achieve decent results with the fan off.

It always pays to make more roast potatoes than you think

you'll possibly need. Any leftovers can be eaten on the way up to bed or kept in the fridge and just picked at with a little salad cream squeezed over the top—or use them to make a quick cheaty Spanish omelet. As a last resort, your chickens will be happy to eat any that you can't manage.

INGREDIENTS FOR TWO
- 1 kg/2 lb good waxy potatoes (I use Maris Pipers)
- Vegetable oil

This is a really simple way of cooking them and removes all the need for parboiling and preheating the fat and all that gubbins. Cold potatoes, cold oil, cold tray, hot oven. Simple.

Peel the potatoes and chop them into appropriate sizes. Sometimes I slice them down their length through their thinnest side and then run the peeler around the cut edge to knock off the sharp corner. This will give them more of a uniform look, quite fancy for a roast spud.

Take a tray that's large enough to accommodate them, without being overly crowded, in a single layer. It should be quite low-sided to help the heat to get all round the potato. Pour in just enough vegetable oil to give them a coating. Add the potatoes and use your hands to turn them over and over in the oil until they are covered on all sides. Put them in the oven at the same time as the chicken.

They should be ready by the time the chicken is done and rested.

NOTE   Don't under any circumstance turn the oven temperature down towards the end of the cooking time. The potatoes will lose their crunchy surface. If they're looking like they're going to be overdone, it's better to take them out of the oven and leave them uncovered until five or ten minutes before you want to eat. Then just pop them back in the oven to get hot again.

STUFFED CHICKEN LEGS

This is pretty much my favorite thing to do with a chicken leg. If the idea of buying whole chicken—and the necessary butchery and boning—is just too much for you to contemplate, ask your butcher to do it. He needs to remove only the thighbone for you.

The stuffing mixture I've listed will give you far more than you need for the pair of legs in question. I've done this because if you shop at the supermarket this is the sort of quantity of pre-packed ground veal that they sell. Very few butchers will have ground veal just waiting for you to walk in and ask for some. They'll therefore have to put at least a pound of meat through the grinder especially for you; understandably they'll be reluctant to do less for you.

Worry not; the mix makes excellent meatballs. Just put what you don't use back in the fridge and use within a couple of days. To make the meatballs, take the leftover ground mix and pinch off tiny amounts, no bigger than marbles—I like them to each be only a mouthful. These need to be rolled around in the palm of your hand into little balls. Place them on a plate as you go and put that back in the fridge for at least an hour. Then, poach them for about fifteen to twenty minutes in a decent plain tomato sauce (either buy a jar or make your own) and serve with spaghetti or linguine.

If you're sufficiently organized, you could remove the thighbone at the same time as you separate the leg from the chicken. Put it and the heel (more of which below) to one side, to be added to the stockpot with the rest of the carcass.

If you'd rather not use veal, try a 50/50 mix of beef and pork, or, at a pinch, ground chicken—although, personally, I detest the texture of minced poultry.

INGREDIENTS
FOR TWO PEOPLE
- Two whole chicken legs (thighbone already whipped out)
- One glass Madeira or vermouth (depending on whether you prefer sweet or dry sauces)

- Butter
- A small amount of the stuffing (see below)

You'll need a small sharp knife. First thing to do is to remove the thighbone. Start by cutting down to the bone on the short side of the leg (that is the side that was attached to the chicken, its "inside leg" in tailor's terminology). Carefully work your knife around the thighbone until it can be held quite separately and is only attached at the knee joint. Don't panic; common sense will get you through this. Holding thighbone in one hand and drumstick in the other, bend the leg backwards to dislocate the knee. You'll need to cut through the dislocated joint. Work the knife around any remaining flesh that is preventing you from removing the bone. The thighbone should now be free of the leg.

At the bottom of the leg, position the heel of your heaviest knife upside down just up the drumstick from the ankle (cutting edge facing upwards). Give the bone a quick tap to break it. Then work the knife through the break to separate the heel from the drumstick; check for any shards of broken bone. Another way to cut through the bone is with chicken shears. I've got a pair but can seldom be bothered to use them—or more specifically clean them afterwards. This break has the double benefit of shortening the leg when it's served and freeing the tendons in the drumstick from the ankle. When it cooks, the drumstick meat will shrink up the length of the bone, leaving half an inch or so of exposed bone. If you're put off by the task, ask your butcher to do it while you're there or just let it be.

Season the inside of the leg with just a little salt and pepper. Take some stuffing and roll it into a small cigar shape. It's going where the bone used to be. So it should be about as long as the bone you removed but can be a little thicker in diameter. Reshape the leg around the stuffing and seal it up, either by using a darning needle and heavy thread or, a quicker alternative for something of this size, run a couple of cocktail sticks through the skin to keep it all together. Put it in the fridge to rest for at least an hour.

Melt some butter in a pan that can be transferred straight into a hot oven (200°C/400°F/gas 6) and when the butter stops bubbling, gently fry until golden. Start by cooking the side that you have been operating on. This helps it to seal quickly. Transfer to the oven and cook for another fifteen to twenty minutes, turning once or twice to help it brown.

When ready, remove to a warm place to relax. If there is an excessive amount of fat in the pan, remove some using a spoon. Put the pan back on the cooker and turn up the heat until sizzling. Add the wine and reduce down to a nice thick sauce consistency. You can monte (just a fancy word for this whisking process) in some fridge-cold butter to help thicken the sauce if you like. It may not need it—but the butter *must* be cold or it won't work.

I think it's best served with some oven-roast wedgie chips (fries) and a green salad.

FOR THE STUFFING
- 450 g/1 lb ground veal
- One crushed clove garlic
- A handful stale white breadcrumbs (or finely crushed water crackers)
- A generous pinch dried oregano
- A handful finely grated Parmesan cheese
- One egg

Mix all the ingredients together in a large bowl with salt and pepper, using your hands to make sure it's all thoroughly integrated. Use for stuffing the chicken leg or for making into meatballs.

WEDGIE CHIPS

Cook in exactly the same way as Excellent Roast Potatoes but cut the potatoes lengthways into thick wedges (normally about eight per spud), leaving their skins on. Sometimes I sprinkle a little dried oregano on when they're done. These are so good that they're the only type of chips (fries) that I cook at home.

PIRI-PIRI CHICKEN

These days our new culinary influences come from all over the world. No longer do menus change based on the wishes of army officers returning from the Raj, bringing us mulligatawny and kedgeree. Chefs in London are as likely to have trained in the kitchens of Sydney and Melbourne as anywhere else. The Aussies' own lack of culinary traditions allowed them to draw from all around them and, "hey-pes-to," we have Pacific rim cuisine in West End restaurants. Half the British pubs (at least the ones that serve food) seem to specialise in Thai food. The pizza and the hamburger are currently battling it out for world domination. (I'd put my money on pizza—currently ahead by a nose, 'cos those burger pushers are getting such bad press right now).

These days anyone with fifty quid in their pocket can hop on a plane, physically eat on any continent they like, and be home in time for tea. I've only twice travelled outside Europe (a weekend in New York—the Big Apple—and a student bus trip round Morocco), yet I've eaten all around the world. Gastronomically speaking, the jet engine has made the planet a small place and the supermarkets have been only too happy to sell us all these imported goods. The world is now our oyster (with Thai dipping sauce).

So why is there so, relatively, little interest in what's almost on our doorstep? And why when we do come over all pro-Euro do we stick, almost exclusively, with France and Italy? I know Spanish food is supposed to be the next big thing, but they've been saying that, for what, ten to fifteen years now. All those new Eastern-block EU members, will they have any effect on what we'll be cooking in a few years time? I doubt it! Stroganoffs and borscht... I'm struggling to think of another ...oh, got it—goulash.

Portugal is another great case in point. Lots of people speak Portuguese. Half of South America at least. But where are their great national dishes? All still being cooked at home, that's where.

This is a typically bastardized (not much more than a nod of gratitude and thanks for the catchy name) kind of Portuguese dish—but that's enough philosophizing and discrediting it. It's worth cooking all on its own merit—ultimately, that's all that counts. The name piri-piri translates to chili-chili.

From a cook's point of view, the interesting thing about this recipe is the way you broil the chicken. Chicken, like any lean meat, will toughen up the longer it's cooked. Thick meat takes longer to cook than thin meat—that's not arugula science. So what do you do with a fairly thick chicken breast? Answer: you make it thinner. This way it will cook right through in about 8 to 10 minutes under a decently hot broiler. This trick also comes in very handy when barbecuing chicken breasts.

The sauce is a doddle to make, too. I like to use the medium-sized red chilies that seem to be available everywhere. They are hot and fragrant without being vicious in a masochistic way. They are about the size of your thumb. If you like it a bit hotter, then either use more or move up to the smaller peppers. It's a simple point to remember that the smaller the pepper, the hotter it will be. Big red bell peppers are easily eaten raw in salads but I wouldn't fancy popping a whole Thai bird's eye into my mouth. Don't be put off by making the caramel—all you're doing is letting the sugar burn a little, and most people seem able to burn things. Just be aware that molten sugar gets very hot, so don't touch it and definitely don't taste it!

INGREDIENTS
- Two boneless chicken breasts, with or without skin, as you like
- Two medium red chilies or more to taste
- Two biggish cloves garlic
- A generous splash of red wine vinegar
- An inch from a bottle of good olive oil
- Three tablespoons caster sugar
- A few coriander leaves to finish

Start by making the piri-piri sauce. Roughly chop the garlic and chilies (leaving the seeds in) and place them in a small nonreactive saucepan. Add the vinegar and olive oil and bring up to a gentle simmer for a minute or two. Take off the heat and allow to cool completely. Tip the whole lot into a blender and liquefy until it is completely smooth.

Next job is flattening out the chicken. Do this by sandwiching one of the breasts between two large sheets of plastic wrap. Then hit it repeatedly with the palm of your hand. Stop when you've squished it out to about twice its original size and half its original thickness. Try not to make any holes in it and don't worry if the little fillet on the underside detaches itself, just put it back in place. Then do the other one. Place them on a roasting tray that will fit under your broiler.

Leaving half of the piri-piri sauce to one side for later, pour the rest over the chicken breasts and rub into the surface of both sides.

If you're at all nervous about this sort of thing, it may be worth making the caramel and sauce before you cook the chicken. I make the final sauce as the chicken cooks but it does mean keeping your eye on two things at once. It's your call. You'll need a smallish pan, for preference not a black one—it makes judging the brownness of the caramel more difficult. Put all the sugar and a little splash of water into the pan. Put it on a high heat until the sugar turns a pale golden color. At this point you must pay more attention in order to avoid really burning the pan. Watch it like a hawk, shaking the pan a little until it is a mid-brown color. Take it off the heat and see that it gets only a little darker. When it is nearly the shade of a horse chestnut, tip in the remaining half of the piri-piri sauce. It will splutter and spit and the sugar will go into a horrid solid mess (do please be careful). Return the pan to the heat and let the sugar dissolve once again. Stir with a metal spoon to help it along. When it is once again smooth, remove from the heat. It will need to cool a little before you can eat it, so don't even bother with keeping it warm.

Place the chicken under a preheated (to maximum) broiler. The chicken will take 8 to 10 minutes. It may take more or less time depending on your broiler. When the underside of the chicken is starting to go opaque, turn the chicken over to finish it off. Roughly speaking, you want to have about two-thirds of the cooking time on the skin/presentation side and one-third on the bottom.

To serve, simply place it on a plate next to a pile of plain basmati rice. Spoon the finished piri-piri sauce over the chicken and sprinkle with a few roughly chopped coriander leaves. A salad of leaves or raw vegetables is the side order of the day; definitely *not* boiled vegetables.

QUEEN OF PUDDINGS

I've always been frightened of making most things meringuey on account of all that whisking that I'd have to do by hand (have I yet mentioned I don't have a food processor or electric whisk?). I finally relented and made some meringue. I've found it takes just five minutes, tops, and have been making sweet fluffy meringues of every variety ever since. When I think of all those egg whites I've let slide down the plug hole over the years . . . it fills me with (mild) self-loathing!

The almost unique thing about this pudding is that it uses both parts of the egg. The yolk goes into the custardy base and the white gets whipped to a froth for the top. Very frugal indeed.

That frugality is carried forth into the custard, too. Instead of being a set (i.e. baked) custard proper, the sort with much cream and many yolks, it is thickened with breadcrumbs. Another canny use for that rapidly hardening, soon to be moldy loaf.

Every recipe I've found for this (and there are very many but all almost exactly the same) has suggested using raspberry jam or blackcurrant jelly. Those that suggested raspberry jam suggested sieving it to remove those pips. I agree. You don't want them interrupting the sublime smoothness of this pudding. I have still got several jars of homemade damson jelly (my father-in-law has a very healthy damson tree) and so I use this more often. It does the job very well and I think I like the damson more than the raspberry, but not as much as the blackcurrant. In fact, there are few occasions that I prefer any fruit to blackcurrants. There is simply no arguing the fact that blackcurrant ice cream is the very-best, all-time-winner, champion-of-champions variety. You don't agree? Then you're wrong—go eat your Häagen-Dazs.

The practicalities of timing and making this pudding fit rather well with eating a main course. Have the custardy breadcrumbs ready baked and sitting around with the jam already on. An hour or two of waiting won't harm it. The meringue can be made up to an hour in advance. I've found that meringue will wait—but woe is you if you think plain whisked egg whites will hang about. After about ten minutes of inactivity they start to droop and will revert to a little runny puddle in the bottom of the bowl. Fortunately meringue is more forgiving. But don't assemble the dish until it's about to go in the oven—the warm base will melt the jam/jelly (good) as well as the meringue (bad).

INGREDIENTS
SERVES FOUR
FOR THE CUSTARD BASE
- 125 g/4 oz fresh white breadcrumbs—real bread please, sliced white is unacceptable for this dish
- One heaped tablespoon of caster sugar
- Contents of half a vanilla pod or a few drops of vanilla essence, or use vanilla sugar (see page 247)
- Grated rind of one lemon (optional)
- 450 ml/¾ pint of milk
- 50 g/2 oz unsalted butter
- Three egg yolks

FOR THE MERINGUE
- Three egg whites
- One tablespoon caster sugar

TO ASSEMBLE
- One big rounded dessertspoon of your favorite fruit jam or jelly (see above)
- A little caster sugar to sprinkle over the top, about a teaspoon

Start by making the breadcrumbs. Put the bread (crusts removed) into a food processor and blitz—or patiently chop them by hand with a sharp chef's knife. Place them in a large bowl, mix in the sugar, vanilla, and lemon rind (if using). In a little sauce pan, bring the milk and butter up to a sufficient heat to melt the butter—don't let it boil. The butter will look all blobby and horrid floating, as it will, on top. Don't worry, that's normal. Pour the milk and butter over the breadcrumbs, mix it well in, and allow to cool until tepid. At that point beat in the egg yolks. Now pour this mixture into a lightly buttered baking dish. I use a 900 ml/1½ pint oval gratin dish but use any shape you like; it shouldn't be too deep, ideally the custard should be about 1.25 to 1.8 cm/½ to ¾ inch thick. Bake it in the preheated oven (180°C/340°F/gas 4) for about 20 minutes. Maybe more, maybe less, it just depends. Don't worry about it developing a bit of a skin, that'll help with the final assembly.

Whilst this is baking, make the meringue. Whisk the egg whites in a spotlessly clean bowl. There must be no trace of yolk amongst the whites either. It may help you to separate the eggs individually into little cups to avoid any broken yolks contaminating the bowl. Once they have reached a soft-peak stage, add half the heaped spoonful of caster sugar. As they stiffen up, add the other half and whisk that in thoroughly. Stop whisking when the whites have reached a good firm peak and look as white and glossy as a cheap satin wedding dress.

Once the custard is ready, gently spread the fruit jelly all over it. Times change and recipes for such things as sweet puddings are becoming less sweet. I find the idea of using two or three times this amount of jelly/jam quite appalling. I think this is enough, but if you want to use more, use more; at worst you're being a tad unfashionable with your sweet tooth. If you have a really firm jelly on your hands, it may help things along if you apply some gentle heat in a little saucepan to slacken it off before you try spreading it.

Now it's time to pile the meringue on top—don't waste your time poncing about with a piping bag—just shovel it on. But do try and get a few wispy peaks that will go a nice brown color in the oven—don't make it a smooth dome, in other words. Rough it up a bit. Sprinkle the last little bit of caster sugar on the top and put it in the oven to go a pleasant shade of brown—about 10 to 15 minutes but keep half an eye on it.

Serve it as hot as possible with lashings of cold thick cream.

SPOTTED DICK AND CUSTARD

How we used to laugh about this at school. I doubt today's preteen children find time for such silly puerile humor. They're all too busy exercising their thumbs texting each other.

Any self-respecting school kitchen or office cafeteria in the UK will have a spotted dick tin. I brought one once. I've still got it, somewhere: never ever used it. Wrapping it in a clean tea towel and poaching it is all you need to do. I reckon a proper spotted dick should have the raisins evenly distributed around the inside. If you want to add some chopped apples or other ingredients, you'd be better off rolling it (just like Swiss roll). But then it's become a roly-poly.

The key here is to make a proper sweet suet pastry. It's the easiest pastry to make, bar none. In a big bowl mix 225 g/½ lb suet, 500 g/1 lb self-rising flour, two tablespoons of caster sugar, and a pinch of salt. Add 500 g/1 lb of good seedless raisins. I sometimes use a mix of raisins, sultanas, and a little candied lemon peel but, nevertheless, 500 g/1 lb fruit in total. Make a well in the center of the dry mix and add a little cold water. Cut this together with a palette knife or spatula, adding more water as necessary until it forms a really stiff ball of dough. It may need a little more water depending on just about everything from the type of flour to the weather. Just add some if needed but remember this is best when kept stiff.

Turn this out onto a floured work surface and manhandle it into a sausage shape. Do remember though, it has to fit comfortably into a pan of water to cook. I use my fish kettle to poach this, so consequently I'm happy for mine to be quite long.

Roll the pudding up in a wet dish towel and tie a knot at each end (Christmas-cracker style). Steam or boil for two and a half hours.

Unwrap it, cut into thick slices, and serve with hot home-made custard.

PS. I understand that the Politically Correct Dinner Ladies (sorry, Dinner Persons) now call this a "Spotted Richard."

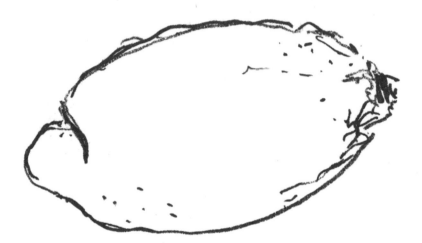

Jane Grigson

Charcuterie and French Pork Cookery

Jane Grigson

CHEZ PANISSE VEGETABLES 🍅 ALICE WATERS

LEGENDS of TEXAS BARBECUE COOKBOOK   WALSH

THE RIVER COTTAGE COOKBOOK

HUGH FEARLESSLEY- WINNSITALL

The Cooking of South-West France

A TALE OF 12 KITCHENS   JAKE TILSON

French Toast
Chicken Pie with Winter
Vegetables
Real Coq au Vin
Roast Chicken with Nutmeg

FEBRUARY

Moroccan Tagine with
Preserved Lemons
Hamine Eggs
Chocolate Almond Cake
Lemon Curd
Rhubarb Crumble and Custard

ebruary is unquestionably slap-bang in the middle of winter. I know that the snowdrops are blooming and the daffodils will be yellow by the end of the month, but it always *seems* colder than January. And in the last few years at least, it has had most of the winter's snow. The shortest month of the year never has the decency of feeling like it.

There are few seasonal new culinary treats in February. Forced rhubarb, some peculiar "niche market" oranges and that's about it. And the game season ends—much to my disappointment and my wife's delight. So, it's a choice of more things to do with cabbage, leeks, and roots or go back to the supermarket and buy some green beans from Kenya, some asparagus from New Zealand, or tomatoes and peppers from the under-sea-level hydroponic-glasshouses of Holland.

Fortunately for me, I like cabbages, just not the boiled-to-a-pulp, wallpaper paste sort of thing that you probably had at school. I'm talking about crisp crunchy Savoys, slow, carefully stewed red cabbages with the last of the Bramleys peeled, chopped, and added towards the end, and even those odd little pointy-topped green cabbages will find a welcome home in my kitchen.

The comfort food continues: stews, stews, casseroles too, plain good honest grub. If I'm not serving some fresh seasonal vegetables then I'll opt for something preserved. Preserved lemons from Morocco make a tagine into something more than a lamb stew that is oddly flavoured with cinnamon and ginger. Peas and broad beans, both fresh from the freezer, when added to a little sweated onion and a few scraps of carrot make a fabulous veggie side dish to the Sunday roast lamb. Liquefy any leftovers for Monday night's soup or just reheat it with a splash of cream to lubricate; it's good served with a chop. Actually, lamb at this time of the year is rather good. I like its flavorsome maturity—spring lamb has its place but lamb that is nearly mutton will get my vote nine times out of ten.

Using the freezer is, I think, absolutely fine. I'd rather eat some frozen British raspberries at this time of year than some that are on the outward leg of their one-way long-haul foreign holiday. And where would we be without those frozen peas? Apart from them, my little freezer just contains the usual tub of vanilla ice cream, a tray of ice cubes, and some odd scraps in unmarked bags.

February is the month for beef bourguignon and its sister act, coq au vin. Justly, these have become world famous regional French dishes, but, to my mind, no better than say, Lancashire hot pot. The French, it seems, just have better global PR (foodwise). We are all too eager to forget our culinary roots . . .

Potatoes can be placed whole in the oven next to the casserole and baked just as slowly, about two hours for a nice big one. The best way I've ever cooked a jacket potato is to put some large ones into a cold oven, letting them warm up with the oven. That step is important because you don't want to prick them (it lets out the moisture that creates steam) and putting cold unpricked potatoes into a hot oven will, likely as not, cause them to explode. To serve them, remove carefully from the oven, place delicately on a serving plate or clean chopping board, and then just punch them quite lightly and just the once. The skins will rupture and open and a head of steam will billow forth. This saves all that messing about cutting a cross in the top of them, fluffing them up, having your little knob of butter slide off the hot knife before it gets to the potato, and so on. I don't know that the punching makes them taste any better, but it will (at least and if only for a while) help you forget about the crappy weather.

FEBRUARY'S DIARY

SUNDAY 2 FEBRUARY
Snow melting now. Hens happy to be able to range over the grass again.

MONDAY 3 FEBRUARY
Am now pretty much set up for my first ever incubation. Rented Brinsea polyhatch incubator for £30 (might buy it though). Just need to sort out brooder enclosure. Have arranged some time with dad to do some carpentry over the next few days. No hurry though —at least 21 days until it's needed. 5 eggs today—black pudding omelettes for lunch.

TUESDAY 4 FEBRUARY
Snow has now all melted, just the melting remains of the snowman we all made. Hens happily peck away at it. I guess everybody loves sorbet.

WEDNESDAY 5 FEBRUARY
Went to Bury St Edmunds for the weekly fowl market to buy some fertilised eggs—very disappointing. Came home empty handed.

THURSDAY 6 FEBRUARY
Plan B was to get some eggs from an enthusiast/breeder. I phoned Keith but he suggested delaying it until after the weekend. The cold weather had, all but, stopped his birds from laying.

TUESDAY 11 FEBRUARY
Collect eggs from Keith first thing. Arranged incubator in my study. Set 48 eggs. Very excited.

SUNDAY 16 FEBRUARY
I found Alice stuck on the wrong side of the fence wandering around in the neighbor's hedge. I left her for an hour to see if she'd find her own way back. No chance. Eventually got her back and gave her some banana. Chickens clearly do not like to be grabbed by the leg and then dragged through a hedge backwards.

TUESDAY 18 FEBRUARY
Eggs have been 7 days in incubator. Did first candling. Eleven eggs infertile. Phoned Keith and asked why all the Light Sussex/Silkie Crosses were infertile. "I guess the cockerel just doesn't fancy the Silkies," he said. Fair enough.

FRIDAY 21 FEBRUARY
Spent most of the week using up odd hours here and there making a new henhouse. What madness! It must be cheaper to just buy them. Third time I've done this. Each time I say never again.

SATURDAY 22 FEBRUARY
Fell asleep watching Alien on the telly. Had VERY scary dreams about what was happening inside the eggs in the incubator downstairs …

FRENCH TOAST

My copy of *Larousse Gastronomique* (which subtitles itself "The World's Greatest Cookery Encyclopaedia," an entirely reasonable claim since it runs to 1193 pages) tells me that French toast is also known as *pain perdu* and has been formerly known as *pain crotte, pain a la romaine,* or *croûtes dorées.* Whatever, it is largely the same as our own eggy bread, but the stale bread is first soaked in some milk, itself sweetened with a little caster sugar, before being quickly passed through some beaten eggs.

Larousse further recommends serving it with custard (yum), jam or fruit compote. It is a very special way of using up the last scrapings of the previous autumn's homemade jams. Toast from the toaster seems much too mundane for such a sad occasion. Once you have run out, try it with a little sprinkling of powdered cinnamon instead. To drink—a short, strong black coffee.

INGREDIENTS
- One slice of stale white bread per person
- One egg per person
- A generous splash of whole milk
- A level teaspoon caster sugar per portion

Pour the milk into a large plate, one that is large enough to allow the bread to lie completely flat in it without the edges being forced to curl up over the rim. The bread *must* be stale and from a proper loaf. Fresh "plastic" white bread just won't work.

Get a frying pan nice and hot.

Using a fork, beat the egg in another shallow plate (or the same one depending whether you're cooking just one piece or starting a brunch-time production line). Season the milk with a pinch of salt and the sugar. Soak the stale white bread in the milk, removing it before it gets really soggy. Add a knob of butter to the pan and whoosh it around a bit. Quickly, but unhurriedly, dip the bread into the egg, turn it over to coat the other side. The idea here is to give the now sopping bread a nice eggy crust, not to soak the bread in the egg as you would for its poor cousin, Eggy Bread. Slide the dripping bread straight into the pan. Cook until a lovely deep golden brown and then turn it over. You may find that you want to add a little more butter to cook the second side; if so, go ahead.

Et, voila-French Toast. C'est tres bon.

CHICKEN PIE WITH WINTER VEGETABLES

I don't tend to eat very many pies. I think it's the fault of that bloody awful size-ist football chant: "Who ate all the pies? Who ate all the pies. . . ?" If (like me) you are big boned/well upholstered/festively plump/XXL, it gets into your subconscious and that little tune works its magic anytime you find your resolve weakening in front of the Fray Bentos.

A couple of house moves ago, there used to be a baker's shop at the end of the road we lived on. I had developed quite a taste for their warm steak and kidney pies. It all ended abruptly, as these things do, when I bit into a lump of something quite inedible. A foreign object, if you like. My affections transferred to their beef and onion pies. They'd be ready by 10.30, perfect timing for a midmorning break. It became a problem for me. In the end I forced myself to go cold turkey. I'm happy to say I haven't done a Pukka Pie for six years now.

Now, as I find myself standing at the butcher's counter, ogling the fresh rabbits, considering a brace of dressed pheasants or some lovely deep red slices of beef shin, perhaps thinking of buying some spankingly fresh little lambs' kidneys, I don't even consider the neighbourly anaemic steak and kidney pies or the oversize Cornish pasties (I just know those will have sweetcorn and carrots in them!).

Annie has a weakness for proper hand-raised pork pies; she says it's her Derbyshire upbringing. I manage to contain myself until about once a year when I crumble and make a couple of proper pork pies from scratch the hard way. They are so good, and yet such an effort, that I'm cured for another year or so.

More often, and only ever in the winter months, I'll find my-self rolling out a packet of puff pastry to put a lid on a little dish of steak and kidney or maybe some chicken-based thick stew. I only ever use puff pastry; I absolutely adore it. That crunchy brittle flakiness when it's risen at least an inch, although two is better; absolute perfection. It always outshines even the very best shortcrust pastry.

Sadly, I don't have the hands needed to make decent pastry. You need small delicate cold hands for the gifted touch. I have big heavy warm hands that are quite useless for the job. Fortu-nately, you can get very good pastry from the fridge section at the supermarket these days. I normally use Saxby's and prefer to roll it myself rather than buy those prerolled sheets that come like a Swiss-roll with a cellophane filling. Besides, it's fun to use the rolling pin and throw a little flour about every now and then.

I'm not sure if these really qualify as pies in the proper sense, though. I'd always thought a proper pie needed a pastry bottom too. I call these potpies. The other day at the super-market someone in front of me was buying a "Beef and Stout Top-Crust Pie," the same thing that I propose, I suppose. It's a stew in a pot with a pastry lid. I prefer this arrangement with, say, steak and kidney—easy to make and a welcome change (for Annie) from having a few dumplings floating around on top, and so much nicer than even the best steamed pudding. I'll save up my suet intake for the very occasional steamed pudding (with custard, natch).

The recipe for the filling I'm giving you here is open to wild interpretation. The base of it is quite a bit of chicken and a good velouté sauce. I've listed it with some nice winter vegetables. You could very easily drop the lot (except the onion) and substitute some chunks of ham instead or as well as. Or just add lots of leeks, at least one per person. Or go mad with the mushrooms. In the spring or autumn (summer isn't pie time) a plain chicken pie with an indecent amount of tarragon is fabulous . . . do you see what I'm getting at?

They do take an alarmingly long time to make though. The contents must be quite cold before the pastry goes on top. If not, then the butter in the pastry will melt long before it gets into the oven and the pastry will be soggy and will never rise. I often make the filling the day before, put it into the pie dish, and leave it, clingfilmed, in the fridge until the next day.

INGREDIENTS
SERVES FOUR TO SIX
- A good chicken, weighing 1.5 kg/3 lb
- Some stock vegetables for poaching the chicken
- One onion
- One leek
- Two sticks of celery, not the tough outer ones
- A small turnip
- 50 g/2 oz butter
- 50 g/2 oz plain flour
- A splash of double cream
- Squeeze of lemon
- 450 g packet of puff pastry, if frozen ensure it is defrosted
- A beaten egg for construction work and to glaze

Joint the chicken and poach it very gently with the stock veg in just enough water to cover everything. The breasts and wings will take twenty minutes, the legs at least forty. Remove the chicken and let it cool. Let the backbone and stock veg bubble gently for another hour or so. Remove the stock veg and discard them.

Prepare the vegetables as seems sensible: thin slices of onion, sections of leek, segments of turnip, little sticks of celery. These need poaching in the cooking liquid as appropriate. Drop them into the stock as follows: First the turnips, allowing ten minutes, then the leeks, allowing four or five minutes, then finally the onions and celery, just bring these back up to the boil. Remove all the vegetables to the ovenproof pie dish. Chuck away the backbone.

Strain the liquid into a measuring jug. You will need about one pint (600 ml). If you have more than that, put it back in the pan and boil it rapidly until you have about the right amount; if you have less, then just add some warm water to make up the volume.

In a separate pan melt the butter and stir in the flour. Once that has formed into a little ball, start adding the warm stock, just a little at a time. I like to use a small whisk for this; others get on fine with a wooden spoon. As the sauce grows you can be a little more generous with the amount of stock which you add each time. Once all the stock is in, you are well on your way to a beautiful velouté sauce; let this simmer *very* gently (barely a blip) for ten minutes or so to help cook out the rawness of the flour. Add enough cream to color the sauce to a virginal white (but not more than a generous splash) and a squeeze of lemon juice. Salt and pepper to taste. That is a proper velouté sauce.

Place the cooled skinned and boned chicken pieces in a four-pint (two-litre) ovenproof dish with the vegetables. Mix them up a bit. Pour over the warm velouté sauce. It should reach a level about a quarter of an inch (1.25 cm) below the rim of the dish. A little less isn't a problem but flush with top isn't good; if this is the case you may have to fish out a few bits and pieces. Leave it all to go quite cold before proceeding with the next bit.

Preheat the oven to 200°C/400°F/gas 6. Lightly flour your work surface and rolling pin. Roll out the pastry until it is a little bit larger than the pie dish. Cut a little strip off each edge about the width of your finger. Brush with beaten egg and glue it onto the rim of the pie dish. Brush the top of this gasket with more egg and lay the large piece of pastry over the pie dish. Press the edges down with your finger and thumb to seal it tightly shut. Cut a cross in the middle and bend the little triangles upward. You can use one of those little pie chimneys if you have one; personally, I think they look a bit stupid. Generously brush the whole of the top with what's left of the egg wash. Stick it in the middle of the oven for 30 to 40 minutes until the pastry is just the right shade of golden brown. When it's done, leave it for 5 to 10 minutes to cool off a bit before you eat it.

Serve it with boiled frozen peas and sliced carrots or something a bit fancier depending on the occasion.

REAL COQ AU VIN

Midweek supper is a favorite time of mine to see friends—just the four of us eating at the kitchen table. Upstairs, the children are fast asleep. These should be simple, relaxed, easy-going occasions. People don't come round just to eat (hopefully) good food—they want to talk, to smile, to gossip, and to laugh. I cook familiar things, like a carefully made cottage pie or some macaroni cheese, a green salad, and some fresh fruit afterwards. Simple and homely is all that is needed.

For weekend entertaining, I still keep it simple. To start with, a straight forward salad or vegetable dish. Perhaps a baked egg. Followed by something that can be taken out of the oven or straight off the hob. Pudding will be a cake or tartey type of thing that will already be sitting, out of sight, on a serving dish. Just grab some cream out of the fridge in passing.

I adore eating coq au vin. It is good food to be eating with friends. If people are coming round at eight, then (with a little effort the day before) I can start making it at six or seven and will have very little to do once everyone arrives.

There are many differing opinions over how authentically "cocky" the cock in coq au vin should be. If I was blessed with both a farmyard and an old rooster this is exactly what I would do with him once he'd retired. Good cockerels reach sexual maturity at about six months, after which they have about two years of happy "stud" work ahead of them before their virility trails off. Then it's time to look around for a replacement; that is the natural order of things, the young usurp the old. It happens to us all.

When his time comes, he should be cooked very slowly, in much red wine, for three, four, even five hours. The cock, of two or three years in age, is too old and tough to be palatable if you cook him in any other way.

More recently, coq au vin has become a poor excuse of a dish. Most recipes read like this: Fry some chicken pieces, bacon, sliced onions, and mushrooms, add a little flour to thicken the sauce, place it all into a casserole dish, cover with red wine, add a bay leaf and a stock cube, and pop it in a medium-hot oven for forty minutes. Done. Yuk.

I admit that I've cooked coq au vin, more or less like this, many times in the past. Over the last few years I started to experiment with thickening the sauce by pre-reducing the wine and using various other bits of "culinary-wizardry" to avoid that thickened-with-flour sauce. Like many, I used good free-range chicken and had never tried cooking it with a real cockerel.

Naturally, I felt duty-bound to try out this idea of using a real cockerel. I tried in vain to secure an old cockerel. I asked about the one that pecks around in the car park of my local pet shop. I made the mistake of mentioning the purpose. So, no luck there. It was nearly Christmas last year when I asked my butcher if he might possibly be able to get me a mature cockerel? "No problem, Tim." I wasn't particularly surprised; he'd previously got me various joints of mutton, goat legs, veal kidneys, boiling hens, and once a couple of suckling pigs. So, as expected, a good result!

I jointed up the chicken but was a little disappointed by the color of the dark meat. It didn't seem especially dark to me, and I was expecting it to be. I faffed about making a stock from the bits of carcass I wasn't using and then reduced and reduced it. I marinated the cock and cooked it, long and slow. It made an okay coq au vin—a bit shy on flavour and the meat was definitely overcooked.

Early in the New Year I was moaning to Gary, the butcher, about the pre-Christmas cockerel. It turned out that I had, quite inadvertently, purchased a large roasting chicken popular at Christmas time with those I-don't-do-turkey weirdos. In fairness to him, he did point out that I hadn't asked for an *old* cockerel. Whilst they *are* free-range they don't have the depth of flavor that can only come with age. It's just like the difference between lamb and mutton, veal and beef.

I phoned my friend Paul, the cheesemonger, to see whether he could get his hands on a proper old cockerel from France (he had previously imported *Poulet de Bresse* for me). We had a long conversation about the hows-and-whys of what I was after. He said he thought the flavor was more likely to be a result of the bird being properly free-ranging and a decent breed (no modern laboratory invented riffraff), than just its age. He doubted that he would be able to guarantee that it was a two-or three-year-old bird-but he would ask. We agreed that proper old-fashioned coq au vin is now, once again, the dish of the peasant farmer (and his lucky friends) who has the odd old unwanted cockerel shuffling about.

Crucially, I realized at this point that I was in danger of writing a recipe which hinged on an almost-impossible-to-obtain ingredient and that wouldn't be at all clever. So I resumed my previous years of on-off half-hearted improvement of how to do a really good supermarket chicken-au-vin.

I realized that the crux of the problem is this. For the sauce/gravy (whatever you prefer to call it) to be truly rich, it takes long, slow cooking. The average chicken is a young and tender bird that turns to string (as pleasant as a desiccated Christmas turkey) if cooked for any more than sixty minutes or so. The only solution is to enrich, reduce, and intensify the sauce before adding the bird. I try to marinate the jointed chicken for a day, two at the most. The wine/sauce then gets reduced separately before I start cooking the chicken.

I like to slip half a split pig's trotter into this stew—it adds immeasurably to the depth of flavor, even when it's got just one hour to work its magic. If you get a pig's trotter from the butcher, get him to split it for you. Do *not* try to do this at home—you may well lose a finger, possibly several. Most butchers will use their band saw. There is only one guy at my local butcher who uses his cleaver. I have to look away. I normally ask them to split two or three trotters at the same time. When I get home, I bag each half separately and freeze them.

They aren't the sort of thing you remember to put on your weekly shopping list!

Your choice of wine is incredibly important for this dish. You *must* start with a really robust wine. I prefer to use French wine; I've tried it with New World wine (the Aussie shiraz type of thing) and the sauce, like the wine, is big and powerful but lacks the subtle tones. Don't, for Heaven's sake go over-the-top though; Premier Cru would be money down the drain; much better to pour it down your throat. Simple, good, hearty, Burgundy will be brilliant. Look for something that is described as "full bodied."

Finally: cooking times are for a typical, good quality, supermarket bird. If you've got a real farmyard bird then I would expect it would need an extra hour, maybe even two full hours cooking to become tender. Similarly a horrid little factory bird will take less time.

INGREDIENTS
SERVES FOUR
- One good chicken, weighing up to 2 kg, or sufficient leg portions (please don't try it with just breasts)

FOR THE MARINADE
- One bottle of decent Burgundy
- Two outside ribs of celery
- Two medium carrots
- One medium onion
- Six garlic cloves, peeled and leaned on with the side of a knife
- Three or four bushy sprigs of thyme
- Two fresh bay leaves
- Six or seven black peppercorns

TO COOK WITH THE CHICKEN
- One pig's trotter, professionally split in two
- One dessert spoon red currant jelly
- 100 g piece pancetta, or in preference (but quite unlikely) plain salt pork from the belly. Whichever you use, cut it into 1.8 cm/¾ inch cubes (this is a bit bigger than normal).

- A good slug of brandy—a typically generous, drinking measure.
   I keep a bottle of the cheaper stuff just to cook with
- A little, very well-reduced chicken stock or ½ a chicken stock
   cube
- Two fresh bay leaves
- A very small amount of flour for dusting

FOR THE GARNISH
- Two dozen pickling-sized onions
- Two dozen button mushrooms
- A couple of pinches of sugar

This has to be started at least the day before you want to eat it. First, you must joint the chicken. Remove the legs and divide them into two. Remove the ankle joint from the drumstick (chicken scissors or a good sharp whack with a big knife). You must now decide whether you wish to leave the breast meat on the bone, or serve it as a boneless breast, or indeed with just the first wing joint on. I suggest you remove the breast from the carcass once it is cooked, serving it as a single piece-perhaps cutting it into two, if it is very large. I like to serve the two wings cut into their separate joints; don't waste your time doing anything with the wing-tips.

Having done all this, you can either save the carcass for later, freeze it, or, the best option of all, make some stock and avoid the ½ a stock cube in the cooking. In which case, add the pig's trotter to the stock before lifting it carefully out and adding it to the stew later.

Take all the marinade ingredients, roughly chop the onion, celery and carrots, and place them in a large bowl with the jointed chicken. Place in the fridge for at least twenty-four, but not more than forty-eight, hours—just to let the flavours mingle and the chicken take on the red of the wine. Move it all around once or twice to avoid any unsightly "tan-line" marks on the chicken.

The final cooking time in the pot is about an hour. The next bit will take about half an hour *if* you can do two things at once; otherwise leave an hour for it.

Remove the chicken from the marinade. Put all the remaining marinade ingredients into a non-reactive pan (enamel or stainless steel) and bring to the boil, skim any scum off the surface—there will certainly be plenty of it. Quickly turn the heat down to achieve a steady simmer and reduce the volume of the wine by half. Pour through a very fine sieve and set aside. Discard the spent marinade vegetables.

Heat an ovenproof casserole dish, a good-sized Le Creuset is ideal. Pour in just a drop of olive oil and fry the pancetta or salt-pork lardons and the split trotter (unless it's previously been in the stock) until the former are quite crisp, and the latter is nicely browned. Ensure the chicken joints are dry by blotting them with a little kitchen paper. Dust them in a little seasoned flour and pat them between your hands to remove any flour that isn't absolutely essential (too much flour will artificially thicken the sauce and you have gone to great lengths to reduce and enrich it without resorting to the crude use of flour). When the lardons are ready, remove them and keep them safe on one side. You may need to keep the trotter in the pot for a little longer until it is properly browned. If so, just start cooking the chicken around it. Now quickly seal the chicken in the bacon fat that's in the pot. If it needs a little extra oil, indulge it so. Try to avoid cooking the chicken through—*just* brown it. It will certainly need to be done in two, maybe even three, batches. When the chicken is suitably browned, remove it from the pot.

With the chicken, lardons, and trotter all done, tip away all the fat in the pan and put everything except the breasts and wings back in the pot. Pour over the brandy and ignite it. Probably best to take a step backwards about now. Once the flames have subsided, add the reduced, strained wine. Bring it up to a simmer. Skim the scum that inevitably rises—where *does* it all come from?

Add the stock or stock cube (if using a cube, make up with about half a cup of boiling water), the bay leaves, and peppercorns. It is now an hour away from being ready. Put the lid on and let it *barely* simmer for twenty minutes. Remember: long, *slow* cooking.

With thirty minutes cooking time left, add the chicken breasts and wings; watch it come back up to a simmer and, once again, skim any scummy bits.

At some point prepare the garnish. You can do it at the last minute or else sometime earlier in the day, reheating at the last moment. Peel the onions, a tedious job for sure, being careful not to cut the root from the bottom. The straggly bits of root need to be trimmed, but there is a cluster that holds the onion together: leave that intact or the onion will disintegrate. Some people suggest pouring boiling water over the onions for a minute or so to help loosen the skins. If the button mushrooms are a little too big, halve or quarter them. Little button mushrooms are best. Avoid large black-gilled mushrooms at all costs as they may turn your lovely deep-garnet-colored sauce an insipid grey. Any muck on the mushrooms should be cleaned off with kitchen paper; never, ever, wash mushrooms in water.

Melt a knob of butter and a drop of olive oil in a pan and fry the onions, adding a couple of pinches of sugar to help them caramelize. After ten minutes add the mushrooms and cook them together for a further ten or fifteen minutes until there is no further moisture to be forced from the mushrooms. If you've done this at the last minute (actually allow about twenty-thirty minutes cooking time)—great— just scatter them on top of the dish and stir them in. If they have been done in advance simply add them to the pot five minutes before the end. You will in any case need to take the lid off the pot to check for seasoning five minutes before you serve. Adjust the seasoning with salt, pepper, and maybe a squeeze of lemon as necessary.

Remove the gnarly looking trotter from the pot before serving. You can leave it to one side for lunch the next day: in which case, carefully pick all the cold and gelatinous bits off the bone, and then eat them with something—sharp-pickled onions, piccalilli, or English mustard. Or you can (oh, what a waste!) give it to a *very* lucky dog.

The different cooking times for the various pieces of chicken should ensure that the legs are meltingly tender and the breasts should be moist and not in the least bit stringy. The little wing bits will be so well done that they are perfect for sucking clean once you have emptied your plate.

I suggest unfashionably plain boiled potatoes or, maybe, some good stiff mash (not too much cream or butter).

However hard I've tried, I've been unable to get a good result with cooking and then reheating this dish. The chicken *always* ends up overcooked. The best you can achieve, when short of time, is get it all up to the stage of the final hour-long simmer. The chicken has marinated for twenty-four hours, everything is browned, and the wine reduced. Just let it all cool down and put everything together in the cooking pot (onions and mushrooms excepted—they were cooked and should be stored separately). Then put the whole thing in the fridge for another twenty-four hours before simmering it and finishing.

I had, at the time, hoped that this second period of steeping would have benefited the flavor in some way. Sadly, it had no noticeable effect.

VARIATIONS

Elizabeth David is the lone voice I have found who says poach the bird whole in red wine, only then joint or carve it, and simply pour the sauce over the top. I didn't really fancy the look of that.

Delia reckons you can make a pretty decent dish by using dry cider instead of the wine. And who'd question Delia?

You may have noticed the similarity of ingredients between coq au vin and boeuf Bourguignon. They are essentially the same sauce for either chicken or beef. To make the beefy version, forego the chicken and use a pound and a half (700 g) of stewing beef. I prefer a big slab of chuck to any other cut, and I always leave it in very large pieces; serving just two or three pieces per person. You can use beef stock, but chicken stock will do just fine.

ROAST CHICKEN WITH NUTMEG

This is my (slight) variation on a roast chicken recipe that I saw in the

River Café Easy book. As I was flicking through the pages in the queue at the bookshop, I became so excited by the simplicity of this dish that I bought a chicken on the way home and cooked it that very evening for supper.

The nutmeg gives the chicken a fabulous unexpected spiciness. It's best eaten when there's a sudden cold snap outside and your senses crave a little reminder of the festive season—far more satisfying than an imported sneak preview of summertime.

The only downside is that the nutmeg penetrates the chicken so thoroughly that it severely taints any subsequent stock. So, if I'm cooking this in winter, I'll use the stock for something like pumpkin risotto or soup and in the spring, it will go into a cabbage greens and bean soup—both of which would receive a little grating of nutmeg anyway.

I use either my home-made prosciutto or some streaky bacon. I like a lot of ham/bacon with this and I'm just too tight to go and buy half a dozen slices of Parma ham to cook with. In fact one of the great joys of curing my own prosciutto is that it ceases to be a rare treat and becomes something I can cook with both frequently and generously—just like having a plentiful supply of home-grown basil in the summer months.

N.B. Don't substitute either ordinary cured "British" style ham (the pink stuff), or pre-grated nutmeg.

INGREDIENTS
- One good chicken, weighing about 2–3 pounds
- A generous knob softened butter
- Half a whole nutmeg, freshly grated
- As much prosciutto or bacon as you can reasonably fit in the bird
- Half a glass dry white wine

Season the chicken inside with salt and pepper and some of the nutmeg. Rub the butter evenly all over the outside of the chicken, then season with salt, pepper, and the rest of the nutmeg—this will all stick in the butter. Shove the prosciutto/bacon inside the chicken's body cavity. Cook it in the oven (preheated to 200°C/400°F/gas 6) for about an hour, perhaps a little more. After half an hour add the wine. Baste it occasionally. When it looks very nearly done pull the ham/ bacon out of the chicken and leave it in the roasting tin to crisp up for five minutes in the oven. Let the chicken rest for at least ten minutes before carving.

I serve mine with just the juices in the pan and some crunchy roast potatoes (what else!)—normally we'll have something vegetal as a starter.

MOROCCAN TAGINE WITH PRESERVED LEMONS

Some years ago, I was an architecture student at the Architectural Association in Bedford Square, London. It was a fantastic place buzzing with the creative excitement and sheer stupidity that only young people (especially students) possess.

My first year was excellent with two brilliant tutors, Jonathan Sergison and Stephen Bates, and a memorable bus trip around Morocco.

We travelled from Tangiers, through Fez, over the Atlas Mountains, and back up to Marrakech before flying home from Casablanca. We bumped shoulders with donkeys that rattled with crates of Coca-Cola as we wandered around the ancient medina in Fez, took camel rides, and slept in Bedouin tents on the edge of the Sahara desert.

Should you want to go to Morocco, then I recommend doing it without the company of callow students. Or, at least, don't expect to eat remotely well when travelling with the budget-conscious. Everywhere we stopped the waiters would say "We have couscous, tagine, and brochettes." After the second day of this, the food was all utterly, depressingly, hopelessly, dire. The only exceptions were a fried chicken joint in Tangiers (although it was so filthy the floors where actually slippery with chicken grease; the tables and chairs too) and the evening food market in Marrakech. My friend Franz led a few of us to Marrakech's ancient market square just as dusk was falling. All the daytime market traders had cleared up and gone home. There were snake charmers and boys, some soon to be teenagers, selling mint tea from copper urns.

Row upon row of little food stalls had been set up. One man, typically, ran his own, perhaps with an assistant. They would stand there behind their barbecues, vats of hot fat for deep frying, simmering urns, or they'd simply fiddle with heaps upon heaps of salads, passing out good food to locals and tourists alike. All cost just a few pence. The layout of these little emporiums was always the same—the food would be prepared in the most basic of "kitchens" that were seldom more than a gas burner or barbecue and a chopping board with a large pot of water tucked somewhere underneath for the occasional unlikely washing of hands. Customers sat at trestle tables that surrounded the kitchen. Lighting came from little strings of bulbs, which in England would normally have been saved just for outdoor Christmas trees. There was no need to bother with washing plates or cutlery, because there were none. It was served on pieces of brown paper to customers who stepped over a bench to sit at the table. I ate some fabulous grilled goat and simple boiled mutton. I passed on the sheep's head—boiled, then cleaved wide open, right in front of you.

That stall seemed to have very few tourists dining on the delights of boiled brains, tongue, cheeks, and, I assume, eye balls. Mmmm.

The fish sellers were just as busy. The fish was either battered and fried, or simply grilled over more hot coals; either way, it was done right there in front of you once you had made your choice. From memory, I recognized none of the species—mainly small, vertically flat fish. The few that I had were bony, but good. I had eaten enough and had no room for the salad bars or "toothachingly" sweet desserts.

The simple beauty of this place was that each stall served just one sort of thing, and they did it brilliantly. Simple fried chicken was so good that men sat there sucking the bones clean—you won't see that down at KFC. You can wander from stall to stall, jostling for a seat at the busy stalls and ignoring the empty ones. Obviously, it's best to choose those patronized by locals over those full of tourists, the sheep's face stall aside (I must try and overcome these little squeamish prejudices). Regular customers, here as anywhere, will be the clearest sign of quality.

I ate a lot of tagine, sadly none measured up to this recipe. Preserved lemons are absolutely essential for this. You can make this dish with plain ordinary fresh lemons, but it will be more like a southern Italian stew, Sicilian maybe. The lemons can be found in most supermarkets along with the other exotic jars, tins, and packets. Obviously any ethnic foods market will have them. They are also rather easy to make, but beware, like the dried limes the fruits you buy fresh will be rather larger than the stuff that gets put in jars. So use half as many.

When the children are older I'll take the family to Morocco; I can hardly wait for them to grow up. I'll show them the wonderful sights, wander through the medinas, soak up the smells—and this time we'll eat properly.

INGREDIENTS
- Two onions
- A couple of cloves of garlic
- A scant teaspoon (that's a bit less than a level one) of ground ginger
- A pinch of saffron stamens
- Chicken joints for four people
- A few green olives
- A little chopped parsley
- A little chopped coriander
- Juice of half a fresh lemon
- Sliced peel of two preserved lemons

An unbelievably simple recipe all done in one pot: Very finely chop the onions, crush the garlic. Soften these in a little oil. Add the chicken joints and turn them to get a little color on the skin. Add the ginger and saffron and add just enough water to half cover the chicken pieces (assuming they are snug in the pan). Gently simmer the chicken with a lid on—leg pieces will take about an hour, breast half that. When the chicken is ready, add the rest of the ingredients and allow it all to heat through for a couple of minutes.

I think this is better served warm, rather than hot from the oven.

HAMINE EGGS

It's no coincidence that this recipe is right under the Moroccan chicken dish. They go very well together. Allow one egg per person. Also consider making the stew with lamb instead of chicken, in this instance.

It doesn't need a recipe. Simply place the eggs with a few onion skins (save them up for a couple of days) in a large pot and cover with water. Simmer on the lowest heat you can muster, the water should barely blip. Cook them for at least 5–6 hours, maybe even more. They taste quite different from any other eggs you will have eaten, the whites will have turned pleasantly creamy; maybe even a little beige and the yolks will have softened in color to a very pale yellow. The shells will become a remarkable shade of purple, somewhat like an aubergine.

I prefer to serve these cold and let people peel them themselves.

CHOCOLATE ALMOND CAKE

Baking is my number two culinary-ability blind spot. Sushi must rank number one, although I normally discount it on the grounds that, really, it's just precision-raw-fish-assembly, salmon origami if you like, and not proper cooking at all. I don't mind baking; I'm not bad at it; I just don't enjoy it very much. As a result, and without premeditated planning, I always seem to avoid getting round to it.

On the odd occasion when I do bake, it's invariably short-bread—one of my weaknesses. The other times I choose to bake are when I find a really interesting recipe. Like this one that uses only egg whites; it is therefore remarkably handy to have up one's sleeve for when you can't face any more meringues!

It is really just perfectly set chocolate and almonds, dense and delicious. Serve it as a pudding with some crème fraîche, to cut through its richness.

INGREDIENTS
- 225 g/8 oz dark chocolate (at least 70 percent cocoa solids)
- 225 g/8 oz ground almonds
- 225 g/8 oz caster sugar
- Six egg whites
- Butter and flour for dusting the baking tin

Finely grate the chocolate or chop it up in a food processor, if you have one. Mix in the almonds and sugar. Beat the egg whites until they form soft peaks. Fold the egg whites into the chocolate and almonds. Butter and flour a non-stick spring-rimmed cake tin. Bake in a preheated oven, at 150°C/300°F/gas 2, for up to an hour. The cake is ready when it has set in the middle.

Although the egg whites are vertiginously beaten, this is in no way similar to a meringue. The chocolate and almonds are too heavy to allow the cake much in the way of floaty lightness. In fact it's a bit stodgy but less cake-like than a brownie.

LEMON CURD

I've put this recipe into the spring section, simply because that's when I make lemon curd in my house. With its unseasonal ingredients, lemons being imported and available all year round, it could have gone anywhere. The fact is, I normally run out of home-made jams sometime shortly before Easter. In the couple of months that remain before the first of the new seasons fruits can be made into vibrant fresh compotes (I leave full-on jamming sessions until later in the year), this lemon curd fills the gap.

It is deliciously sharp and, as I'm not a marmalade man, it provides that longed-for citrus fruit "kick" in the mouth. I'm afraid I haven't a clue how well this lasts in the jar, as I've never managed to keep any for more than a few days.

INGREDIENTS
MAKES ABOUT A JAR FULL
- Grated rind and juice of two unwaxed lemons, of an average size
- One egg
- 40 g/1½ oz butter
- 50 g/2 oz caster sugar

To get the most possible juice out of a lemon before you cut it give it a good squeeze between your hands or briefly roll it around on a worktop whilst gently leaning on it.

Grate the lemon zest directly into a heatproof bowl. I use a large Pyrex one (some people will go to the trouble of rubbing the surface of the lemons with a sugar lump or two to catch all the essential oils). Squeeze the lemons through a nylon sieve to remove pips and any rogue fleshy bits. Add the juice to the zest. Break the egg into the heatproof bowl and beat it and the lemon together. In a separate bowl, cream the butter and sugar with a wooden spoon and add it to the lemony eggy mix (it will look a bit curdley and horrid at first, but persevere). Place the bowl over a saucepan of barely simmering water—ensuring it doesn't make contact with the water. Stir constantly until the mixture thickens to the consistency of good mayonnaise. Spoon it into a jar and once it has cooled a little, pop a lid on.

It's best kept in the fridge.

RHUBARB CRUMBLE AND CUSTARD

Rhubarb and custard was a favorite of mine as a wee nipper—right up there with The Clangers and Hong Kong Phooey. I am, obviously, referring to the cartoon, all wobbly edges, with a poor "put upon" dog named Rhubarb and a scheming cat called Custard. Oh come on, you must have seen it . . .

Frankly, I couldn't stand the stewed rhubarb that dad grew down by the compost heap and mum cooked. I don't think rhubarb is a very child friendly flavor—my children, who aren't fussy eaters by current standards (i.e. not their grandparents'!), won't touch it either. Now I'm fully grown up, I adore it. Sadly, I don't grow any rhubarb of my own but my father-in-law always has some in a corner of his orchard. I raid that on occasion. But here in February it is time for the forced rhubarb, from the dark sheds up north. Very welcome it is at this time of the year, too.

While plain cooked rhubarb and custard is good, rhubarb crumble and custard is, I think, better. Whether this crumble is better with custard or a big scoop of top notch vanilla ice cream is a moot point.

To simply cook some rhubarb, trim off the scruffy ends from about half a kilo of rhubarb. Then cut the sticks into two-inch (5 cm) long pieces and put them into a pan. I've found a Pyrex casserole to be ideal, but a non-reactive roasting tray with some tin foil over the top will do too. If you feel like it, squeeze over the juice of one orange. But you must sprinkle at least four tablespoons of sugar, or else when you first taste it your face will pucker up to look like a cat's backside with a squeeze of lemon on it. It will still be tart with that amount so you may like to add more. Put it into a preheated oven, set to 180°C/350°F/gas 4 and cook until quite soft. This may take twenty minutes or it may take an hour, it all depends. If you like your rhubarb to be still in identifiable chunks, check it after the first fifteen minutes. Serve it warm with hot or cold custard.

Making a crumble is just about the simplest thing you can do with a bag of flour in the kitchen. I don't normally bother with measuring the ingredients—it's that simple. A good quantity of plain flour, half that quantity again of caster sugar, and enough cold unsalted butter to make it all come together into that crumble. Use your fingers.

For 1 kg/2 lb of rhubarb, I'd use 175 g/6 oz flour, 75 g/3 oz
of caster sugar, and about 75 g/3 oz unsalted butter, with a good
pinch of salt, don't be shy about the salt with this. Simply sift the
flour, sugar, and salt into a roomy bowl, and then rub the cold
butter in until it forms a light crumbly texture. Chop the rhubarb
into 3.5 cm/1½ inch lengths, place them in the bottom of a buttered deep baking dish, sprinkle over about 75 g/3 oz caster sugar
(use a little less if you like it quite tart, more if you've an insatiable
sweet tooth). Now tip the crumble mixture on top of the rhubarb,
but don't press it down—I like the odd little hole here and there
for the pink juices to erupt through like a mini-Vesuvius. Cook
it in the middle of the oven, preheated to 190°C/375°F/gas 5 for
about half an hour.

Let it rest for a few minutes once it's done. I think it's much
better eaten warm than piping hot from the oven; leave it for as
much as half an hour after cooking. Crumble is a particularly
good way of using the later green-stemmed normal stuff from
the garden. I'll happily eat forced rhubarb once or twice a week
whilst it's available, so it gets crumbled, fooled, and baked before
the brief season for it is over.

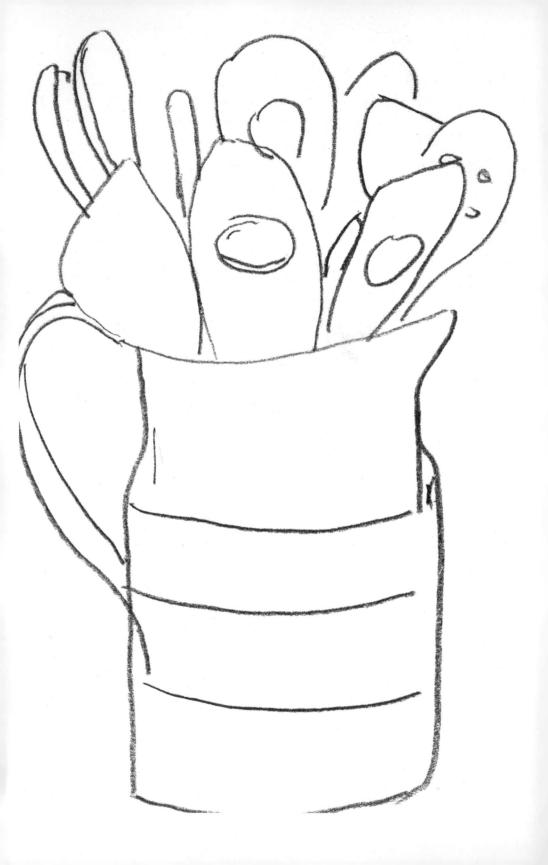

Chicken, Chorizo, and Chickpea Soup
Nettle Soup
Goat's Cheese and Crouton Omelet
Scrambled Eggs with Purple
Sprouting Broccoli and
Anchovies

MARCH

Easter Lamb Stew with Egg Sauce
Coq au Chardonnay
Roast Chicken Stuffed with a
Whole Lemon
Easy Chicken with Lemon
Thousand Year Eggs

March is a culinary no man's land. A foodie desert. Not much to be had. The seasonal cupboard is bare. Little wonder that the Church came up with the idea of Lent for this time of the year. In the years when eating local fresh food was the necessary norm and not a lifestyle choice (and there were a good few millennia of those years), there was no decent grub to be had in March. And so it came to pass that this lean time was deemed a timely reminder of just how bountiful the harvest of a few months hence truly is. There is something fundamentally right about this attitude to our food, even to a near atheist like me (I'm there strictly for weddings, funerals, christenings and Christmas carols). It is, I think, a shame that we are now able to graze on the same food at pretty much any time of the year we choose.

If what you desire is not growing here, then it will be somewhere else in the world. All you need do is pick it unripe, wrap it in plastic, and put it in a 747's cargo hold. When it gets here, unwrap it, put it into another plastic bag, suck the air out and fill the bag with inert gases (to help preserve the goods), then stack it high. I don't like eating this sort of unseasonal, air miles food however tempting it might be in March, and you will never be more tempted that you will be in March. I don't like the fact that many of the agricultural workers are living in abject poverty, I don't like the idea of flying food around the world, I don't like the idea of trucking it all over Europe, and I don't like the amount of road freight that it creates (something like 70 percent of all trucks on the road are food related). I know that if I eat French cheese, or Irish lobster, or Spanish chorizo, or Italian hams, or Jersey Royals or Scottish raspberries, or even a banana then I'm a hypocrite. But I console myself with the fact that these are occasional items, and they are among the very best of what's available. I see little comparison between that and the mountains of green vegetables that get flown in from sub-Saharan Africa every day of the year, just because some people fancy mange trout in December.

Some might argue that for our nation's health sake we should be grateful that they're cooking vegetables at all. I think we should think bigger than that.

Frozen ready meals, pizza from the chill cabinet, those year-round uninterrupted supplies of perfect green vegetables and salads—they all come at a price and, environmental and ethical concerns aside, that "price" is that they don't taste as good as the real thing. Cook something from a few raw ingredients for dinner; a shepherd's pie, a lasagna, a plate of pasta with a good meat sauce, make a pizza from real dough, top it with fresh tomatoes and good buffalo mozzarella, buy a whole lettuce from the supermarket, better still visit a farm shop or go to the market. Become fanatical about lettuce and grow a row of them in your garden. All these things are simple to cook, can be done after a busy working day, and taste fabulous. Some may work out cheaper, others will cost more; that is the price you pay for good quality ingredients.

Real food can't be beaten—it's as good as a meal can get. The fact that it's in short supply in March must a good thing. Abstinence makes the heart grow fonder.

MARCH'S DIARY

SUNDAY 2 MARCH

When working at my desk I heard the first cheap-cheap from inside an egg. WOW! First sign of piping—expect first arrival overnight.

MONDAY 3 MARCH

6.00 am.—Got up early. Nothing happened overnight.

9.15—Got back from dropping daughter at pre-school. One rather sticky dazed-and-confused little chick.

12.15—Got back from school run. Three more arrived in my absence.

3.15—Damn it. Missed the next five too.

11.00—Looked in just before bed-time. Almost all hatched by now.

TUESDAY 4 MARCH

Put all but the newest (wet and sticky) arrivals under "cosy-brooder" in new chicken shed. All seem happy, except two that seem to be unsure on their feet.

WEDNESDAY 5 MARCH

Phoned Keith for advice on lame chicks. Culled the two that couldn't stand up. Upon closer inspection another four had foot/leg deformities. Did them in too.

THURSDAY 6 MARCH

All re maining chicks doing well.

WEDNESDAY 12 MARCH

Chicks seem about half feathered now—lost their yellow chick cuteness—not yet little chickens. Quite unattractive actually. Different size and shape of breeds now very evident.

FRIDAY 14 MARCH

First 5 kilos of chick crumbs gone. Purchased another 5 kilos yesterday. After that it's onto growers' pellets and fresh green grass—all they can eat!

FRIDAY 21 MARCH

Have resolved to finish building nursery run/pen this weekend.

SATURDAY 22 MARCH

Usual boring chores most of the day, didn't find time for the run.

SUNDAY 23 MARCH

Beautiful spring day—took the children to the park, fed the ducks, ice creams all round. Am seriously considering getting some ducks —space allowing—when we move.

MONDAY 24 MARCH

Great weather— chicks should be out enjoying the sun— haven't got the coop built yet though.

TUESDAY 25 MARCH

Gave up on building the coop. Phoned a local chicken shed dealer. He delivered at 6.30 p.m. and put it together for me. It took 10 minutes. I will never again bother with building a coop.

WEDNESDAY 26 MARCH

Put the little chicks out in the new run for a few hours sunshine. Apprehensive at first but all finally left the house to catch some rays in the run. Big chickens and dog very interested in new arrivals. Left the door to the chicken shed open for some good-old-fashioned-airing. Turned my back for two moments and then found the children sitting in the (mercifully clean-ish) litter—throwing it at each other!

FRIDAY 28 MARCH

Unusually overcast, cold, damp morning. Didn't let the chicks out 'til midday. Noticing some distinctly cockerel-y behaviour from some of the chicks. The biggest Light Sussex (boys presumably) are now about the size of a quail.

Original "Five Hens" doing well. Daughter only eats white eggs—not brown; son doesn't care for eggs; give mum and dad most of Angelica's eggs (HUGE). Annie and I like Welsummer eggs best.

SATURDAY 29 MARCH

Chicks have now eaten 10 kg of Chick Crumbs. I weighed them all together (in a box) 5.5 kg. Not a bad "conversion rate," but commercially a disaster. At five weeks commercial breeds would be very nearly at market size and off for slaughter.

CHICKEN, CHORIZO, & CHICKPEA SOUP
(IT'S FROM BARCELONA)

For my second year as an architecture student I chose to be taught by a Spanish tutor. He lived at that time in Barcelona (probably still does) and commuted, via easy jet, every week to teach us! He was quite right about the cost of it—he paid less than one guy who got on the train at Manchester.

That spring term's field trip was, inevitably, to Barcelona to visit the modern reconstruction of the famous Mies van der Rohe pavilion. The building was, in the flesh, a total disappointment but the food was excellent. Carles Muro, the tutor, was, like many Spaniards, a keen lover of good food—he "insisted" on it. During the day, he would traipse us around Barcelona to visit the architectural sites of his choosing. We went up to the roof of a cathedral. As Carles said, "When it rains, as you say 'cats and dogs', up here, it is very beautiful." We visited Carles' mentor Enric Miralles in his gorgeous home just off the Ramblas. He opened some wine for us and chatted for a couple of hours—nice man. We chartered a minibus and took a day trip to the Igualada Cemetery that Miralles had built. (Sadly, since writing this I discovered that he died in 2000, at the age of just forty-four whilst in the middle of building the Scottish Parliament.)

It was on the way back from here that we had to stop for one of Carles' (by now famous) two-hour lunch breaks. First we had to find somewhere to eat. Not as easy as it sounds—Carles would jump out of the minibus and scamper into any number of these little remote village restaurants. Mostly he would get back on the bus shaking his head. Typically it would always take him several attempts to find one that would suit him and, by default, us. It was on this particular day that I first ate chorizo and chickpea soup.

I soon learnt to seek his advice over what to order. "What's good on the menu? Are there any specials? What is typically Catalan? What is that bloke over there eating—it looks good?" Sadly we got on better when talking about food than we did when discussing architecture.

He introduced me to a starter—I forget its name—but he translated it as "yesterday's vegetables." It was just that, yesterday's leftover vegetables—typically chards, cabbages, broad and green beans, with a little onion and garlic added and gently fried in olive oil. It was delicious—a kind of Catalan bubble and squeak. *Mel e miel* was another great find. Simply cheese and honey. Just very fresh plain curd cheese, only a day or two old (I suppose ricotta is the nearest you'd get outside Spain without making your own) with some runny honey served separately on the side. You'd pour this over the top, then dig in with a fork and maybe just a little bread. I also tried grilled spring onions. These are larger than the sort available in Britain, the size of little leeks. The Catalans have a special festival to celebrate them when they first come into season. (Odd that we don't honour asparagus the same way isn't it?)

That little restaurant on the way back from the cemetery served just three or four starters, this chorizo and chickpea soup, "yesterday's vegetables," and a plate of hams and salamis are all that I can remember. One big surprise was portion control. Starters were, by British standards, always huge and main courses quite small. In effect, it was always two courses of roughly equal sizes.

I had this soup, it is brilliant and utterly simple to make, although I make it thicker than the version I first had. I prefer it this way. There are two ways to thicken it. The easier way (and therefore more often used by me) is to mash a few of the chickpeas in the soup. The other, probably more authentic, way is to fry a slice or two of stale bread in olive oil until dark golden brown. At the same time have one or two whole cloves of garlic in the pan, both to flavour the oil and later mash into the soup—these also need to be browned. When you're happy that they cannot take on any more color without burning, remove everything to a pestle and mortar. Pound the bread and garlic to a thick paste, adding a little oil for lubrication if you need to. Add this paste to the soup instead of mashing some of the chickpeas to thicken it.

It's more of an effort, but the reward is greater. It depends on how long you've got. The soup I had, although it was clearly based on chicken stock, didn't have the shredded chicken that I've added here. If you have previously roasted a chicken, eaten every scrap of flesh off it, and only have the bare carcass left to make stock, don't worry, go ahead without it.

Getting the right sort of sausage is the key to this dish—if you haven't got chorizo, cook something else instead. There is no substitute. Chorizo is a dried Spanish sausage that is flavoured with pimento-roast and dried red peppers, which are then ground to a powder. The sausages often have little strings attached to the ends and are hung to dry by these, creating a perfect, simple, and distinctive U-shape. Pimento can also be brought in little jars or tins. Try to get the hot smoked one; it will likely say *Picante* (hot) on the side. It's also an essential ingredient in a Hungarian goulash.

I cure my own chorizo around November. I make some very narrow ones using chipolata casings (ready in about three weeks) and great big fat ones, using beef middles; they take three or four months to mature. Most places will sell the U-shaped sausages or big salamisized ones of two to three inches in diameter. If all you can find is the big-bore stuff you must get them to slice it very thickly for you. Little chunks are needed for this, not thin slices.

If you're fanatical about pulses and want to soak and cook your own, then do so. I find canned goods perfectly useable in something like this.

INGREDIENTS
MAKES ENOUGH FOR FOUR SMALL BOWLFULS
- The stock from two chicken carcasses or one carcass and an extra leg, neck or handful of wings
- One whole U-shaped chorizo sausage, cut into thick pieces
- A handful, maybe two, of little scrappy bits of chicken
- One large onion
- Two teaspoons of pimento, preferably picante
- Two cloves of garlic, crushed

- One tin of chickpeas
- Small bunch of parsley
- A slice of good white bread and extra garlic—optional

Finely slice the onion and sweat in a little olive oil. When they are nearly translucent, add the crushed garlic. Don't put the garlic in too soon or it will burn. Add the pimento and stir it well into the onions and garlic. Everything will magically become beautifully, deeply, colored—a rich earthen red. Add the chorizo to the mixture and, if you are using it, the chicken. Let this gently combine for a few minutes until you see the color of the chorizo change very slightly. Drain the tin of chickpeas and tip about a third of them into the pan. Using a potato masher or a large slotted spoon, set about crushing some of the chickpeas in the pan. Break the chickpeas up a bit to help thicken the soup. It will still have some big lumps and, from the later addition, whole chickpeas in the soup. If you're using the pounded bread to thicken the soup, don't mash anything (see my ramblings on the subject above). Add the rest of the chickpeas. Add the stock and let it simmer for about ten minutes.

Check the seasoning and, when you're happy that all is well, add some coarsely chopped parsley, stir and ladle into your chosen soup bowls. Add a splash of extra virgin olive oil for extra taste if you like it.

Serve with some fresh chewy crunchy crusty bread, a cold beer or a glass of good Spanish Rioja.

NETTLE SOUP

This soup is a paradox. It's dead trendy right now, which surely comes about through the influence of the black-suited urban media-types and yet they'd be unlikely to ever cook it for themselves. Where would you get the ingredients? I'd no sooner eat nettles gathered from the verge of the north circular than truss up a Trafalgar Square pigeon for the oven. And I've never seen nettles for sale—seriously, would you actually *buy* them? So the media set must be eating this soup in their favorite trendy restaurants.

Imagine the farmers' joy as they supply them to the kitchen doors: Selling their weeds!

I can tell you that the soup is delicious. At its best when the young nettles are about a foot tall in spring or very early summer. It's also unusual, obviously organic, and almost completely free. At its simplest it consists of just fresh young nettle tops and gently cooked onions, whizzed up in a blender with a little something to thicken it: a single cooked potato or a handful of cooked plain rice will do the trick. You can add some stock vegetables, a little diced carrot, celery and, garlic if you like. I don't have a blender—I get by with one of those little handheld whiz-sticks. They're great but have their limitations. I'm on my second one now—evidently they are not up to the rigours of making crab bisque.

The biggest problem that you are likely to encounter with this soup (if you're at all like me) is getting over the mental hurdle of taking a carrier bag and a pair of Marigolds or thick gardening gloves out for a walk to pick a nice bunch of weeds to cook for your supper.

When you are picking your nettles, try to find a patch that isn't next to a field in which the farmer may have been using pesticides or chemicals. I also avoid those closest to a footpath, especially where dogs walk! Pick only the top few leaves—they are the tenderest. And rest assured that the nettles completely lose their sting when cooked. My mother suggested: "Grow your own nettles, Tim—they are also good ecologically for butterflies, habitat, etc." There, I passed it on.

INGREDIENTS
- A little knob of butter
- One big onion, finely sliced
- A carrot, two sticks of celery (both diced), a chopped clove of garlic (optional)
- Enough nettle tops to fill your soup pot
- 1–1.5 litres/two or three pints of pale, light chicken stock (or use a good cube)

- A cooked peeled potato or a handful of cooked plain boiled rice
- A little slug of cream

GARNISH (ALSO OPTIONAL)
- A little more double cream
- A few chopped fresh chives

Melt the butter in a big pot and add the sliced onion (also the carrot, celery, and garlic, if using). Cook it gently until translucent—don't let anything brown. Meanwhile give the nettle tops a really good wash, removing any thick stalks—you'll need to don the Marigolds again. Add the nettles to the pot and immediately add about a half to two thirds of the stock. Avoid using a dark brown stock—the soup would end up the unhappy color of mud rather than vibrant green. The nettles will wither as the stock heats up. You must now make a judgement call about how much more, if any, needs to be added. It is always better to have too thick a soup, which can be thinned down later, than to add too much liquid initially—too much will ruin a good soup every time. Bring it quickly to the boil and once bubbling, cook it for only a minute or two more. Liquefy the soup, along with the cooked diced potato or the rice. Once completely blended, return to the heat (through a sieve if you think it's needed) and add a little cream, salt, and pepper. Taste for seasoning. Warm the soup through but don't let it boil. If it's a little too thick add some more stock. If it's too thin—well, you'll know better next time.

Ladle it into soup bowls and, maybe, garnish with a little swirl of cream and chopped chives (don't ever garnish anything with whole chives, they may look pretty but are a real pain to eat).

Serve immediately to intrigued guests.

PS. I discovered, quite by accident, that this soup is also lovely cold (sheer piggyness between fridge and pan one day with some leftovers). Bring it out of the fridge about half an hour before you want to serve it. That is sufficient to take the worst of the fridge chill off it but to keep it wonderfully cool. Stir it well, serve, and garnish it in exactly the same way.

VARIATIONS Use sorrel leaves or young tender spinach leaves instead of nettles. As an alternative to a thickened blended soup try blending the soup without any potato or rice. Add plenty of cooked Arborio or Calasparra rice to make something like a very sloppy risotto, something with the texture of a Risi e Bisi, to which a little blob of homemade minty-pesto would be a nice addition.

GOAT'S CHEESE & CROUTON OMELET

Cheese omelets were the first thing that my mother taught me how to cook and it will probably be the first thing that I teach to my children. However, and despite my earliest efforts in the kitchen, I'm not a fan of the plain cheese omelets; gooey eggs with gooey melted filling does not make my day. This version, however, is one of my absolute favorites.

This is my variation—an update if you like—on an old, rather heavy, classic recipe. The goat's cheese really lightens the taste, adding that slight sharp tang of goatiness that cuts through the heavy cholesterol fattiness of the eggs. The croutons are essential for some textural bite and that satisfying crunch you can actually hear from inside your mouth. I always use a fairly mild, almost bland, goat's cheese. If you use too strong a cheese, the effect is completely overpowering, quite unpleasant in fact.

INGREDIENTS FOR ONE
- 2 large eggs
- A thin slice from a goat's cheese log, not too much
- A thick slice of good white bread
- 8–10 chives
- Butter

Start by getting an omelet pan really quite hot and quickly melt a largish knob of butter in it. Remove the crusts from the bread and cut it into croutons. I tend to use up white bread in the cupboard that is past its freshest and suits the job, ("plastic" sliced white doesn't really do it) but try some baguette, Italian sourdough, ciabatta, whatever else you have. Fry the bread until you have golden crunchy croutons. Crack the eggs into a cup and lightly fork them, then add a little seasoning. Remove the croutons and put them on a piece of kitchen paper so that any excess fat can drain off quite happily. Wipe the pan, add a little fresh butter, and pour in the eggs. Because the pan is quite hot from the croutons the egg will cook extra quickly, so deftly move the eggs around in the pan until they're close to being set. Avoid scrambling them. Scatter the croutons and crumble the goat's cheese over the top and sprinkle with the chives.

Fold directly onto a plate, serving it immediately.

SCRAMBLED EGGS WITH PURPLE SPROUTING BROCCOLI & ANCHOVIES

Purple sprouting broccoli is, without doubt, the best of the spring vegetables that you'll get in the shops, at the market, or are able to grow in your garden. Since there will be a few more hens laying by now, I'll be looking at more eggs than I know what to do with. It was, therefore, kind of inevitable that the two got together one day. The anchovies add that little extra which moves this into the realm of proper "grown up" food, rather than posh nursery fodder.

The PSB only needs to be steamed for about 5 minutes. At that point I check it for doneness by sticking the tip of a knife into the thickest bit. It should go in easily but may require a bit of a shove. If not, leave it just a little longer. As always, try this out first on a raw piece so you have something with which to compare the cooked piece. (You could always just hoik out a piece and eat it!) Once the little florets at the top start falling off, the vegetable is ruined. Boiling seems to bring this about sooner. Some people swear by their microwave for cooking vegetables. I swear at them, and haven't owned one for nearly ten years now.

On the telly, I recently saw the fishy chef Rick Stein saying that he likes to chat about scrambled eggs with young chefs who want a job working for him. I'm not currently after a job there but, should you get into conversation with the Codfather of Cornwall, here is my top ten of helpful tips.

- Use the best eggs you can get hold of. Ingredients matter.
- Never cook more than two eggs per person, whether it's for scrambled eggs or an omelet. You wouldn't really want to eat three boiled eggs or three fried eggs, so why scramble that many?
- Always use a non-stick pan. Cleaning the remnants of scrambled eggs from a normal pan is a Sisyphean task.
- Put a knob of butter and a splash of milk or cream into the pan first, and then break the eggs directly into the pan. Don't bother whisking everything together in a little bowl first. This way saves on unnecessary washing up.
- Only add the necessary pinch of salt (you should know that Rick does not favour Maldon) and grind of black pepper once the eggs are broken up a bit. If you add seasoning to the whole eggs, then as you start to scramble them the seasoning tends to remain in clumps. If you add salt to beaten eggs and leave them to stand for a while, it makes the yolks go runny and thin.
- Use a wooden spoon or a plastic spatula—not a whisk, or indeed anything else. These eggs are best served when they have some visible curds and aren't simply pureed set eggs— as many people mistakenly think are best.
- Stir the eggs regularly, but not constantly.
- As the eggs start to come to your chosen consistency, remove the pan from the heat and continue to stir. The heat within the eggs will continue the cooking away from the heat. Better to pop them back on the heat for a moment more than to cook them to a horrible solid lump.
- Find out how people like their eggs before you start cooking them. I personally prefer mine loose, almost as a runny sauce. My wife insists hers are cooked through, nearly solid.
- Always serve them immediately. Scrambled eggs will not wait around.

For this dish, I normally make up some toast to serve it on. That way it's more of a midweek supper. Alternatively, forfeit the toast and serve it as a starter. For supper allow 200–225 g (7–8 oz) of PSB per person, as a starter about 100–150 g (4–5 oz) of PSB is plenty.

INGREDIENTS, PER PERSON
- Purple sprouting broccoli—see above for quantities
- Two eggs
- Two or three anchovies (optional)
- A slice of toast, but maybe not

Start by cooking the PSB. I suggest you steam it for five minutes or so, but boil or microwave it (urgh) if you prefer. As that's happening, make some toast.

Warm a suitable non-stick pan. Once the PSB is done, and not before, scramble some eggs (see above). If you like anchovies, stir one or two (per person) finely chopped ones into the eggs just before serving.

Since I like my eggs runny, I put the PSB on the toast and then pour the eggs over the top. Since Annie likes her eggs firmer, I put them on the toast and pile the PSB on top. Either way is delicious.

EASTER LAMB STEW WITH EGG SAUCE

This sauce for this stew isn't a million miles away from an Italian carbonara sauce. I like to serve it with plenty of fresh parsley and generous squeezings of lemon juice, *a la Avgolemono*. It is at its absolute best when made with very young lamb—around Easter time, and for a couple of months after that. Later in the year there are many better things to do with the more mature lamb you will be buying. In deference to its Italian origins I often serve this, as they might, without an accompanying carbohydrate on the plate. That would have come in a previous course; a simple risotto, some pasta, maybe a small bowl of simply dressed ravioli, or some pesto-coated gnocchi. Eat that followed by a perfect green salad or some simple, plainly dressed vegetables. Then, when you serve this, be sure to have a little crusty bread on the table to dip in the sauce and eventually use to wipe your plate clean. If you want to be altogether more British about this, then nothing more adventurous than plain (stiff-ish) mash or a jacket potato with a knob of good butter in it will do nicely.

When buying the meat, I suggest you ask the butcher for some leg of lamb. If you use shoulder, it will be good—but perhaps a bit too fatty for this delicate sauce. Pieces of fillet may be too dry. Either way, I have found that it's worth asking for a lamb's tail or two to add to the pot (your butcher will most likely just give them to you). You'll need to trim most of the fat off before you use it but the flavour it will impart on the stew is glorious. But don't throw it out before serving—it's well worth nibbling on after you've finished everything else. You will find a surprisingly large amount of delicious meat on a lamb's tail.

Try to buy the meat on the bone or at least in one large piece. It is always best to dice it yourself when you get home. Carefully cutting the meat along its natural muscular seams is far preferable to a butcher's quick knife. I've also found that I prefer cubes of meat in my stew that need cutting with a knife into two or three once on my plate. I think the meat tastes better when cooked in larger pieces and it prevents any chance of that lazy-fork-only eating style so beloved of the Americans.

INGREDIENTS
MAKES ENOUGH FOR TWO
FOR THE STEW
- About 450 g/1 lb (boneless weight) of leg of young lamb, diced into two-inch (5 cm) cubes
- The leg or shoulder bone it came on, preferably a tail or two as well
- One smallish onion, very finely chopped
- One clove of garlic, very finely chopped

- A glass dry white wine
- A bay leaf

FOR THE SAUCE
- Two egg yolks
- Juice of one whole juicy lemon
  A good handful medium-chopped flat-leaf parsley

You will need a good heavy-bottomed casserole dish with a lid that can go straight on a hob. A Le Creuset pan is ideal. Simply place all the stew ingredients in the pan, all together. Add a twist of black pepper and generous pinch of salt. Bring it all slowly up to the heat and cook it on the hob at a very gentle heat, barely a simmer, for about 1½ to 2 hours, give or take a bit. As always, skim the horrid foamy bits off the top.

You emphatically do not want to brown the meat, although after two hours it will naturally have turned a little brown. The onions and the garlic will completely melt into the sauce; they will all but disappear. The majority of the cooking liquid needed will come from the lamb and onions themselves. But do, please, keep checking on the stew and stirring it as it cooks. You may need to add a little water if it starts to dry out. Conversely if it is too wet when the meat is ready, then remove the meat with a slotted spoon and turn the heat up high, reducing the liquid rapidly to the desired few tablespoonfuls. Return the meat to the pan before proceeding with the sauce. If there is a lot of fat in the pan, tip the pan up to an angle and carefully spoon most of it off the top.

When the stew is ready remove it from the heat. It's important that the pan isn't too hot, if it's a big cast-iron one and has just come off a hard-boil, it will quickly scramble the eggs. Separate the egg yolks from the whites and beat the yolks gently with a fork. We don't need the whites for this dish. Squeeze the juice from the lemon and combine with the yolks. Tip this into the stew and stir to combine everything together. Given only the heat in the pan and of the meat itself, the yolks will thicken slightly.

You will have a delicious eggy-lemony sauce that will completely coat the lamb—the sauce should thicken to about the consistency of double cream. Dip a finger in to taste and add salt and pepper or even more lemon juice as you see fit. Either sprinkle the parsley over the top or mix it into the sauce—your call. Eat without delay.

COQ AU CHARDONNAY

My anchovy-intolerant friend, who recently emigrated to Australia, inspired this dish. When asked what she would like to drink, she would say "any white wine—anything except chardonnay." Now it seems the Australians have a name for her; she is an ABC drinker—Anything But Chardonnay. If this ABC prejudice takes off over here—and apparently it's pretty big in Oz right now—we'll need some recipes to drain the wine lake which nobody will want to drink anymore.

This recipe is surprisingly different to coq au vin, although it started from the same point. I started by using white wine instead of red and just kept dropping ingredients until I was left with chicken stewed in white wine with some onions and mushrooms. The cream saves it from being a chicken chasseur that has lost its tomatoes.

It's a good spring time recipe for when it's still dark when you get home from work and you crave something comforting but haven't the time to make up a big rib-sticking stew. Also, the almost complete absence of fresh vegetables in it makes you less miserably aware that little is growing apart from cabbages and purple sprouting broccoli (cultivated mushrooms, I'm told, are kept in the dark . . . etc, and so are one truly unseasonable vegetable-slash-fungus).

INGREDIENTS
SERVES FOUR
- Four good chicken joints—preferably whole legs
- A little plain flour for dusting
- One large onion
- Three average sized cloves of garlic

- 200 g/7 oz button mushrooms
- Most of a bottle of chardonnay (it doesn't have to be Australian)
- One bay leaf
- 150 ml/¼ pint double cream or a little cold butter or beurre
  manie to thicken the sauce with
- A little fresh chopped parsley, an optional garnish

Put a casserole-type dish (I use my smaller Le Creuset for this) on the heat, and let it get properly hot. Take about a heaped tablespoon (or just grab a handful) of plain flour, put it on a plate, and season it generously with salt and a little pepper. Roll the chicken joints, one at a time, in the flour and remove any excess by jostling the chicken from one hand to another (envisage the world's least-entertaining juggler). Add a little cooking oil and a big knob of butter to the pan and, once sizzling, fry the chicken pieces until just the right shade of golden brown. Remove them with a slotted spoon to a waiting plate, leaving the fats behind in the pan.

Whilst that is cooking, finely chop the onion and the garlic. Put the onions in the pan and gently fry them, without coloring, until they become translucent. Add the chopped garlic, and mushrooms; let these both, slowly, lose their rawness—but don't expect the mushrooms to go properly brown. Try not to rush all of this; it needs to be done slowly so that the flavours concentrate, mingle, and develop. When you are happy that all those ingredients are getting along nicely with each other, reintroduce the chicken pieces and add the wine. Turn the heat up to maximum, bring it to the boil, hold it there for a few moments, and then turn it down to a gentle simmer. Add the bay leaf and maybe a little more seasoning. Let it cook, lightly bubbling, with the lid on—but gapingly ajar—for about twenty to twenty-five minutes for breast pieces, perhaps as much as double that for good leg meat. After that cooking time, the wine should have reduced but without being at all syrupy. If it starts to look too dry, add a little splash of water.

The sauce will now need to be thickened a little. This is much easier to do if you take the chicken out of the pot for a few moments. Use a slotted spoon and keep the chicken warm, on a plate, under a piece of tin foil. It will be fine there for a few minutes. It won't get cold. I thicken the sauce with cream, cold butter, or beurre manie depending on my mood. Choose either method 1, 2 or 3 from below.

If you want to use cream, this is technically the easiest to pull off. Simply add about 150 ml (¼ pint) of double cream to the sauce, stir it in, and turn the heat up a little to let it reduce a bit. Put the chicken back into the pot, turn the chicken pieces in the sauce to ensure they are nicely coated, taste for seasoning, and serve.

If you fancy the richest possible sauce, it has to be butter. Take a block of butter out of the fridge—it has to be cold—cut a bit less than half of it (approx 100 g/4 oz) into little cubes and whisk them quickly into the sauce; you may not need them all. The sauce will magically thicken before your very eyes. Abracadabra. Check for seasoning, adjusting as necessary. Don't, whatever you do, let the sauce boil as it will split and become like runny butterscotch. Because this sauce is a little temperamental, I put the chicken straight onto plates and pour the sauce quickly over the top. Then serve immediately.

The most calorifically frugal way to thicken this sauce is with a little dob of beurre manié. This is far simpler than it sounds. Take about a teaspoon of plain flour and, in a little bowl, rub it and a large knob of butter together, using your fingertips. The butter must be at room temperature and quite soft, otherwise you'll be well on the way to making crumble. Keep rubbing until they have formed a thick paste. Just drop this doughy blob into the sauce, then whisk like billyo. If you added plain flour straight into the pan, it would form horrible lumps but, by combining it with butter, you will have a smooth thick sauce. The flour in the sauce needs to cook for a few moments to fully thicken up and lose the rawness of the flour. Taste the sauce and add a little salt or pepper as needed. Put the chicken pieces back in the pot to coat them with the sauce. Then put them onto plates or a serving dish.

Don't forget to sprinkle on a little coarsely chopped parsley to garnish, should you want to. Please don't ever add a whole sprig or, even worse, a little bunch as garnish to your food. This is a stupid restaurant affectation. As such it has no place in your homely kitchen.

I like this with potatoes: baked, mashed, or sautéed, and a plain green bitter endive salad on a side plate. And what else to drink but a glass of cold, crisp, cheeky, buttery, oakey, smokey, *"mmmm, yes, it smells like Sandi Toksvig running through nettles in a shell suit on a dewy spring morning"*—Australian chardonnay!

ROAST CHICKEN STUFFED WITH A WHOLE LEMON

I first tried out this recipe after reading it in one of Marcella Hazan's excellent books. Sometime later I spotted it in the *River Cafe Easy* book. This can't really be called plagiarism since it is a well-known Italian recipe. I mean; you couldn't accuse Gary of nicking Delia's idea of steak and kidney cooked together in a pie, could you?

There are slight differences in the recipe given. Marcella manages to shove two lemons into a slightly larger chicken. I suppose it also depends on the size of the lemons. Have a little peer inside your chicken and see if one or two will fit. Maybe even try some out for size. It won't matter if you don't end up using the second one, as long as you don't put it back in the fruit bowl— give it a good rinse and keep it for cooking in something else (make sure you don't pierce it first!). Rose and Ruth add a few sprigs of thyme—that's gilding the lily a bit, I think.

Whatever, it is a fabulously good way to cook a little chicken. Simple and delicious. And if the recipe isn't already in your repertoire, believe me you should have it.

INGREDIENTS
SERVES FOUR
- One smallish chicken, about 1.3–1.4 kg
- One unwaxed lemon, about the right size to fit snugly in the chicken's cavity

Wash the bird inside and out. If there are any of those globules of fat inside its bum flaps, pull them out and bin them (or make some schmaltz, q.v.). Season generously with salt and pepper inside and out.

Give the lemon a good squeeze, either in your hands—or roll it on a worktop whilst leaning on it. Prick the lemon all over with a skewer or carving fork—don't use a knife. Push the whole lemon inside the bird and seal the opening with a couple of wooden cocktail sticks. That is the important thing. The lemon must be sealed inside otherwise you're just cooking an ordinary roast chicken.

Marcella, Rose, and Ruth all say this chicken does not need any oil or butter: "The juices of the lemon are sufficient to stop it from sticking." Errm, nope, not in my kitchen. I've found I have to rub a little butter or olive oil (albeit a fraction of what I'd normally use) all over the bird. I place the chicken on a shallow tray, breast side down to start with, and roast the chicken towards the top of the oven, preheated to 200°C/400°F/gas 6. Turn the chicken over after about twenty to twenty-five minutes. It will take about the same time again to be fully cooked. Serve with the juices.

If you want some roast potatoes, these will need to be done in a separate dish.

EASY CHICKEN WITH LEMON

This is brilliant. An easy option, a concept really (not that I'm suggesting it's concept food), for making a quick dinner in about thirty or forty minutes. No fuss, very little trouble.

It is absurdly simple: Jointed chicken pieces, a lemon, some olive oil, and a few herbs. Place all those things together in a roasting tin and then put it in the oven 'till it's done. Good, tasty chicken just does not get easier than this.

INGREDIENTS
- A whole chicken jointed into eight pieces or sufficient pieces to feed four
- One lemon
- Olive oil
- A handful of herbs of your choice, see note below

Take the chicken pieces and place them in a roasting tray. Cut a lemon in half and squeeze the juice all over the chicken. Add the exhausted lemon halves to the pan. Dribble a little olive oil over the whole lot—just enough to coat everything. Add some seasoning. Rub everything together to make sure all the flavorings are evenly distributed. Place in the preheated oven, at 200°C/400°F/gas 6, and roast for twenty-five minutes. Remove and add the herbs. Return to the oven for a further ten minutes.

The chicken is ready when it is well browned and the sauce (such as it is) is a sticky, unctuous mess underneath the chicken—add a splash of water if it's too dry. Use a skewer to check the legs are done if you are at all nervous or unsure.

HERBS

The above recipe is perfect for summer's delicately leaved herbs such as basil or tarragon. The more wintry herbs such as sage, thyme, and rosemary can all be added at the beginning. Use basil, tarragon, or thyme separately. Use sage and rosemary either alone or combine the two together. Fresh bay is a good lonesome choice too. If you don't have any fresh herbs, don't use dried. Sparingly add a few fennel seeds and flaked dried chillies. For a south side of the Med feel, try a little ground cinnamon and a teaspoon of honey at the end.

The astute amongst you may have noticed the similarity of ingredients between this recipe and the Summer Herby Roast Chicken. It's no coincidence. This is *even easier* to cook since the separate joints lead to a reduced cooking time and obviate the need for any carving. I know that some people have a fear, bordering on phobia, of carving. So, that's another problem solved.

THOUSAND YEAR EGGS

These aren't to be confused with the Chinese Hundred Year Old Eggs. They are boiled then buried in the ground until they putrefy. Apparently, quite a delicacy … Sounds nearly as bad as that other Asian taste sensation (oh, what's the bloody name of it?) where they boil up eggs that are partly incubated. Knock the top off and you have a two-week-old embryonic chick inside. Remember—they hatch at three. I saw it on telly once—some bloke was extolling the delicious mix of soupy fluid and delicate crunch. No, I don't think I'd eat it either.

This recipe is for a children's Easter treat. Simply hard boil some eggs; place them in cold water, bring to a rolling boil, and keep them there for five minutes. Take them out and let them cool naturally.

Now the fun starts. Traditionally strong tea was used to add some coloring to the eggs. Now we have food dyes in many different colors, so I say use them! The more numerous the colors the better (individually, of course, don't mix them all together) and the more garish the better; greens, oranges, pinks, and definitely blue. There is something very surreal about eating blue food—it always reminds me of chef's plasters.

Mix up some dyes with water. I generally use some cups or little plastic bowls. The mix wants to be quite strong. Roll the hard-boiled eggs around on a clean work surface causing the shells to crack all over. Place the eggs in the dye for a minute or two. Rinse briefly under cold running water and peel off the broken shells. The dyes will have seeped through the cracks giving the egg a sort of crazy paving effect. The eggs now look at least a thousand years old, maybe more. Perhaps try it with just one egg before committing yourself to a whole batch.

Baked Eggs with Tarragon
Oven Baked Sticky Wings
Wild Garlic Omelet
Duck Breast and Chicken Liver
Ragu with Peas

APRIL

Poached Chicken Breasts with Morels
Sautéed Legs with Lentils and Bacon
Salami or Pancetta Carbonara
Toad in the Hole
Boozey Prunes and Custard

pril's great. I adore it. The clocks have gone forward—so it's still light in the early evening. The fields have lost their winter brown and are a vibrant uniform green (albeit as short as a Marine Corps hairdo—so no possibility of seeing a fleeting, windy shimmer). Also it'll be the first time in the year to sit outside, in the garden, with a cup of tea. City dwellers once again get the short straw and have to settle for drinking their grande-skinny-lattes on pavement tables.

The month kicks off with a few trees starting to bud and the early fruit trees in my father-in-law's orchard will begin to blossom (the plum we call Early Rivers is reliably the first). By the middle of the month, most of the daffodils need dead-heading. By the end of it, they'll all be gone. However their departure is compensated with the sight of the native hedgerows beginning to turn green with leaf and white with blossom. I found a recipe for hawthorn-bud pudding a couple of years ago, but haven't got round to it. The nettle soup remains a must-try of the season.

April is a strange month for food. By the end of it you could almost think it was summer. The range of vegetables has opened up, but just as they're starting to arrive (and I expect it's entirely to do with the certain knowledge of the impending loss) I have a sudden flurry of interest in cooking those big hearty winter dishes, especially, and for whatever reason, the ones I didn't get round to cooking over the previous few months. A colder day is all the excuse I need to make oxtail stews; maybe sweetened with prunes, or in the Spanish way, with chunks of chorizo sausage, and beef daubes. Spread a little Dijon mustard onto crusty rounds of baguette that have simmered for the last few minutes on the top of the stew and soaked up whatever fat rose to the surface. Steak and kidney, toad in the hole, and coq au vin, they have all been round for dinner this April. I miss them over the summer months, but then there is so much more to look forward to.

Cambridge is blessed with a grower of asparagus who does it under glass so it can be had locally quite early. I know it's a little sinful to grow *and water* such crops artificially—but then consider the waste involved in this little escapade: Last November I saw a sign under some purple asparagus that read "NEW SEASON'S" in a supermarket. It was fresh off the plane from New Zealand! Now, *that* I do consider to be very wasteful—bordering even on the obscene. So, with only a little guilt, I tuck into my first of many plates of asparagus at the start of April. The normal outdoor stuff can be had from about the third week, depending on the weather, although it is with some sadness that, by then, I will have eaten the last of the purple sprouting broccoli. The first of the summery salads will be on my plate—sure it will be the tiny immature thinnings from mum's raised beds rather that the real grown up thing. But I'm not complaining . . .

The little chicks are having a fabulous time in the better weather. They've been getting out and about, enjoying the fresh grass. A couple of the Light Sussex (the biggest breed I hatched) have been growing tremendously. Inevitably the subject of whether to eat them or not has surfaced. A pair of them would make a magnificent brace of little spring chickens (perfect poussin-sized). Annie awarded them a reprieve by pointing out that it would be pretty daft to eat a whole one each of this size when, if we waited a couple of months, one good sized cockerel could feed four or five people easily. It seemed like a sound argument to me. Only later did I realize that she'd already named them! And, I suppose a bit like a pet rabbit, we can never bring ourselves to eat chickens that we have named.

APRIL'S DIARY

TUESDAY 1 APRIL
Recent sunny weather has ended abruptly. Kept the chicks in their shed all day. Absolutely foul—wind, rain, no sun at all.

MONDAY 7 APRIL
Blimey! The Light Sussex chicks are now fully twice the size of the Marsh Daisy chicks.

THURSDAY 10 APRIL
Angelica laid a freakishly small egg today—about half the size of a normal egg. Will cook it at the weekend—ideal toddler size egg?

SUNDAY 13 APRIL
Bacon and eggs for family breakfast. Very disappointed to discover that Angelica's tiny egg was, in fact, only white, no yolk at all. Spent the day imagining the vast fortunes to be made in California if she continues this freakish behavior.

THURSDAY 17 APRIL
Weather excellent 27°C. Chickens basking in it, digging inappropriately placed dust-baths for themselves.

FRIDAY 18 APRIL
Put the little chicks into the big (new & empty) hen house after dusk last night. Let them out after breakfast. Although they haven't roamed far—they are clearly enjoying their liberty.

BAKED EGGS WITH TARRAGON

These baked eggs must be, just about, the most unfashionable thing in this book. I can't recall when I last saw some on a restaurant menu or glimpsed some ego-chef on the telly cracking an egg into a ramekin, garnishing it, and slipping it into the oven. They're due for a revival, not because food fashion (like flares) is cyclical— but because they taste so good.

The interesting thing is what you add to them. There are two or three different variations scattered throughout this book, according to the seasonality of the additions. The first and simplest is a classic and couldn't be easier. I normally serve one egg per person as a starter but it's up to you. I suppose it depends on what you're cooking for the main course and on how hungry your friends are. If you want to serve two, you would be better off using gratin dishes rather than ramekins.

INGREDIENTS
SERVES FOUR (SEE NOTE ABOVE ON PORTION CONTROL)
- Four eggs
- 5 tablespoons double cream
- A sprig or two of tarragon

Springtime brings the first fresh tasting shoots of tarragon. At this time of year you don't even need to bother with stripping the tarragon leaves from their stalks. Place a sprig or two of tarragon in a small non-stick milk pan with the cream. Bring the cream to a boil and reduce only slightly—we're aiming to infuse with tarragon flavours rather than thicken, or clot, the cream. Set aside for ten minutes or so. Remove the stalks from the reduced cream. Season the cream quite generously with salt and pepper. Finely chop the damp tarragon leaves (no thick stalks please) and add to the cream. Butter four small ramekins and pour a little of the green-flecked reduced cream into the bottom. Carefully break an egg into each ramekin. Pour just a little more of the cream on to the top around the yolk. Bake in a preheated oven (150°C/300°F/gas 2) for 5–8 minutes, until the whites are set but the yolk remains runny. Place each ramekin onto a side plate and serve immediately.

N.B. I don't normally bother with using a bain marie, I find I get perfectly good results without them. The trick is not to have the oven too hot.

OVEN BAKED STICKY WINGS

This is a slight variation on something that my dear late friend Rebecca Hemsley used to serve at parties. She made them with little cocktail sausages. I remember her rolling them out on Guy Fawkes Night (now there's something worth celebrating!) to be followed by a very creamy pumpkin soup. They're an absolute doddle, can be mixed up in advance, and left to marinade in the baking tray. As long as they're covered, keep them in a fridge, pulling them out only once the oven is warm. Hot party food (or TV munchies) doesn't come much easier.

I can easily eat my way through a dozen of these and still want a proper meal later.

INGREDIENTS
FOR TWO DOZEN WINGS
- Twelve whole chicken wings, to yield twenty-four pieces
- Two tablespoons runny honey
- Two teaspoons French mustard
- One big sprig fresh rosemary
- At least one tablespoon Worcestershire sauce, maybe more
- A little sunflower oil

Split the wings into their separate joints. Keep the tips for stock or for adding to a roasting pan to improve some gravy at a later date.

Pull the rosemary leaves off the stick and roughly chop them. In the roasting tin that you intend to cook the wings in, simply mix together the honey, mustard (with or without grains, as you prefer), a generous splash of Worcestershire sauce (depending on your fondness for it), the rosemary, and the oil. Add the chicken wings and push them about to enrobe them completely in the sticky sauce.

Roast in a preheated oven, at 200°C/400°F/gas 6, for 30-40 minutes until the wings are really very sticky and the sauce has dried out almost entirely.

VARIATIONS Rebecca's original version used cocktail sausages instead of the chicken wings. Rather than using mass-produced cocktail sausages, go to your butcher and buy some of the best chipolatas. Once home, simply pinch then twist them in the middle. Then cut them in two with a sharp knife.

WILD GARLIC OMELET

Down south, wild garlic is at its absolute best in April, maybe a little later as you go further north.

Whilst swotting up on the subject, I found that in addition to the normal ways of using it as a (surprisingly un-pungent) wild salad leaf, one person recommended putting some sliced leaves into a peanut butter sandwich. I'm writing this recipe out of season, but in a few months time, when I can pick some, it will be the first thing I try.

Last year there was a really big wild garlic patch near the house—I'd pass it every morning walking my daughter to school. Each time I saw it I'd think, "I'll let the leaves get a little bigger, another day or two." Then, one day, I took a carrier bag and pair of scissors with me, ready to harvest just enough leaves for a couple of omelets at lunch time. When I got there, someone had snaffled the whole lot. Every last leaf! Gone! Now, I know it grows wild but it must certainly be bad manners to clear the whole site, leaving nothing for anyone else. So please, when you're out collecting your wild leaves or foraging the hedgerows, don't be selfish; leave a little for the next person.

This is a really simple omelet to make, much the same as any other. What makes it so special is the seasonal wild leaves within. Just a handful per person is plenty.

INGREDIENTS, PER PERSON
- A few wild garlic leaves
- Two eggs
- A couple of knobs of butter

Take the garlic leaves and slice them across into thinnish strips. Heat up your favorite omelet pan. Put in a knob of butter and tilt the pan to cover the bottom with the melting, foaming butter. Introduce the sliced leaves to the pan and move them around gently with a fork. They just need to wilt slightly, no more. As this is happening, break the eggs into a little bowl and whisk them lightly with the fork. Add a little seasoning. Take the leaves out and put them on a side plate. Add the second knob of butter, if necessary, and then the beaten eggs. As the eggs start to set, push the edges into the middle, using the tines or side of a fork, as you prefer. Once it's rumpled up a little but not yet cooked, reintroduce the garlic leaves. Once the omelet has set to your liking, slide it onto a warm plate, flipping the trailing edge over to form a half moon. Eat immediately.

VARIATIONS
You may prefer to add the wilted leaves into the egg mixture so they are evenly distributed throughout the omelet. That's fine—I just prefer mine this way.

DUCK BREAST AND CHICKEN LIVER RAGU WITH PEAS

It's important that you understand I am referring to a ragu sauce, the Italian generic name for a meat sauce, rather than Ragu Sauce—which is something red and available in jars.

This is very, very similar to a straight Bolognese sauce, except that it uses duck breast and chicken livers for the meaty bits. It elevates the familiar classic from "bed-sit student" spaghetti to sophisticated sauce. If you want to go for the more normal Spag Bol sauce, simply replace the breast and livers with a pound (maybe a pound and half) of minced beef or veal or beef and pork mixed together.

The duck breast *must* be hand chopped. I once cooked this for eight people and (being basically bone idle) asked the butcher to put the meat through their grinder. It was a complete disaster. Instead of having succulent toothsome little cubes of meat, the whole sauce took on the texture of a child's sand pit. Poultry just doesn't make good mince—the texture is all wrong—that's why there are no recipes involving ground chicken in this book.

The chicken livers can be frozen, but it's relatively easy to buy them fresh these days, so why not do that? They, too, must be hand chopped into little cubes. Don't fret about this too much, there's far less meat in this dish than you would think.

The peas are essential to this dish (and are a pretty good addition to a bog standard Bol sauce). They add sweetness, as well as color and bring one of your five daily fruit or vegetable portions to your plate.

INGREDIENTS FOR FOUR PEOPLE
- Two large onions
- Four sticks of celery, taken from the heart
- Two large carrots
- A bunch of flat leaf parsley
- One duck breast, such as Barbary, skin removed—keep the skin
- About 200 g/7 oz chicken livers
- A glass of full fat milk
- A glass dry white wine
- One 200 g tin of Italian plum tomatoes
- Maybe a bay leaf
- Extra virgin olive oil
- A 500 g packet of your favorite pasta shape (I favor linguine)

- A couple of handfuls of frozen peas
- A generous quantity of freshly grated Parmesan

All the chopping is done as you are cooking. No *mis en place* required. This helps hurry things along considerably and, since I enjoy using my knives, this is no chore at all.

Put a roomy heavy-bottomed saucepan on to get warm. Pull the fatty skin off the duck breast; it will come off quite easily with a good tug. Add it to the pan along with a little of the olive oil. There's no need to cut the skin up, you'll be removing it later anyway once it has surrendered most of it delicious fat.

Finely chop the onions and add them to the pan. Next, finely chop the celery and add that to the pan. Peel and cut the carrots in half lengthwise. Cut those halves again to make long quarters. I like the sweet taste of the carrots in this sauce, but not the look. Doing it this way and then removing them, prevents the sauce from looking like something you would find pancaked onto the pavement outside the Student Union bar during fresher's week. The carrots are also delicious on their own, gently reheated the next day, with a little olive oil and a light sprinkling of sea salt. Now finely chop the parsley, including the stalks (unless they are very tough) and add that to the pan.

That lot needs to cook very gently, and without browning, for at least fifteen to twenty minutes. Whilst that's happening you have plenty of time to chop up the duck breast. Either cut the breast down its length as finely as possible, and then cut all those pieces across, as finely as possible, or alternatively adopt the Maitre d'-making steak tartar approach. This requires two large sharp knives. Put the meat (you'd be wise to chop it up a little bit first) in the middle of a chopping board. Now cross the knives above the meat to form a vertical X. With the two blades touching, slide the knives apart (not together—think about it), whilst keeping the tips of the blade on the board and the blades touching each other. The meat that gets caught between the two (the bottom of the X) has no option but to be cut. Reshape the meat and repeat until the meat is quite finely chopped. When the vegetables are ready, turn the heat up, add the chopped duck breast, and stir it around a bit. Check over the livers for any green bits, removing any that you might find. Chop the livers as you did the duck and add them to the sauce. Stir it all for a little while until the meat has taken on a little color.

Add a generous amount of salt, stir it again and add the milk. Boil this rapidly until the milk has all but disappeared. Add the wine, let it boil for a few moments before reducing the heat and adding the tomatoes (you may find it helps the tomatoes to taste even more like tomatoes if you add a *tiny* squirt of ketchup). Add a bay leaf if you have one handy.

You must now establish a gentle simmer and leave it to reduce down to a thick, light brown sauce. This can take up to three hours. It will need regular stirring, especially towards the end to make certain nothing is sticking.

When you're ready to eat, cook the pasta as you like it, *al dente* or maybe a little more. Boil, or saute in butter, some frozen peas (only use fresh if they are really, really fresh). Fish out the carrots and the shrivelled-up duck skin. Grate a generous quantity of fresh Parmesan and put it in a bowl. Drain the pasta and return immediately to its cooking pot. Add most of the sauce to the pasta and mix it all together. Divide this onto suitable plates, and add just a little more sauce (try to avoid the cowpat look). Then sprinkle on a little Parmesan and scatter the peas on the top.

Finish, as is traditional, with *THE* River Café garnish— "drizzle with a little extra virgin olive oil."

POACHED CHICKEN BREASTS WITH MORELS

Next time you find yourself needing to cook a pig's trotter that you'd like to serve whole at the table, here's a handy tip: Tie it up tightly in a bandage and then wrap that firmly to a piece of 2x1 timber the same length as the trotter. The wood will need to have been well boiled beforehand to extract any nasty woodish resins within. The reason you must go to all this trouble is that, without something firm to keep the trotter straight, it will curl up into a misshapen arthritic-looking fist as it cooks.

If you slip a boneless skinless chicken breast into some water and poach it, however gently, for 15–20 minutes it can curl up into a dry contorted little ball about half its original size. Like the trotter, for best results, the chicken breast needs attaching to something for it to keep its shape. Fortunately for us, chicken breasts can arrive on the bone.

I very seldom buy anything other than whole chickens. It is with similar infrequency then that I ever cook a whole one. I apologise for the fact that I keep banging on about buying whole chickens throughout the book, but it is, I think, an important point to be made. It's not just an old fashioned thrifty tip for the budget-minded householder—it makes sense on a gastronomic level too. Breast meat benefits from different cooking styles and times to the legs and wings. They are seldom interchangeable. It's a peculiarly Anglo-Saxon obsession with eating white meat only. How often have you heard people ask for chicken tikka marsala *white meat only?* Most of Asia favours the more flavoursome dark meat. The Chinese go to the extreme, and the extremities, in pursuit of flavor: they have a penchant for chicken's feet. They are on the menu at most proper Chinese restaurants (the sort that are full of Chinese people, not Jerry and Margo types ordering menu C, with an extra portion of crispy duck, please). One of my brothers lived in Singapore for a year; he told me how the Singaporeans happily snack on a bag of chicken's feet as we might eat a chocolate bar. According to the USDA website, in 2001 China imported 473,078 tons of American chicken feet, and that figure was 20 percent down from the previous two years. I couldn't find any quoted tonnage for Chinese consumption of Chinese-produced chicken's feet. I really would not want to count how many chicken's feet there are to a metric ton. It's safe to assume, there's quite a lot.

I normally butcher a chicken by first removing the legs and then the wings. The ankles and wing tips are taken off and put aside (ideally with the giblets) for the stockpot. I then run a sharp knife or maybe my chicken scissors (like big bladed garden secateurs) down the sides, between the breast and the backbone. This leaves me with what is known, in Bernard-Matthews-speak, as a "Crown Roast," The backbone also goes into the stockpot. That crown roast (just the two breasts still on the bone, with skin attached) can then be roast as it is (25 30 minutes in a hot oven), or, indeed, as we need for this, poached. The fact that it is still attached to the breastbone means it retains its shape whilst cooking *perfectly*. Additionally, unless you're very skilled with a knife, you'll probably get more meat off the bone once it is cooked than when it is raw.

Home economics and butchery tips aside, on with the recipe ...

Fresh morels are in season around about April/May. They are quite unlike any other mushroom—not just to eat but to look at, too. They are pointy topped and taller than they are round. The surface is exactly like an open-pored dark-brown sponge or, maybe, a little cone of inside-out brown tripe. This can make cleaning them a bit tricky. I use one of Annie's old make up brushes.

This is likely to be the least of your problems with fresh morels. Chances are that you won't find them anywhere—seemingly, every fresh morel gets dried. Fresh ones are almost as hard to find as hen's teeth—you'll need a very good greengrocer and he will probably have to order them for you. That's fine, because dried ones are marvelous and easy to reconstitute. If you can get hold of fresh ones, use your common sense re quantities. Don't add them to the sauce—just fry them quickly in a little butter and serve separately at the side, nestling alongside the sauced chicken breast.

INGREDIENTS
SERVES TWO
- 10 g of dried morel mushrooms
- One crown roast of chicken
- A generous splash of cream

- A slug of dry vermouth, Noilly Prat in my house
- A few parsley leaves
- Two egg yolks or a little beurre manie to thicken the sauce

Begin by soaking the dried mushrooms in enough hot water, just off the boil, to barely cover them. They will need 30–40 minutes soaking. At the end of that time, strain the mushrooms and discard the soaking water. I know, I know; almost everyone says keep the soaking water for stock, soups, adding to mushroom risotto— whatever. But I remember seeing Giorgio Locatelli on the TV making mushroom risotto; "Never, never, never use the water" he said. So, the next time I was soaking some mushrooms I tasted the water. *Disgusting*—tastes like dishwater—why have I been using it all these years? A little splash of mushroom ketchup does the job much more pleasantly.

Wash the chicken breast joint under plenty of cold running water. This will help reduce the amount of foamy scum on top of the poaching liquid—not something the Environmental Health Officer would recommend you do, but then he's more concerned with "chicken-splashers" than a nice clear stock. Place the chicken breast joint into a snug-fitting pan and simmer in lightly salted water for about twenty minutes; more or less may be necessary according to the size of the bird. Remove the breasts and wrap them up in a double layer of tin foil. They will keep perfectly warm for ten or fifteen minutes.

Skim any foam from the poaching liquid and turn the heat up high. Leave the lid off and reduce the poaching stock to about a cupful. If you have a significant amount of water to start with, just drain some off until you have about three cupfuls to begin with. Once you have the reduced amount, add enough cream to turn the poaching stock a pleasant white. Add the rehydrated dried mushrooms. If you are thickening with beurre manie, now is the time to whisk that in. If you want a richer sauce, use the egg yolks. In a little bowl whisk the egg yolks until creamily smooth, then add a little of the cooking liquid, whisking as you do so. Remove the cooking liquid from the heat and pour in the loosened egg yolk. Whisk like crazy. Do not reheat the sauce; the heat in it should be enough to thicken the eggs slightly. If not, only then should it go back on a *very* gentle heat. If it boils, the eggs will scramble.

You can now either add the chopped parsley to the sauce or keep it for sprinkling over the top. Or, indeed, do a little of both.

With a sharp boning knife remove the breasts whole from the bone. Remove the skin. Either serve them whole or slice them on a slant into three or four pieces. Put them on a plate and spoon a good quantity of the finished creamy mushroom sauce over the top. I like this served with simple sauteed potatoes or a little mound of plain boiled basmati rice.

Serve with a thin wedge of lemon at the edge of the plate.

SAUTÉED LEGS WITH LENTILS AND BACON

There is, almost obviously, two separate bits to this meal—the chicken and the lentils. It's not one pot cooking. They are cooked entirely separately and only meet each other on the plate. An arranged marriage, if you like. Bit like bangers and mash.

There are many ways to cook the chicken. A proper sauté would involve dusting the chicken with a little flour, seasoning and then shallow frying the joints in vast amounts of clarified butter. Best to use a wide, shallow, lined, heavy copper pan for maximum authenticity. It could also be grilled—either under a normal domestic grill, or over hot coals. My personal favorites are either to do a quick roast in the oven, or if it's a boneless breast, flatten it and grill it (like the Piri-Piri Chicken). I've found a quick roast of the various joints to be the simplest way; least amount of fuss, maximum flavour, and you get a few juices and fats, in the bottom of the pan, that you could almost call gravy. By adding a little moistening alcohol (white wine, sherry, or vermouth) and a bit of vigorous scraping of those crunchy bits that have burnt onto the bottom of the pan, you will have all the gravy you, or I, will ever need. Just perhaps, it may need a squeeze of lemon too. Cook the legs this way and the bacon gets thrown in that pan as well.

These lentils are a cinch. I don't particularly like cooking dried pulses. All that pre-planning—"leave to soak overnight" as the books say. How long is that? Do you put them into soak as you're making dinner or on your way up to bed? Do you drain them just before you need them, or at lunchtime, or when you get up in the morning? Will they be ruined if you oversleep? I know it's uncharacteristically pedantic of me, but I worry too much. These lentils obviate all anxiety, for these are Puy lentils. Not only are they the easiest to cook, but they are the tastiest of the lot, too. The only down side is that they're about the most expensive. This is so easy that it's a regular dinner for us during the colder months.

INGREDIENTS FOR TWO
- Two chicken portions (legs or, if you must, breasts)
- Two thick slices of pancetta or thickly cut dry-cured smoked streaky
- Fresh herbs from the garden (at this time of year that's likely to be just sage, rosemary, and thyme)
- 5 oz Puy lentils
- Two cloves of garlic
- One sprig of fresh sage
- A splash of white wine, vermouth, or dry sherry

Place the two chicken legs in a heavy-bottomed roasting tin. Season them with salt and pepper and smear with just a little olive oil. Add a few chopped fresh herbs; at this time of the year I keep it simple with just a little sage and perhaps some rosemary from the garden. If you can only get dried herbs, stick to just fennel seeds. If you're cooking it later in the year, you may have a greater choice available. Try to avoid a little sprig of everything, though. I feel herbs are at their best when they're boldest. Place the chicken in a preheated oven (180°C/350°F/ gas 4), they will need 35–40 minutes total cooking time (20–25 if you use breasts).

Next get on with the lentils. Put the lentils in a saucepan; add sufficient cold water to cover them and then add about an extra inch on top. Add the whole garlic cloves and a sprig of sage. Bring them quickly up to a boil and then reduce the heat to a gentle simmer. They will take about 25–30 minutes.

About ten minutes before the chicken is ready add the bacon-or pancetta-lardons to the chicken pan. If you want them extra crunchy it may be wiser to cook them separately—that they come out a little chewy and not fully crisp doesn't bother me on this occasion.

When the chicken is done, remove it from the pan. Place it to one side and cover with a piece of foil. The legs will be fine like this for at least ten minutes. Carefully remove the lardons from the bottom of the pan and put to one side probably with the chicken. Add the splash of alcohol to the roasting pan and put the pan over a burner or hob. Scrape away at the bottom to dislodge the good stuff that's stuck there. Don't over-reduce this—just warm it through. Drain the lentils and remove the garlic and sage. (Sometimes I add the cooked garlic to the sauce and just smash it down with a wooden spoon.) Toss the bacon into the lentils and mix well in.

Serve each chicken leg with the saucy scrapings poured over and around it (it will be just a few spoonfuls) and a little pile of bacony lentils next to it. The lentils will now benefit from a little coarse sea salt and a River Café garnish.

SALAMI OR PANCETTA CARBONARA

I have heard many conflicting stories about the origins and the naming of this classic simple dish. My favorite one is that the Carbonari first made this dish. The Carbonari were the Italian peasants who would make charcoal for artists around the time of the Renaissance. It was a poorly paid job, coppicing the willows down by the river and then cooking the wood in huge ovens to turn it into charcoal. They would surely have been as black from head to foot as a miller is white from his flour.

The story goes that, like most poor people then, they would have had a few hens pecking around and so had a few eggs handy. Then, by adding a little scrap of bacon to the pasta, it was transformed into the plate of food we knock-up today. Whether they added the obligatory Parmesan or not, I couldn't say. The best bit of the story is that lots and lots of black pepper was always added to disguise the fact that the airborne soot from the ovens would land just as readily on the food as it inevitably did on everything else.

The classic pasta shape is spaghetti, but I most often use linguine and sometimes one of the tube shapes—such as penne, a smooth-tubed version if I can find it.

CARBONARA WITH PANCETTA

With the exceptions of Bolognese sauce and a meaty hare sauce for pappardelle (much like jugged hare), I never make any pasta sauce that takes longer to make than you need to bring the water to the boil and then cook the pasta. It is a good plate of food when you come home tired and hungry—and all in little more than the time it takes for a frozen meal to rotate and go ping.

Pancetta is Italian bacon and is particularly good, essential even, for this. Most large supermarkets now sell pancetta, either on the deli counter or in amongst the bacon. If you can't get it and are thinking of using ordinary waterlogged bacon instead, don't do it. Cook one of the other variations!

If you're mug enough to buy some jar of carbonara sauce at a supermarket, you'll find inside a pseudo-cheesy white gloop with tiny little scraps of bacon-style-product suspended in it. This sauce is nothing like that: it is just creamy eggs, good toothsome perfectly sized crunchy Italian bacon and good pasta. *The River Cafe Cook Book* (the first, blue one) originally encouraged me to drop the cream and use egg yolks only. The splash of white wine is a little tip I picked up from a Marcella Hazan book (think Italian Delia but with a bigger, worldwide, following!). I cooked this for years without it and it's still excellent. This just makes it a little better.

INGREDIENTS

SERVES FOUR AS A BIG MAIN COURSE, SIX AS STARTER

- 500 g linguine
- Eight egg yolks
- 400 g pancetta, cut into lardons
- Generous handful of grated Parmesan
- A small glass of white wine

Turn the grill on. Bring a large amount of water to the boil in a heavy-bottomed pan and add plenty of salt. Select a suitably sized roasting tin that will fit under the grill. Splash a little olive oil into the tin, add the pancetta, and place under the grill. Give it a shake about half way through to make sure it's crunchy all over. When it's cooked take the pancetta out with a slotted spoon and put to one side. Pour the wine into the pan with the bacon fat and olive oil. Now apply some heat (either back under the grill or on the hob) to reduce the wine to almost nothing.

Meanwhile break the eggs, separate the yolks—discard the whites, or reserve them for something else. Beat the yolks lightly with a fork. Don't add so much as a splash of cream—it doesn't need it. Season the egg yolks with plenty of pepper and the merest pinch of salt (the pancetta will be quite salty). Add a generous handful of finely grated Parmesan to the yolks—this is now your sauce. When the pasta is done to your liking, drain it, reserving a little of the cooking water, then return it to the pot in which it was cooked. Add a splash of the hot water to the cold eggs—this thins the eggs slightly, beginning to cook them and reduces the chance of scrambling the eggs. Pour the sauce over the top of the pasta and stir it in quickly and thoroughly. The heat of the pasta and the pan itself will be quite sufficient to cook the eggs. Do not be tempted to turn the heat back on or you will have scrambled eggs. Keep stirring the pasta until the sauce has thickened—it will do. Add the pancetta and all the bacony winey juices. Stir again.

Divvy it up onto warm plates to serve immediately. Obviously add a little more Parmesan on top.

CARBONARA WITH SALAMI

This is very much the same as above. Sometimes I have home-made salami to use for this, at other times I visit the deli. I get the salami cut into really thick slices almost 5 mm/⅕ inch thick. When I get these slices home I cut them up into long thick, square-sectioned, matchsticks—lardons, really. I tend to fry the salami instead of grilling it. Habit, I suppose. I'm sure either would do fine.

I favour mild salamis for this and ones that are quite young. Salamis get drier and drier as they get older. I don't know how old commercially produced ones are when they are sent for sale but my own ones are best for this between two and three months old (about February through April).

INGREDIENTS
SERVES FOUR AS A BIG MAIN COURSE, SIX AS A STARTER
- 500 g linguine
- Eight egg yolks
- 400 g plain salami, such as di Napoli
- Generous handful of grated Parmesan

The exact type of salami you use isn't that important—but it should be a favorite and fairly plain one, without herbs and of a fairly coarse texture.

Then follow the recipe above, obviously using the salami in place of the pancetta. I don't normally bother with the wine for this variation.

TOAD IN THE HOLE

There was a recent TV survey of the nation's favorite food, you know the sort of thing; *"I'm an Entree—get me out of here"* To vote just dial 0898 555-1 for Roast Beef, 0898 555-2 for Toad in the Hole... (calls cost no more than £8.50, 2p from each call goes to chari-dee). As I recall, and please don't quote me on this, Toad in the Hole was the only thing in the top ten, apart from toast (huh?) and chocolate that wasn't some part of a traditional Sunday lunch. And yet the toad is nothing without its Yorkshire pudding hole to hide in, which most certainly is very much Sunday lunch.

My point is that, for a while now, people have been writing about the virtues and benefits of comfort food, most of which I agree with. What I think they really mean (those few weirdos who voted for toast excepted) is in fact the archetypal Sunday lunch of old England. Obviously roast beef and the Yorkshires, but also roast lamb and mint sauce or roast pork with crackling (so crisp that it just might shatter teeth) and some apple-sauce—freshly made that morning from the orchard windfalls. And roast chicken—an old fashioned, slow growing, big bird with lots of flavor—surrounded with chipolatas, rolls of crisp bacon, homemade herby stuffing or a second gravy-boat full of milky white bread sauce. That's comfort food to me; all the family seated round a big dining table, plenty of good homecooked food, and dad carving the joint. Trifle or steamed puddings should follow.

I think these idyllic days are disappearing for good. The Sunday lunch is the last chance for families to sit around a table and eat homemade food—with the telly turned off. Fewer and fewer people these days bother with cooking Sunday lunches like that. Even if they do it's a sorry little joint from the supermarket and some frozen Aunt Bessie's that go ping. Maybe that's why Toad in the Hole has such a place in our affections. It's that comforting crunch of Yorkshire pudding—but made easy—with sausages. Anyone can do it—even the defrosters and the microwavers.

Opinions vary as to quite how high the pudding should be. I like mine to have risen a good couple of inches at the sides of the dish, but still have a quarter inch of cooked, yet slightly soft almost cake-like, batter in the middle for the sausages to nestle in.

I always use chipolatas for this. I know some people prefer big fat bangers—but they then need to be precooked, but not on the top side or that bit will burn and, you know what, that's just more effort than I'm prepared to expend on this. If you do get caught wanting big fat snarlers, try poaching them first. Just drop them into plenty of boiling water, let them come back to the boil, and turn the heat off. Leave them in the water for 5–10 minutes. They will tighten up nicely into that classic sausage shape: slightly ovoid and with a gently curvy bend to them.

One thing that I am prepared to do for this, though, is take the trouble to get the scales out and measure things carefully. Normally, in the kitchen, I just wing it and everything turns out fine—but this is baking. As I've said before, baking is just about the only area of cooking that needs to be measured. It's chemistry. I went through a particularly defiant stage (it lasted about two years) when I didn't even measure the ingredients for Yorkshire puddings—but the cumulative effect of each time getting a little further away from how the proper recipe looks and feels left me with a very low rise pudding indeed.

INGREDIENTS FOR TWO
- Beef dripping or sunflower oil
- 125 g/4 oz plain flour
- A big, big pinch of salt
- Two eggs
- 150 ml/¼ pint full fat milk (if you want a lighter, slightly crisper batter use half milk, half cold water)
- Eight top quality chipolatas or six fat sausages

Turn the oven to 220°C/425°F/gas 7; then put in a heavy-bottomed roasting tin (Le Creuset is good for this) do it now, so it can heat up with the oven.

To make the batter, measure the flour into a big mixing bowl. There really is no need to sift modern flours. Add a really big pinch of salt, two even. Quickly disperse this in the flour with a swish of your fingers. Break the eggs into a second bowl and add all of the milk (or milk and water mixture). Beat this with a big whisk. It really won't take long, so why bother with an electrical appliance. Once that is smooth and custard-like pour it straight on top of the flour and salt. Whisk, whisk, whisk. Lump free won't take long—but don't over-do it.

I find that, by the time the oven has heated up, at least 20–30 minutes have passed. If you have a good oven that does it quicker, then make the batter first, it needs to rest a little while. Take the hot pan out of the oven and add your chosen fat—don't be shy with it. Use beef dripping for the best flavor, sunflower oil if you've an aversion to such wonderful things. Please remember that beef dripping is, apparently, better for you than butter. There needs to be an ample covering of it in the bottom of the pan. Put the pan and the fat back into the oven to let the fat heat up. Now's the time to de-link the sausages from each other—all good butchers' sausages come well-connected.

When the fats are starting to pop with excitement in the oven whip it out and pour the batter in. Move the bowl around over the baking tray laying ribbons of it into the fat in any pattern you like. This seems to help the batter to rise and reduces any tendency for it to stick. Now place the sausages into the batter, keeping them away from the edge of the dish, but not letting them touch each other. Put the dish back into the oven for 25–35 minutes, depending on your oven and your preference for a golden-brown or nut-brown pudding.

I'll serve it with most things: Green vegetables and onion gravy in the winter, some whole roast tomatoes in the summer. Heinz baked beans any time.

BOOZEY PRUNES & CUSTARD

Good Sauternes can cost a fortune. It would be completely wasted on this recipe. Either buy a cheap Sauternes or use one of the New World sweet dessert wines. You're likely to have been put off the very idea of prunes, either as a result of school cooking or from sitting next to a German on holiday at breakfast time (ham, cheese and prunes at breakfast time? No thanks, Helmut). Put these prejudices aside—this is a simple and gorgeous dessert that is also a sophisticated way to end a meal.

Place 300 g/12 oz pitted prunes in a bowl. Pour over half a bottle of Sauternes wine and leave to macerate for twenty-four hours. After that, transfer the prunes and wine to a saucepan. Add two tablespoons of caster sugar, half a vanilla pod, scraped out (or use vanilla sugar, page 247), a piece of lemon rind, and an inch or two of cinnamon stick. Bring to a simmer for five to ten minutes. Then let it cool. The flavor will improve considerably if you leave it for another day or two before eating.

Remove the flavoring bits and pieces before serving with a few spoons of the wine syrup and some cold custard.

VARIATION Try using a full-bodied red wine (something like a Barolo—not a sweet Aussie Shiraz) instead of the Sauternes, but use double the amount of sugar.

Poached Egg with Sorrel
Egg Mayonnaise
Paella
Asparagus Carbonara with Penne
Chicken Caesar Salad

MAY

Simple Roast Poussin
Coronation Chicken
Mayonnaise
Ultimate Club Sandwich
Baked Custard

There's something about May. Perhaps it's the most optimistic month of the year. Even at the start of it, you can easily go outside without a coat on; lunches outside are a more common occurrence (probably asparagus—yum, yum!); seeds get planted in the ground; and the tomato plants on your windowsill are now actually starting to look like tomato plants, even though they're only a few inches tall.

But what gets me most excited, tickled pink, happy as a hippo in a waterhole, is the butter. It is the first time of the year that the butter can really be spread straight from the dish! I know that this seems a little thing to get so excited about, but it is the cumulative little pleasures, such small delights that, when added together, make a person like me feel happy and content.

Another little source of happiness in May is when mum starts to turn up with some proper home-grown salad leaves. A few years ago, dad made two or three raised vegetable beds and they have been fantastically productive ever since. If they were mine I'd be inclined to grow vegetables the whole year round—not the ordinary stuff though (I would need a smallholding just to keep the family in potatoes and onions). If I had the space, I'd plant the interesting things that you can't always get in the supermarkets; borlotti beans; Florence fennel; interesting varieties of squashes; pumpkins and beans; an array of weird and wonderful greens. I'd also grow those things that are at their best when just picked: asparagus, broad beans, and, of course peas. If you grow your own peas, not only do you have the sweetest, tenderest peas but, as they start to grow, the pea shoot thinnings will make a fantastic risotto. And you can't buy *those* in the shops. Mum is happy to just do salads and herbs in the summer, with a couple of tomato plants in the greenhouse. I'm happy to help out with her surpluses.

One of the disappointments about moving house next month is that I've missed a whole year to get started on growing some vegetables. Also, just over the garden fence here looking towards the village church, there is a strip of land (about half an acre, I suppose) that isn't used. I'd been in touch with the owner who was happy to rent it to me for the hens. I also quite fancied doing a bit of the River Cottage thing—getting a polytunnel, digging a vegetable patch and maybe even buying a couple of little pigs to fatten up. Now we're moving—so that's gone out the window. We've been looking over in Suffolk for the archetypal "Little Pink Thatched Cottage," preferably with a couple of acres of land. The trouble is, it seems, that everyone else wants exactly the same thing over there. Still, at least I can find a little happiness in spreading the butter now.

MAY'S DIARY

FRIDAY 9 MAY
I'm not certain—but I'm pretty sure—we used to have five Marsh Daisy chickens, now there are only four. More likely that it went for a walk through the hedge and lost its way than a fox strike. Dunno.

TUESDAY 13 MAY
Have decided there are too many chickens roaming around the garden. Also, getting fed up with looking at the Araucanas and Light Sussex. Phoned the chicken lady (who sold me the original five hens) she'd like to buy them. Agreed to swap them for feed!

WEDNESDAY 14 MAY
Went to do the chicken exchange. Took six chickens—came back with five different ones! Three Welsummers, two Blue Andalusians. They are much smaller and just off the heat lamp. Put them in the (now empty) nursery run. Had to pay real money for the three bags of feed.

FRIDAY 23 MAY
One of our neighbors would like to buy some chickens for their youngest son's fifth birthday. Seems he's been looking over the fence hopefully and, when asked what he'd like for his birthday, he said "chickens!" More use than a couple of rabbits.

SATURDAY 24 MAY
Too much poo all over the garden. Must do something about it.

SUNDAY 25 MAY
Have purchased some moveable hurdles to keep chickens enclosed. Fenced off one corner of the garden. They still have plenty of room.

POACHED EGG WITH SORREL

The new season's sorrel should be hitting the shops by April, expect to see it all through the summer. It's dead easy to grow. Just avail yourself of a sunny spot in the garden and a packet of seeds. Do what it says on the seed packet. It's the sort of vegetable/salad leaf that seems to turn up at farmer's markets. I guess it's seen as a bit different and the growers can then charge a bit of a premium.

I've partnered it here with a poached egg and serve it on a toasted muffin. I like muffins; they keep their shape and, when laden with butter, retain their bounce much better than a thick slice of toast ever could.

INGREDIENTS

PER PERSON

- A handful of sorrel leaves, rinsed and cleaned of any grit
- One poached egg
- One muffin
- Butter

As you are poaching the egg, get a small frying pan hot. Also start toasting the muffin in a toaster or under a grill. I normally three quarters toast the muffin and then, once everything is nearly ready, push it back into the toaster for a final thirty seconds. When it pops up, it is toasty perfection.

Because you only want one piece of muffin, instead of cutting the muffin in half, try cutting the thinnest possible amount off the top. Chuck the unwanted thin piece away. This will leave you with a toaster-ready muffin that is at least three quarters the thickness of the original one. Check it will fit in your toaster though.

Once the egg is nearly done, chop the sorrel very roughly. Put the muffin back in the toaster. Put a big knob of butter in the frying pan and add the sorrel. Move it around a little. As soon as the muffin pops up, butter it with a ridiculously generous amount of butter. Put it on a plate. Pile the (by now perfectly wilted) sorrel on top of the very buttery muffin. Put the poached egg on top of that. Three things in a little tower. Sprinkle a little salt and add a twist of pepper over the top.

Eat without delay.

VARIATIONS It's unbelievably good with hollandaise sauce generously poured over the top, but this is meant to be quick food—hollandaise is never that. I find that with plenty of butter on the muffin, you're half way there, so I just don't bother.

EGG MAYONNAISE This is another of those classic eggy starters that everyone overlooks. I suppose that's because it's now considered a bit unfashionable. For the life of me, I don't know why because, done properly, it is absolutely gorgeous.

It's springtime and the first of the year's lettuces will be appearing. They'll be glasshouse grown or progeny of the polytunnel. I'm not too bothered as long as they're grown locally, aren't wrapped in plastic, and haven't spent three days on the road being driven all over Europe. Eating food that's been flown in from the tropics is, quite literally, bananas (except they tend to travel by boat).

To get the right consistency of yolk in the softly hard-boiled egg, I add my eggs to warm water and boil, hard, for five minutes. It really doesn't matter if they're a bit squishy—better that than hideous hard-as-bullets, grey-ringed yolks. The only other thing to remember is that it is better to use up your older, less fresh eggs if hard-boiling them. Because the white will have evaporated a little—eggshells are air-only-porous (somebody, somewhere must know a proper word for that?)—the shell will be much, much, easier to peel. It's not a disaster if the eggs are fresh, but you'll be unlikely to manage a neat job when peeling them.

Most times I add some finely sliced little cornichons to the leaves to give it that little vinegary tang and a bit of crunch. If you don't like these tiny gherkins and want something a bit plainer, just cut some skinned and deseeded cucumber into suitably small cubes.

For the decoration and garnish I like to stay fairly true to the classic. A lot of people seem to dislike anchovies, and if in excess I can understand why. Here they are used sparingly to add a salty fishy punch to what is otherwise a fairly plain but well constructed plate of food.

INGREDIENTS
SERVES FOUR AS A STARTER
- Six large softly hard-boiled eggs, left to go entirely cold
- One quantity basic mayonnaise, the stuff in the jar is too stiff for this
- A reasonable quantity of favorite salad leaves (I like Little Gem, but anything with a bit of fresh crunch in them)
- Twelve cornichons
- Six pitted black olives
- Six anchovy fillets
- A little cayenne pepper

Peel and halve the hard-boiled eggs down their length. Shred, cut, or tear the salad leaves, as you prefer. Dress the lettuce with just a little olive oil, but be very sparing—the mayo is the main dressing. Arrange the leaves on the plates. If you happen to have elongated plates that are made for the job, so much the better. Slice the cornichons down their length and then halve them again. Scatter onto the leaves. Place the halved eggs in a row across the center of the plate, yolk side down, i.e. domed side up. Carefully spoon the mayonnaise over the eggs. Cut the anchovies in half down their length and make a crisscross pattern over the eggs. Cut the olives in half and place on the center of the egg. Dust with just a little cayenne pepper. Serve with plenty of crusty bread.

PAELLA This is, pretty much, the Spanish national dish.
Any Spaniard I've spoken to is as passionate about it as an

Englishman is about roast rib of beef with Yorkshire pudding; maybe more so. That said, I've had a couple of terrible ones in Spain, many good, and some superb. Like most holiday food it has made it back to British shores—sadly it hasn't traveled terribly well. I would never consider eating one indoors—it would be as wrong as roast beef by the swimming pool in the middle of summer. Way, way out of context. That limits paella to summertime food.

At its simplest, it is rice and saffron, with a few essential vegetables and whatever scraps of meat or fish are lying around the kitchen. I've eaten it in beach bars and posh restaurants and, on one notable occasion, in someone's home in Barcelona, but the best paella I have ever eaten was in a tapas bar in Ibiza. We were the last customers in the place and the chef had just knocked up a large one for the staff's lunch. It wasn't even on the menu but they were happy to sell us a couple of platefuls. I'm not a fan of the fish-only paella—too many fiddly little bones. That Ibicencan one had (cheap) shellfish and rabbit joints it in—my favorite version. Chicken and shellfish is nearly as good and is more likely to be happily eaten by your guests. I can't understand people's reluctance to eat rabbit (my wife included). I suppose it's those anthropomorphic childhood tales from Beatrix Potter that have people thinking "awww" instead of "delicious."

I've previously made paellas for two in a frying pan, and fed four from a casserole pot. Despite many resolutions made in the departure lounges of Stansted and Gatwick, I still haven't brought home a proper big paella pan (I'm thinking two or three feet in diameter). The trouble is that they need to sit over two or more burners in the kitchen or, if you're cooking outside, you need a good campfire. I recently bought a big freestanding wok burner that works off bottled gas—now I've got no excuse not to get a proper pan. The good news is that I saw one in my local "trade" kitchen supply shop. I will buy it for myself for my next birthday present and cook paella for, about, thirty at my birthday party. No excuses now.

I normally use Calasparra rice. This is Spanish-grown rice "suitable for paella," as it says on the packet. I also use this to make risottos—so I guess you could use Arborio instead. You absolutely cannot substitute basmati or other long grain rice. The meat/fish and vegetables are here just to enhance and "lift" the rice a little. This dish is all about the rice—don't forget it!

INGREDIENTS
SERVES FOUR, VERY GENEROUSLY INDEED
- A really generous pinch of top quality saffron
- One large/two medium onions, finely chopped
- Two or three cloves of garlic, finely chopped
- Two chicken legs, chopped into little pieces (see below)
- One red pepper, deseeded and cut into little strips
- 500 g/1 lb Calasparra rice
- About 1.75 liters/3 pints light chicken stock, boiling water and a good cube will do
- A handful of peas, frozen are fine
- Some mixed shellfish: prawns, mussels, and clams—a small bowlful in total—preferably still in their shells. Any beards and barnacles removed
- A splash of dry vermouth such as Noilly Prat

Start by soaking the saffron stamens in a little hot (not boiling) water. If you are chopping the chicken legs up yourself, you'll need a cleaver or a pair of chicken shears. It's probably easier to get the butcher to do it for you. Either way, check the ends of the bones to remove any splinters. I aim to cut a whole leg (drumstick and thigh) into five or six pieces. I like the pieces to be small enough to pop a whole one into my mouth to give it a gentle chew and a working-over with my tongue, before discreetly spitting the bone out into my hand. I can then hold it and gently nibble to remove any last bits of flesh that are still attached. If you must, just use drumsticks or jointed wings, but please, not pieces of breast meat. The rice needs the flavour from the bones.

Get the paella pan hot over a medium-high heat. In a separate pan heat the chicken stock up to a gentle simmer. Pour in a really good quantity of olive oil and add the chopped onions. Stir these around to prevent them burning. You're looking for a nice soft texture and the lightest of golden colors. Now add the chopped garlic, and almost immediately, the little chicken pieces. Once the pan has recovered its heat, add the pieces of red pepper. Keep cooking and stirring until the chicken is a pale golden brown and the peppers have softened up a bit.

Tip the rice into the paella pan. Add the soaked saffron stamens and their dark yellow soaking water. Stir it around to make sure all the grains are lightly covered with saffron, olive oil, and chicken fat. Add about three quarters of the stock to the pan all in one go. Add some salt and pepper. Give it all another quick stir and then leave it alone. Don't keep stirring it—it's not a risotto.

Moderate the heat (as best you can) to provide no more than a gentle simmer. The total cooking time for the rice will be twenty-five to thirty minutes. If all the stock has been absorbed before the rice is done, add some more. You may well need all of it by the end—depending on how you like your rice cooked.

After about twenty-five minutes (as the rice is very nearly ready), stir in the peas and scatter the shellfish across the top. Add a little splash, no more, of vermouth at the last minute. Once the mussels and clams have opened the dish is ready.

To serve, try and get a fair selection of everything on each plate. It's a complete meal in itself so there's no need to serve anything else with it. You may well have had some Spanish omelet and a green salad to pick at whilst it was cooking. I tend to eat what I can with a fork first and then go in with my fingers. Things then get very messy with all the shells and chicken bones: It's all part of the fun. Serve it with plenty of paper napkins.

ABOUT THE SHELLFISH The usual rule of thumb applies when choosing mussels and clams: discard any that are open when raw and any that remain closed when cooked. If you're using prawns these will have already been cooked

and only need heating through. Don't use tiger-prawns (often the only raw prawns you can buy) as they're utterly tasteless and wrecking the environment where they're farmed. If you've managed to get hold of some razor clams, I suggest steaming them first and then removing and chopping the meat before adding it with the other shellfish (discard the mouth end). Always avoid crabsticks—they are the saveloy of the seabed. I'm particularly fond of squid; use whole tiny ones if you can find them or cut bigger ones into largish flat sections and criss-cross the surface with a knife; they'll roll up into little tubes as they cook. Don't cut them across to make squid rings; it's a cliché and looks really naff. I once ate paella with lots of lobster in it. I can't say that it was any better or worse that you'd expect—just a lot more expensive!

ASPARAGUS CARBONARA WITH PENNE

Carbonara sauce is really nothing more than eggs tossed over hot, just-drained pasta. The heat of the pasta cooks the eggs just enough to make the sauce. Most commonly, it's used to coat spaghetti and is partnered with crisp lardons of pancetta or bacon. The Italian version of bacon and eggs at dinnertime, I suppose.

If I'm passing a good Italian deli, I find it impossible not to drop in and stock up on all those weird shapes of pasta that you simply don't find in the supermarket. I am especially fond of tiny smooth penne and the shape (I don't know it's name, and I'm too lazy to go and look) that is a long thin tube—it's about the same size and shape as the tube bits from two Bic biros stuck together, end to end. Dried pasta lasts for months and months, so chances are you'll use it all up at some point.

Asparagus is one vegetable that is blessed with a well-understood season. People know that, like fresh English strawberries, it will be around only for a while—just a couple of months—and then be gone. This suits me just fine. I can indulge and satisfy my gluttony for this vegetable with a passion that, between you and me, crosses the line to obsession. There are, of course, many ways of cooking it: Steam it and serve it with a wedge of lemon amidst a little slick of olive oil. Steam it and serve with a little anchovy butter (just anchovies and butter beaten to a paste). Dip it into a simple tonnato sauce. Put it on the barbie—its season coincides with the first few tentative barbecues of the year—it is amazingly good just slapped on the grill, pulling it off before it blackens. Serve it on some crostini, also from the 'que, which has been quickly and lightly rubbed with a clove of raw garlic. It can be poshed up when served with a rich hollandaise, fingerbowls and big starched napkins. For less fussy finger food I steam it and pour over a little melted butter and a sprinkle of flaky sea salt. And, of course, just use it instead of soldiers with a boiled egg.

It just happens to be a coincidence that the end of the asparagus season coincides with my birthday—so the last chance to eat some sees me barbecuing it for friends. Then, it's gone.

I find asparagus so good on its own, such a special ingredient, that I always make it the main event of that course. So it never appears in a "medley of vegetables" next to a lamb chop (the concept of a medley is in itself far too country house restaurant, square black plates and mango coulis for my kitchen). Here the asparagus has become the main course by adding pasta and eggs. In season I will eat this at least once a week, just a big plateful of this and a chunk of bread, sat in front of the telly. Nothing for starters—no room for pudding.

INGREDIENTS

SERVES FOUR AS A BIG MAIN COURSE, SIX AS A STARTER
- 500 g/1 lb penne
- Eight egg yolks
- Two bunches asparagus spears (preferably not the really fat ones)
- Generous handful of grated Parmesan

Snap off the stump end of the asparagus and discard. Slice the good piece to be the same size and shape (obliquely cut) as the penne. Put the water on to boil, add some salt. Separate the eggs and beat the yolks until smooth. Cook the pasta. Just as you think the pasta needs only another minute or two add the asparagus to the boiling pasta. Assuming the asparagus is fairly fresh, a minute (90 seconds at most) will be sufficient cooking time—it should remain fairly firm. Keeping a little of the cooking water to one side drain the pasta and asparagus and return to the pan—don't put the pan back on the heat. Add some salt and pepper, turn the pasta/asparagus over. Add a good splash of the hot cooking water to the eggs, this thins the eggs and starts them cooking (much the same way as you would make custard). Then add the eggs, water, and Parmesan to the seasoned pasta—turn it all over again. The heat of the pasta will be sufficient to take the rawness out of the eggs; they won't be cooked solid but will produce a delicious creamy sauce to smother the asparagus and pasta gently. Serve it topped with more grated (not shaved, please) Parmesan. I don't drizzle any oil over this dish but go ahead, if you like.

CHICKEN CASER SALAD

"Caesar Salad" seems to be on the menu of probably half the restaurants in the country. The whole world loves a Caesar salad. And the whole world thinks it knows how to make the best one, ever

Me too.

Every chef tries to reinvent the Caesar; some see it as a green salad with bits on. Some are okay, some are plain wrong, and every now and then a genius pulls something special out of the hat. To my mind the foul-mouthed failed-footballer Gordon Ramsay got it completely wrong in his book *Kitchen Heaven.* His version of the Caesar—with bacon, maple syrup and *boquerones* (sweet pickled anchovies) may make a great salad but it has nothing, *at all,* to do with Caesar. My favorite reinterpretation of what a Caesar can be, was thought up by Thomas Keller, chef-owner of The French Laundry in the Napa Valley (it is frequently voted the world's best restaurant). He turns it into the cheese course.

A crisp crouton is mounted by a Parmesan cheese custard, topped with a little pile of shredded romaine lettuce, and a Parmesan crisp. This all sits on a dab of traditional Caesar dressing—the anchovy bit. I have to admit I've not eaten it, but what he's done there strikes me as genius. Fussy, yes—but genius nonetheless.

My own bit of titting around with the recipe is confined to the contentious anchovy; I used to put chopped anchovies into the dressing and whisk it all together. I have now settled, simply, for a splash of anchovy essence in the dressing. This way it is much easier to taste the dressing as you go along, adding a little more fish juice if it's not strong enough. Although, if I'm making it for Annie and me, then I will add a couple of coarsely chopped fillets, straight into the bowl.

Why does the poor little anchovy attract so much animosity? A good friend once refused to speak to me for nearly a whole hour, after I forgot to make her salad separately, without any anchovies. Apparently even after I had picked them off the top she could still taste them! The situation was made worse by the fact we were all on holiday together at the time. It's best to check that everyone likes anchovies before making this dish.

Annie and I were out for dinner a while ago with two friends Susie and Steve. She always orders the Caesar salad—every time. She tasted her Caesar and immediately left it alone. I wondered what was wrong. I asked her, and tasted it myself. It was nothing more than "past it" lettuce with a lot of gloppy, slightly garlicky, mayo on it. No Parmesan to speak of, no evidence of eggs, no croutons and, of course, no anchovies. The waitress apologised and cleared the salad away, but then came back from the kitchen to say that she had spoken to chef, who insisted "that is the way we do it here." Unbelievable.

It's a really simple salad and is made a bit lighter by toasting (grilling really) the croutons rather than frying them. Buy, or pick, the lettuce the day you're going to make it—the fresher the better. The chicken is an addition that makes the salad a supper. If I were serving it as a starter, I'd leave the chicken out.

INGREDIENTS

MAKES A STARTER FOR FOUR
- Two cos lettuces
- Some slices of good white bread—enough cut up to make sufficient croutons to go round
- Two eggs, at room temperature
- Extra virgin olive oil, about an inch (2.5 cm) depth out of a normal sized bottle
- Parmesan cheese
- Anchovy essence
- A squeeze of lemon
- One clove of crushed garlic
- One clove of garlic, halved lengthwise
- One, maybe two, poached chicken breasts (optional)

First make the dressing. Separate the eggs, putting the yolks into a large bowl. Do what you like with the whites—they are redundant here. The bowl must be big enough to serve the salad in or, if you are plating the salad, at least big enough to mix it all together. Add a generous squeeze of lemon to the eggs, also the crushed garlic, and only a little salt and pepper. Pour in a tablespoon of anchovy essence and a little olive oil. Whisk it, then add a little more oil; keep whisking and adding oil until it is the consistency of engine sump oil (or double cream, if you prefer more culinary similes). Taste the dressing. If you think it would benefit from a little more of anything, adjust as you see fit.

Next, prepare the croutons. Evidently I'm the last person in the world to fanatically count calories—I just prefer these slightly lighter croutons to the traditional fried versions. You can do them any way you like, but I would suggest you give these a try—at least once in your life. This idea came to me after a summer of grilling "ready-to bake" ciabattas on the barbecue, rubbing them with some fresh raw garlic, then drizzling them with oil. Much the same way as you make crostini, I suppose. Heat an overhead grill to its maximum. Remove the crusts from the bread and rub a little of the good olive oil onto the surface of the bread. Adding the oil now makes the croutons more like fried bread and less like toast. Leave them under the grill until golden, then turn them and do the other side. When they're done, rub the other split clove of garlic on them, one side only will do. Cut them into your preferred size of crouton. Using a good serrated knife will help reduce their tendency to shatter, even so, cutting them after toasting will give the croutons a more random appearance. If you want them all the same size and uniform shape, cube them before toasting—but the garlic rubbing will be tedious.

Tear the cos (also called romaine—same thing) lettuce into sensible, mouth-sized pieces. Put them in the bowl with the dressing. Being very gentle, simply toss it around to coat it evenly; use your hands.

Serve the lettuce on four plates and grate some Parmesan over the top. You might prefer it mixed in with the dressing; I don't. I suggest you use the coarsest side of your grater to give the cheese a bit of a toothsome bite. Please don't use a potato peeler—the age of Parmesan shavings has been and gone. Ghastly. Sprinkle the croutons over the top of the salad.

If you are using the chicken breast, poach it gently for twenty minutes in lightly salted water, and let it cool completely. Remove any skin and bones, then slice it thinly across the grain. Lay a few pieces gently on top of everything else.

VARIATIONS I recently tried a version of Caesar
that used white crab meat instead of chicken. Not too much though. It was delicious, a more moderate fishy feel, a real crowd pleaser.

PS. My anchovy-intolerant friend (I think she has even self-diagnosed herself as "allergic") has no idea that anchovies are a key ingredient in Worcestershire sauce. I take great delight in making her as many spicy Bloody Marys as often as possible.

SIMPLE ROAST POUSSIN

Once, for a very dear friend's birthday party, about twenty people gathered together in a decent Italian restaurant (a south-London, neighborhood kind of place). I ended up sitting next to a woman whom I'd never met before. We both ordered poussin stuffed with almonds (it was lovely). The moment the whole roast little bird was placed before her she went mad. "I can't eat that—look, it's a whole bird—I can even see where its feet would have been—I'm almost a vegetarian, you know!" I suggested that she sent it back to the kitchen and ask them to carve it for her. But, no, it was too late. Nothing could be done about it. The poor little bird was dead, and she'd seen it. She couldn't possibly touch it.

To this day, I still don't understand that incident. The menu clearly said "Whole Roast Poussin, Stuffed with Almonds." So there could have been no surprise there. Then to get upset that something had died in order to be put on her plate—and then to leave it. All rather disingenuous. It's just plain weird behavior from a grown person.

So, take it from me: don't serve roast poussin, quail, partridge or, indeed any whole bird to people who may have slightly wobbly constitutions or vegetarian leanings.

The principles for roasting poussin are exactly the same as roasting any other game bird. Season, lubricate, and put it in the oven. Like their big brother, the large roast chicken, they can be prone to drying out. A piece of bacon or turning the bird upside down generally takes care of that.

A poussin will obviously take any of the flavorings mentioned elsewhere, so there's no big recipe and list of ingredients, but I tend to keep it simple and go with just herbs and lemon or perhaps be a bit more trad and serve it with roast potatoes, bacon, and bread sauce in the winter.

Season each bird, rub with butter or oil, and roast in a preheated oven (200°C/400°F/gas 6) for 20-30 minutes. I like my poussin slightly overcooked, so that the meat falls very easily off the bones: I want to eat it, not arm-wrestle it.

CORONATION CHICKEN

I shan't start by boring you with the historical details of who invented this or for what occasion—oh, all right then—it was the Queen's Coronation Lunch in 1953, and Constance Spry and Rosemary Hume of Le Cordon Bleu Cookery School in London came up with it. It subtly reflected the fading Empire that she had just inherited, our historical links with India (her mother had been the last Empress of India), but also looked forward to a brighter modern future. As it was, it proved such a hit at cold buffets that it became a cliché and was then consigned to the culinary store room, the place where all over-used recipes go (it was filed next to Chaud-Froid Chicken). Fifty years to the day later, at a celebratory lunch, she was, apparently, served a "Thai-scented" chicken curry—kind of inevitable, and truly a sign of the times. What a vacuous gesture, what a pitifully ill-conceived and ignorant nod to the past.

If you look at the original recipe—and I think it was the original that I managed to dig up—it has tomato puree, sautéed onions, tinned apricot halves, and *red* wine in the list of ingredients. At the opposite end of the complexity scale, some sandwich shops simply dismember imported boiled chickens, dice them up, and mix in a load of mayo and some curry powder, spread the bread with hydrogenated marge and some over-sweet mango chutney, and add a bit of lettuce: Taadaa. One Coronation Chicken sandwich—and all for the price of one hour's take home pay on minimum wage that the kitchen staff get.

I started out with the original recipe and, along the way, changed but updated a few things here and there to suit a more modern mouth and contemporary expectations. It has evolved into the recipe below—Queenie would still easily recognize it, though—I promise—no lemon grass or kaffir lime leaves! I was astounded how, with a little care and attention, Coronation Chicken is a truly superb cold buffetstyle centrepiece. It is deep and complex, quite far removed from the sickly slick of orange mayo-ed chicken that you find inside even a very good sandwich.

You can, if you like, use mango chutney instead of the apricot jam. In fact, unless you are using the very best apricot jam I suggest that you do just that to add the necessary fruity sweetness (you wouldn't believe how little of the headlining fruit there is in cheap jam—it's largely just apple pulp and sugar). The curry powder should be plain, bog-standard, common-or-garden, nothing-special-whatsoever-about it curry powder. It will probably come in a little jar that just says "Curry Powder" on the label, and can be found hiding in amongst the herbs and spices. Failing that, choose Madras powder rather than tandoori. I prefer not to do the current favorite "in" thing and replace the mayonnaise, either wholly or in part, with yogurt of some sort. Nor do I make my own mayonnaise for this, or use reduced-fat mayo: it's fullfat, wide-boy, Hellmann's Original in my fridge, and that's what I use here. If you do want to do the drizzle and whisk thing, just look up my recipe for mayonnaise below.

It makes far more sense—admittedly you will need the time—to poach your own chicken. You could buy a cooked chicken—and this is the only occasion that you can even consider buying a boiled chicken that has been painted brown to give it the appearance of looking "roasted." Just remove the skin and skip over the instructions on poaching. If you do poach the chicken, then you will have a stock, and a chicken carcass, which adds up to . . . free soup! Just strip the meat off the chicken, save a little for the finished soup, and put the carcass back into the stock for another hour or so. Finish it off with some seasonal vegetables and little pieces of pasta.

I normally make this for when I'm entertaining "buffet style." Yes, I know that a buffet is as out of fashion as kippers for breakfast and carpet slippers, I know—but, good grief—it makes everything so much easier for the cook. It is no fun at all to be the person preparing a sit down meal for more than eight (maybe ten) people and there are occasions when just putting a well-chosen selection of good food for people to pick at and to return to for seconds is the ideal option. I am not of the opinion that a buffet should be groaning with many various assorted cold meats, quiches, poached salmon, coronation chicken, cold sausage rolls, and, inevitably, chicken drumsticks. When I do serve a buffet, there will be one, two at the most, main meaty-things, a huge spankingly fresh green salad, a carbohydrate salad, potatoes of some sort, beans or couscous, and some good fresh bread. If coronation chicken is making an appearance, then there must be a rice salad. simply cooked plain white rice, dressed at the last moment with a light vinaigrette, tossed with some nuts, raisins, and then finely chopped spring onions or perhaps coarsely chopped parsley flung on top. Keep it simple. Follow this with trifle or a tart of some sort and cheese afterwards and you will have very happy, well-fed guests.

INGREDIENTS
ENOUGH TO MAKE THE CENTREPIECE FOR A BUFFET OF EIGHT
TO COOK THE CHICKEN
- Two good chickens, each about 1.4–1.5kg
- Stock vegetables; onion, carrot, celery—all roughly chopped
- One bay leaf

TO MAKE THE SAUCE
- One small onion, finely chopped, or a similar quantity of shallots
- One dessertspoon general purpose/Madras-style curry powder
- One dessertspoon passata or thinned down tomato paste
- Two glasses of good white wine
- One bay leaf
- 300 g/10 oz full fat mayonnaise
- 200 ml/7 fl oz whipping cream
- Three big tablespoons of apricot conserve (best quality you can find) or sweet mango chutney
- Roast flaked almonds and coriander or plain watercress to garnish

Start by cooking the chickens. Rinse them, inside and out, under a running tap. Put them into a roomy pot and add sufficient cold water to cover. Remove the chickens from the cold water and put to one side. Bring the water to the boil, and then put the chickens, and stock vegetables, back in the pot. Bit of a palaver, I know. My theory goes that, if you put the chickens into boiling water, more of the flavor stays in the chicken. If they are brought up to the boil in cold water, then the flavor ekes out into the water; that is why it is done that way for soup and stock. It is a difficult theory to prove, with real scientific certainty, but it makes sense to me; so that's how I do it. The bit with putting the chickens in, adding water, then removing the chickens, is so that you have the correct amount of boiling water in the pot—*Eureka*. Skim off any scummy foamy bits that rise to the surface and simmer gently for about thirty minutes, until the chickens are cooked. Remove the chickens and let them cool. For goodness sake, keep the stock and make some soup or a risotto later.

Heat a little butter or oil in the frying pan and add the *very* finely chopped onions or shallots—they must be finely chopped because they should almost disappear into the sauce. Sweat them down until completely translucent—but not colored at all. Add the curry powder and fry that for a minute or two, add the passata, or thinned tomato paste, and let it catch a little on the bottom of the pan. It will turn from red to brown, this is important for both color and flavor. Add the wine, bay leaf, a little salt and pepper and, if the wine is very dry, a pinch or two of ordinary white sugar. Bring it to the boil and keep it there for a minute, then turn it down to a simmer and reduce it to a thin syrup consistency— five or ten minutes should do. Let it cool completely.

In a roomy bowl, beat the whipping cream to soft peaks. In another bowl mix the mayonnaise, apricot jam, and cold, reduced curry sauce together. Fold this syrupy, jammy, curried mayo into the stiffened whipping cream.

Joint the chicken, remove all the skin (give it to the dog) and hand shred or chop the meat into suitable single bite-sized pieces.

Remember that one joy of this is that it can be eaten holding the plate in one hand and the fork in the other, so the pieces should be small enough not to need further knife-work. Put a little of the sauce, which should have the consistency of fairly thick cream, to one side. Toss the chicken in the remaining sauce and taste it. Add a little seasoning if it needs it.

Put all the saucy chicken onto a serving plate, or into a bowl. Spoon the remaining sauce over the top, and cover with plastic wrap until ready to eat. At the last minute, I like to fling plenty of roasted flaked almonds over the top and sprinkle, a little less generously, with roughly chopped coriander. Staunch traditionalists would garnish with a bunch or two of watercress.

If you can make this up on the day (and so avoid bunging it in the fridge) it will taste much, much fresher. If that means getting up at three in the morning, on the day of your daughter's wedding, to start cooking—furgeddaboutit! Make the sauce and cook the chicken the day before but don't combine it all until just before you head off to the church.

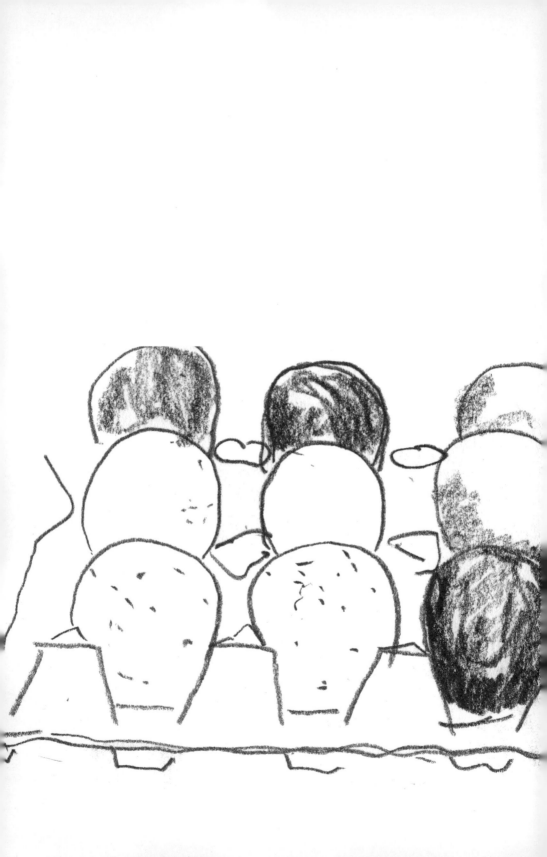

MAYONNAISE Mayonnaise is about just two
things, really fresh eggs and the right oil for the job.

The eggs must be the best you can lay your hands on. Free
range definitely, organic if possible. If you're really lucky they'll
come fresh—as-fresh-can-be from your own hens. This isn't just
food-writer rhetoric (we collectively always seem to stipulate free
range/organic these days), you'll be eating raw eggs—so here,
even more than normal, it pays to get the best.

About the oil: using only extra virgin olive oil for mayonnaise,
is almost always, a mistake. It's got too much flavor in it. There
are very few occasions which warrant such a strong and pungent
mayonnaise. Allioli, the Spaniard's favorite excuse to eat lots of
raw garlic, is one of them—the Provencal rouille another. I now
always use plain sunflower oil. I used to use groundnut oil (another name for peanut oil) for such plainer things in the kitchen.
I dismissed all those crazy peanut allergy scares as dreamt up by
hysterical, over-protective parents and more likely to be caused
by junk food diets than any mere whiff of a peanut. I changed
my opinion, pretty sharpish, when I had to find a doctor at nine
o'clock one Sunday morning because my two-year-old son had
come up in a massive rash after finding some of Annie's peanut
butter on toast. So, I don't buy groundnut oil anymore.

The other thing I'd urge you to avoid is the dreaded "vegetable
oil." This is nearly always made from oil seed rape. I know this
won't bother the townies one bit, but please—we country folk have
to live with all those hideous yellow fields. The rape seed plants
have begun pillaging the hedgerows and have started to grow wild.
It looks horrible and it *stinks!* Drive past a field in full flower and
it smells exactly like one of my very worst sneezes ("not very nice,"
says Annie). If you use it to fry with, it will give off the worst whiff
of any of the cooking oils. So, if you buy that and your house stinks
of rancid cooking oil, you've only got yourself to blame.

In my kitchen there is a bottle of extra virgin olive oil. This is
really good stuff used for salad dressings and the occasional final
garnishsplash on a plate. I pay at least twice what I could do in

order to make sure it's top quality. I then use it very sparingly. Next to this there's an ordinary olive oil; nothing fancy, certainly not extra virgin. This stuff comes in a big five-liter can at the supermarket or from under the counter at my friend Paul's deli. I then decant some into a clear glass wine bottle and stick one of those little pourers, the type they use in cocktail bars, in the top. I use this for almost any occasion that requires cooking with olive oil. Extra virgin is full of impurities, which, in part, is what makes it taste so good, but it will burn and turn acrid when over-heated. If you don't believe me, just heat a little of your best extra virgin stuff up to a good shimmer, keep it there for a little while, then just let it cool down in the pan. Taste it once it's cold, alongside some of the unheated oil, for reference. Most of the subtlety and aroma will have gone and you'll kick yourself to think of the money you've wasted over the years.

Finally there is the sunflower oil. Again, I buy this in as big and inexpensive a bottle or can as possible and decant it. Given that I also use real beef dripping and occasionally duck fat (as and when appropriate), I only need buy a few bottles of extra virgin olive oil each year, almost all of which gets used in the summer.

If you've tried making mayonnaise before and it hasn't worked, the most likely reason for failure is that the egg yolk and the oil were at different temperatures. Equally possible is that you simply added the oil too quickly at the beginning. Least likely, these days, is that the egg was stale. There are ways to go about saving a curdled mayonnaise. You could try whisking a fresh yolk in a clean bowl— and then slowly add the curdled mayonnaise—but, frankly, I think you might as well start again. The most useful tip is simply to whisk in a teaspoon of tepid water. That normally works and I've had to use it on occasion when I've been in a hurry. More haste less speed.

If you keep your eggs in the fridge (and you shouldn't be doing that anyway) remove them at least an hour, preferably more, before you start making the mayo. Make sure the egg, oil, bowl, whisk, even the vinegar and mustard, are at a comfortable room temperature before you start. In my kitchen the cupboard under the sink can be pretty chilly on all but the hottest days. I've frequently needed to run some warm water over the stainless steel bowl just to bring it up to a sensible room temperature. I cannot over emphasise this point about everything being the same temperature.

It really isn't practical to make less than this amount of mayo.

- One egg yolk
- about 150 ml/¼ pint of sunflower oil (maybe change to extra virgin olive oil)
- One teaspoon white wine vinegar or a squeeze of lemon juice
- Pinch of salt

Into a spotlessly clean mixing bowl, put the egg yolk. Lightly beat it with a wire whisk to break the yolk down. Then start adding the oil very, very, *very* slowly. Literally just a few drops at a time—you'll want to rush it but you must resist this temptation. Only once there's as much oil as egg yolk in the bowl, can you start to speed things up a bit. Just keep adding more oil and whisking. Be patient. You will end up with a lovely yellow dollopy sauce certainly able to stand up for itself and a bit thicker than you are used to. Only now should you add vinegar, salt, mustard, lemon juice, whatever you like to adjust the taste for the intended purpose. This will then thin the mayo down to a more normal thickness.

Job done.

ULTIMATE CLUB SANDWICH

The Club Sandwich shouldn't be that difficult to make. It isn't. Like all things that are simple, it's all about getting the ingredients just right and doing it properly. At its simplest, the Club Sandwich is no more than a BLT with some chicken in it. At its most complicated (read: misguided, ill-conceived manifestation of some poor chef's inner turmoil) it can become an abomination. I've seen some dire ones in my time. The absolute worst—and I'm not kidding about this—was ordered by a friend of mine whilst we were on holiday; it was a veritable tower of ingredients including bacon, lettuce, tomato, and chicken. So far so good—but here's where it starts to go horribly wrong: spring onions, green peppers, pickled beetroot, quartered gherkins, and a thick slice of tinned pineapple. (I hope you'll agree that's certainly one ingredient too many.) But what I haven't told you is that instead of the usual two, or possibly three, slices of hot toast used in any normal Club Sandwich this one had four slices, of crust-removed toast, both granary and white bread. The sandwich was left uncut because then (and I'm actually laughing as I write this) the chef, using a pastry cutter, had cut a hole out of the top piece so that you could look through into the top of the sandwich and see his final addition: a fried egg!

If you think that's the recipe for the Ultimate Club Sandwich then I'm afraid you're about to be disappointed. What I like is the simple basic one. Just chicken, bacon, lettuce, and tomato. Lubricated with some good butter and homemade mayo, this is a sandwich of unsurpassed excellence. These ingredients are a perfect match for one another and, if you make it with three pieces of toast, like a double-decker, you have exactly enough for a light lunch or simple dinner in any season except darkest winter. The bacon must be the best you can find and cooked to a crisp. Many like to grill or fry the chicken breast—I find this is too much fried stuff—just lay the bacon on a low-sided baking tray and roast in the oven. I prefer a succulent, moist poached piece of chicken—if you want more fried crunch, just add more bacon. Needless to say, it's at its best with fresh tomatoes from your own greenhouse and a lettuce from your own vegetable patch—but that's not the reality for many people. Please just choose carefully, and choose local, un-bagged stuff if you're at the supermarket!

INGREDIENTS FOR TWO SANDWICHES
- Two chicken breasts on the bone, a crown roast in other words
- Six or eight rashers of dry-cured smoked streaky bacon
- Two or three properly ripe tomatoes
- Fresh crunchy green lettuce of your choice (please, not iceberg)
- Six slices of wholemeal bread
- One quantity of homemade mayonnaise

Bring a large pot of lightly salted water to the boil. It must be sufficient to cover the chicken breast joint as it poaches (see the Coronation Chicken recipe for tips on poaching chickens). It will take about 20–30 minutes of gentle simmering, depending on its size. Leave the skin on whilst it cooks. Only once it has cooled down a little should you de-skin and take the flesh off the bone.

Whilst this is happening you can make the mayonnaise (turn back a page or two) and assemble the rest of the sandwich.

Cook the bacon as you like it. I prefer it crisp. Slice the tomatoes and discard any excess juice that exudes from it. Finely slice the lettuce to make shreds. I never like to use the universally preferred iceberg—but Annie loves it. Here's a tip; if you're going to use the whole iceberg hold it in the palm of your hand with the root pointing downwards. Slam it onto the kitchen worktop. This will break the inedible root off in one piece. It can then be pulled out whole without any need to resort to knife-work. I saw that used as a crucial plot device in an Alan Alda film once.

Cut the warm chicken breasts across their grain at a slightly oblique angle—or simply carve them off the crown roast as you might a Sunday roast.

Only when everything is ready should you make the toast; three pieces per person. This is also the only occasion (apart from smoked salmon) that I will even consider eating wholemeal bread. Butter and mayonnaise each piece as generously as you dare. On top of the bottommost piece layer half the amount of chicken, then all the lettuce, then half the bacon. Next the middle piece of toast, then the other half of the sliced chicken, then all of the tomato, then the remaining half of the bacon. Top it off with the final piece of toast. Cut the whole sandwich in half on the diagonal with a sharp serrated knife. The last thing to do is hold each wobbling tower together by stabbing them with a cocktail stick—preferably the sort with a little tassel on to help you see it. Eat immediately whilst the chicken, bacon and, most importantly, the toast are still warm.

BAKED CUSTARD

Boil the kettle. Warm the oven to 150°C/300°F/gas 2. Whisk together two whole eggs, two egg yolks, 75 g/3 oz of caster sugar and a tiny dash of vanilla extract (or substitute a little vanilla sugar, page 247). Put 425 ml/15 fl oz of double cream and 200 ml/7 fl oz of full-fat milk into a saucepan and slowly bring to a simmer. Remove from the heat, and slowly add the warm cream/milk to the cold eggs. Keep adding and gently whisking until it's all incorporated. Pour all this (through a sieve) into a shallow gratin dish. Set this into a larger dish and pour in the hot, but not boiling, water to come half way up the side of the gratin dish. This little water bath will protect the custard from the direct heat of the oven. Cover the whole thing with a piece of baking parchment and place in the middle of the hot oven. It may take anywhere between a half hour and a full hour. I like this custard to set up quite firmly, with very little of the wobble about it. Two slices for me please!

VARIATIONS
Finely grate some whole nutmeg over the top for a classic addition. Or substitute the milk with a reasonable Sauternes—add another egg yolk to help it set.

Perfect Breakfast—Bacon and Eggs
Chicken Croquettes
Salad Niçoise
Barbecued Chicken with Open-Secret
Barbecue Sauce
Spatchcocked Poussin.

JUNE

Spanish Omelet
Dead-Posh Egg and Cress Sandwiches
Teeny Tiny Tea-Time Meringues
Prairie Oyster
Classic Sherry Trifle made with
Custard

June is the best month of the year. It's got my birthday, my wife's birthday, our wedding anniversary, and both our children's birthdays all crammed into the second half of it. People kindly send us cards announcing "HAPPY EVERYTHING!"

It's also got the longest day of the year. And Le Mans. I love going to Le Mans—it must be Britain's biggest annual barbecue event, *and* it takes place in France. Apparently 80,000 plus Brits travel down there—that's more than most Grand Prix. The roads are awash with beautiful sports cars. Most people pitch a tent in one of the many campsites around the circuit. Aston Martins, Caterhams, Ferraris, Lamborghinis, Morgans, MGs, Porsches, TVRs and tents—it's a surreal sight. Everyone barbecues. Some do it quite modestly with a few bangers and a little disposable jobbie—others treat it like a military invasion, taking vast barbies and setting up field kitchens under canvas.

Much of the official catering comes off the barbie too. Merguez and frites in a bun is my favorite. Not to be trusted, however, are the *andouillettes*. These are innards sausages—grizzly chewy affairs. I'm partial to most offal, but I try to avoid these.

Back in Blighty the barbecue season is really hotting up too. The supermarkets have special promotions of charcoal, sausages, burgers and (seemingly) every spare chicken drumstick in the country racked up on their aisle ends—"Gondola displays" they call them. They're all well and good; but what about cooking a thick beef rib steak, the sort that has a bone, feeds two or three people, and needs carving before serving. Or, similarly, a butterflied leg of lamb—bone removed and opened out to produce a tattered-edged, flattish slab about one square foot in size. These can be treated to some Moroccan spicing or, more popularly, spiked with garlic, rosemary and some little chopped bits of anchovy. Chicken is great on the barbecue. Cook whole legs for a change—cut a few slashes down to the bone to help the marinade and the heat properly penetrate the flesh. If they're cooked through slowly enough, then you should be able to rip them apart at the knee joint. If you must cook chicken breasts, thin them down, beat them flat, and treat them to some piri-piri sauce. Thai pastes make great marinades—just buy a jar (my Burmese curry paste works a treat too). Once cooked, squeeze over some lime juice and cover with fresh chopped coriander just before serving.

And don't ignore the vegetables. It doesn't have to be just sweetcorn (cook them with the leaves still on until they blacken, peeling the burnt husks off, and smothering the tender cobs in melted butter when they're ready). Try wrapping some red onions up in tin foil and cooking them long and slowly on a cool edge of the barbie (first cutting a cross into the top and shoving in plenty of garlic butter). At some point in June you'll eat the last of the English asparagus. Mine always goes on the barbecue—hopefully we may get one last meal of it after we've thrown our Happy Everything party.

JUNE'S DIARY

MONDAY 2 JUNE
Those damned Marsh Daisies keep flying over the fence. Maybe because they are no bigger than plump pigeons. Looked up how to go about clipping wings in books. Tried it out. No use at all.

SUNDAY 8 JUNE
I woke up thinking one of the children was quietly crying in their sleep. But no—it was a Marsh Daisy cock. Deep and quiet—I'd expected them to be shrill and loud, like a bantam.

TUESDAY 10 JUNE
Butthead (Beavis & Butthead are the two Light Sussex cockerels) started crowing this morning. Quite loudly. May pen them up and start to fatten on a mostly corn diet. Annie is not keen on the idea ...

WEDNESDAY 11 JUNE
Counted the chickens at lights out—lost another Marsh Daisy. This time I'm sure.

THURSDAY 12 JUNE
AWOL Marsh Daisy turned up this morning. Didn't see where it came from. It just arrived back home. Was awake at 6.00 a.m. and heard the cockerels crowing. ... can't decide how to cook them.

FRIDAY 13 JUNE
Annie flatly refuses to eat any of them. She's gonna phone around a few places and see if she can shift some of them. Planning on taking ten or eleven with us when we move to Suffolk.

SATURDAY 14 JUNE
Got rid of lots of excess chickens to a breeder who had been recently visited by a fox. Left with ten hens for us, and three hens for the little boy who lives down the lane's birthday present (honestly—that's where he lives—down the lane).

MONDAY 16 JUNE
Chickens have a bloody poor sense of timing: Angelica has gone broody. It takes twenty one days for eggs to hatch and there are just twenty-five days to go until we move house! Aargh! If I want to take advantage of her broodiness and hatch some chicks, I'll have to be very quick about setting them under

her. Anastasia (the other Maran) is pining for her sister's company—lying about all day next to Angelica's broody coop.

TUESDAY 17 JUNE

Finally managed to find half a dozen fertilized eggs from a breeder in Bedfordshire. Miles away. So took the children out to Woburn Safari Park on the way—unsurprisingly it seemed bigger when I went there as a child! At the breeders I paid £10 for 6 eggs! three Araucanas, two Welsummers, one Light Sussex. Popped them under a grateful Angelica when we got home.

WEDNESDAY 18 JUNE

Found Anastasia dead in the coop this morning. Buried her under the crab apple tree. Decided the children were still too young to be introduced to death. I'm surprised by how much it has saddened me.

THURSDAY 26 JUNE

I candled the eggs again. They all look duff to me. I phoned the guy who sold me the first lot of fertilized eggs (back in January). He's got some in the incubator that should hatch Sunday/Monday. I'll check them again—and, if I'm certain they're duff, I'll take the eggs out and slip some day-old chicks under her.

SATURDAY 28 JUNE

I took the eggs inside to the airing cupboard. In its full darkness the candle showed that five of them were okay. One unfertilised Araucana egg. Only £2 down the drain, what a relief.

MONDAY 30 JUNE

Shit! Let Angelica out for some food and a poo. As always, closed the door behind her but forgot about her for 40-50 minutes. Fingers crossed the eggs didn't get cold.

PERFECT BREAKFAST— BACON & EGGS

It may very well be the same the world over—I can't be certain—but in most households, what gets served up for breakfast is the most habitual meal of the day. Frequently it's the same, day in, day out.

When I started writing, working at home, friends were worried I might start missing out on the social side of office life—water-cooler chit-chat and all that. Surely I missed the banter about, say, football, EastEnders, and celebrity reality TV shows? "No, NO, and good God NO!" The next question would always be the same, "So, what's so great about being at home all day, then?" Well, what I enjoy most about the way I work now, is, in this precise order; seeing so much of my wife and children, being able to grow my hair long and not shave for days on end, and simply having the time to decide what to have for breakfast each and every day.

I think most people would quickly agree that having the time to see more of the family is something to treasure. And I know I'm deluding myself to think that growing my hair long and having a beard makes me look like Steve McQueen during the years which he spent living in a beach house with Ali McGraw. And I'll bet most people give breakfast barely a second thought.

But believe me, having the time to come downstairs, look in the fridge, see what's in the larder, weigh up some possibilities, and then decide on what you feel like eating that morning is a very great luxury indeed. No longer is the choice an "either-or" between toast and a bowl of Sugar Pops—the choices become endless. Pancakes—thin plain ones with lemon and sugar or thick American ones with maple syrup or fresh berries? Crisp bacon from the grill in a toasted sandwich, French toast with a little sugar and cinnamon on top or a grapefruit? Maybe in summer, some quickly made fresh fruit salad or half a papaya quickly scooped out and simply filled with Greek yoghurt and topped with sticky runny honey. Or perhaps, if the hens have been busy, some scrambled eggs on toast with a little scraping of Marmite.

A boiled egg (better still, two), with thinly cut soldiers. Coddled eggs, poached eggs, fried eggs. Amidst all these possibilities, a bowl of Cornflakes becomes a pleasant, deliberate choice, no longer a rushed chore on the way out of the door. Thus, it is Sunday morning *every* morning in my house these days.

Thanks to Dr. Kellogg and, I'm sure, their in-built convenience, cereals are now the most popular breakfast choice in this country. Anecdotal evidence suggests that the French, too, have long since wised-up to the convenience of the cornflake. The all-butter croissant is now their Sunday treat and is more than likely pulled out of the freezer section at a hypermarche than collected from the village patisserie.

I thoroughly enjoy stopping at a lay-by snack-wagon for a bacon sandwich and mug of tea every now and then, especially if I've been up since before dawn and am already a hundred miles from home. How do those dreadful chains of roadside eateries stay open? Does the wayworn-travelling-professional consider an "Olympic" sized breakfast to be as much part of his life as his BMW, gold cards, and a round of golf?

For me, pretty much the perfect English breakfast is not the Full English, the Full Monty, or whatever you call it—I find all that just too much to eat before about eleven a.m. A few rashers of brittley-crisp streaky bacon and a perfectly fried egg, maybe two, settle my matutinal rumblings and set me up for the day like nothing else can. It's my regular birthday treat.

PERFECT BACON

The bacon should preferably be dry-cured. This means that the whole side of raw pork belly (for streaky—or loin for the other cut; back bacon) was treated with dry salt and not immersed in brine (salted water). The brining method traditionally allows the pork to retain much more moisture. Sadly these days it is often a cover up for brine *injected* bacon. Here, the pork is simply injected with brine (quite legally)—adding weight—and so making it worth more money. This is the completely rubbish bacon that weeps a white sticky mess into your frying pan. Sure, it's cheap—that's because so much of it is just salty water. The best commercially available bacon I've found in supermarkets is the Duchy Originals dry cured bacon. It will cook to be crisp and tasty, but it is expensive.

I like to cure my own bacon (full instructions on how to make your own bacon in my next book). When that runs out—normally around late spring/early summer, because I never seem to make enough—I'm blessed with an excellent local butcher. They make all their own bacon (and know how to mature a damned good rib-eye of beef). Obviously one of my big concerns about moving to Suffolk is to get a good supply line going again. Some parents worry about the local schools in the neighbourhood they're moving too. I have the added worry of finding a decent butcher.

Annie has been getting a little short tempered with me when, after driving over to look at yet another house, we'd go off and reconnoitre another butcher. In the end I got lucky. Ruse & Son in Long Melford, five miles away, is a small family-owned butcher (fourth and fifth generation, Henry and Oliver, are now working there). Mr Ruse cures whole bellies of pigs that have been slaughtered by him on his premises—they still have a small abattoir behind the shop. He then smokes them over oak chippings. He also makes an excellent Suffolk cure, blackened with molasses, which isn't so much to my taste.

I suggest that bacon is often better grilled—if there is any brine to seep out the bacon won't boil. If it's dry cured and perhaps a little too salty, then the salt will run off, along with the fat, into the pan below. The choice of streaky or back bacon is yours.

PERFECT FRIED EGGS

As always with something so simple, there are so many different ways to do things. The way I cook fried eggs is this: add just enough butter to a non-stick frying pan to prevent the egg from having any chance of sticking. I like to fry the egg so gently that not so much as an air bubble erupts through the white surface. Just keep the temperature really, really low. Given enough time the white will set completely and the yolk will still be utterly runny but without any raw snotty white around it.

Then there is also the "greasy spoon" school of thought. Here you have quite a bit of fat in a frying pan (for maximum authenticity use lard). The egg is broken straight into it. The fat is hot enough that the white instantly splutters and bubbles up. And it'll turn the whites brown at the edges. Additional fat is then flicked over the top to set the white that clings to the top of the yolk.

There are occasions that you may want to flip the frying egg over, "over easy" they call it in America. There are only two occasions I can think of. The first is if you're making a fried egg sandwich: Two buttered slices of cheap white bread, one fried egg in the middle. Delicious. The second is if you happen to be frying an egg for my wife.

You may want to have a double-yolk fried egg instead of two fried eggs. The way to "make up" a double-yolker from plain, ordinary, single-yolk eggs is to take a small bowl and break the first egg into it—separating the yolk from the white, yet putting both parts into the bowl. Then break the second egg over the sink and allow the white to disappear down the plughole (or keep it for something else, if you're feeling both organised and thrifty). Carefully add the second yolk to the first egg. It seems a palaver to separate the first egg—but, if you don't, the second yolk will just roll off the centre of the other egg, once it is in the pan; and remain there, at the side, all-lonesome.

I prefer a little squirt of ketchup; others will go straight for the brown stuff. That's it. Simple. Great. Just drink some OJ and tea or coffee with it—as you like.

CHICKEN CROQUETTES

There are recipes in this book that can be made with leftover bits of chicken. Chicken soup demands a carcass, and anything that needs cold chicken—rice salad, Caesar salad—can (at a pinch) be made with leftover plain roast chicken. What I mean by "leftovers" is the sort of thing that normally gets given to the dog—little scraps of chicken pulled off the cold carcass, too small to be able to do anything substantial with. Proper leftover dishes stretch the handful of choice scraps to provide another whole meal or at least a substantial snack.

I am enormously fond of these little croquettes. I make them whenever I get the chance. I found them in *The River Cottage Cookbook* (Hugh calls them *croquetas de gallina)* and, whilst they might not be my favorite recipe from that book, they are certainly the most cooked.

Every other recipe which I've come across features chicken bits mixed with breadcrumbs or mashed potatoes and whole eggs. Those can end up a bit stodgy. These, however, are bound with a *very* stiff béchamel. The contrast between the crisp crunchy outside and the melting, smooth chicken within is astounding. If KFC ever put these on the menu, I'd eat there twice a week.

The really canny cook will always make a little more béchamel sauce than is needed. My children demand macaroni cheese at least once a week, so I make a little extra sauce and fill a tiny Tupperware tub before adding the cheese. Having that sitting in the back of the fridge makes this recipe a doddle to prepare.

I've left some things, such as the garlic, nutmeg, and herbs, out. I'm always dipping these into something hot and spicy so I don't miss those at all. Serve a little bowl, or ramekin, of your favorite dip in the middle of a plate, surrounded by these hot croquettes. Try your favorite chili dipping sauce, blue cheese dressing (my recipe for this is tacked onto the bottom of Buffalo Wings), some pungent Alioli, or even a little of the left-over sauce from your most recent Indian takeaway.

INGREDIENTS

- A handful of cold chicken, very finely chopped
- Some cold béchamel sauce
- An egg, to coat
- Dried breadcrumbs (the sort you buy in a box)
- Vegetable oil, for frying

Mix the chicken and the cold béchamel together. Add plenty of salt and pepper. Pinch off little bits, about the size of a walnut, and form them into little croquette shapes. Put them on a plate and place them back in the fridge to get cold again—half an hour should do it. Start to get some oil hot enough for deep-frying (drop in some bread and see how quickly it browns). Beat the egg on a plate and pour the breadcrumbs out onto another. Roll the croquettes in the egg, then the breadcrumbs, and place to one side. When the oil is hot enough fry the croquettes until a pleasant shade of brown. Place on kitchen paper to absorb the unavoidable excess of oil, before eating very quickly. They don't last long.

VARIATIONS I've previously made these with either rabbit or pheasant to very great effect.

SALAD NIÇOISE Usually, the dwarf beans keep bringing me back—back to salads and back to Salad Niçoise. We're all familiar with ordering something "for the last time" almost every time I eat a Salad Niçoise, I vow that I should send it back (it's that bad). Then the months pass—as a rule, not more than four or five—and once again, I'll be ordering the large salad with *tonnato* (my apologies to John Irving for that).

Salad Niçoise suffers more cheffy abuse than any other salad—even more so than Caesar. Dwarf green beans, tinned *tonnato* (just plain tuna in English, but, you'll find it's increasingly commonplace in pretentious Italian menu parlance), cold potatoes, all sorts of things get thrown at what really did ought to be a simple summer salad of fresh vegetables just picked from the garden. I like those little green beans enormously, but they are never cooked properly; either cooked 'til they're soggy or barely blanched and quite decidedly raw. Neither is at all good.

Of all the many abominations out there, I'll single out the Gas-tropub's favorite way of serving a Salad Niçoise for top honors. It comes with side orders of pomposity and snobbery; it deserves your scorn and derision. I'm talking about the salad with all the usual suspects and then a slab of chargrilled tuna balancing on top. You know, sashimi raw inside and a neat criss-crossing of singe from the chargrill on top. Aaaargh!

I like my Salad Niçoise to be a riot of little early summer vegetables. I prepare it when the first tiny English broad beans make an appearance. At first they need only be podded; eat them raw they're so good. As the summer slips by they must be podded and blanched, no need to peel them; they're still so small. As their season is about to end they need podding, blanching, and peeling—the skins become tough little leather jackets (feed those bits to the hens). Some red and/or yellow peppers—chopped quite small. Cucumbers deseeded and diced, black olives, spring onions, and big red tomatoes.

And then the radishes—as small as you can find, and cut as thin as you possibly can. I used to actively to dislike radishes but now I adore them. Try growing your own—they are the easiest of all edible plants to grow. I've found that one of the great joys of being a grown-up is when natural inquisitiveness leads you to an appreciation at least—if not a full blown love affair—with food that you would never have touched as a child. Tomatoes, courgettes, runner beans, Marmite, and now radishes are all things that simply were not on my plate twenty—or even ten—years ago.

I don't always use tuna in my Salad Niçoise. Unless I have a really decent tin of tuna to hand—something like the Ortiz brand—then I'd rather leave it out. You can get a more pleasant fishy hit from a few judiciously used anchovies. And even cheap anchovies are more pleasant than rubbishy tuna tinned in brine.

As for the tomatoes, I'll use whatever is to hand—but most importantly, whatever variety they are—they must be ripe. Big Jack Hawkins, tough-skinned knobbly Marmondes, elongated San Marziano or Borghese plums, Elsa Craig, Tumbler, tiny wee Gardner's Delight—all are worth seeking out. If I've got some from a friend's greenhouse—great, otherwise farm shops that grow their own, greengrocers, and even supermarkets will have a good selection of tomatoes in the summer. Try to avoid any imported ones, and recognise "vine ripened" tomatoes as the marketing scam that they are. I've found, quite subjectively, that they taste no better. The only area of improvement is the smell, and that only comes from the branch and emphatically *not* the tomato. A British-grown tomato that's had its face in the sun and its roots in some proper soil is what you're after in the summertime.

This salad is worth starting a while in advance—whatever the provenance of your tomatoes they will benefit enormously from the treatment outlined below. Whether you indulge the tomatoes so, or not, the vegetables will take a surprisingly long time to chop, especially if you need to peel the beans. It's knife therapy on a hot summer's day.

This much would be a main lunchtime salad for four.

- Two big ripe 'beef' tomatoes or an equivalent weight of plum or cherry tomatoes
- A sprinkling of dried oregano and a pinch of caster sugar (optional)
- A small bowlful (once podded) of fresh, young broad beans
- One yellow pepper
- One red pepper (optional)
- Ten or more radishes
- Three or four spring onions
- One cucumber
- A small handful of black olives
- Anchovy fillets to taste—say, eight
- One egg per person
- A small tin of good quality tinned tuna, in olive oil
- A small bunch of basil

FOR THE DRESSING
- One mashed clove of garlic
- A pinch of caster sugar
- A little splash of red wine vinegar
- A bigger splash of best quality extra virgin olive oil

First the tomatoes. I like to skin them and cut them into bite-sized pieces—in the case of little cherry tomatoes, I just halve them. I then remove and discard most of the seeds and slush inside. (I know this is tasty stuff and the likes of Marco and Gordon would turn it into a little freebie soup micro-starter; *un petit* tomato consommé. I guess Heston might use it to make a granita, or, possibly, Corn Flakes.) Place the skinned and deseeded tomatoes in a small bowl and add a little dried oregano, a twist of black pepper, a pinch of caster sugar, and a little glug of extra virgin olive oil. Leave this to macerate for at least an hour, two or three is better. Make sure they are cool—but not in the fridge. Before adding these to the salad drain off most of the juice.

As I said somewhere above, if the broad beans are positively nursery sized just pod them and use them raw, any bigger just quickly blanch them, later in the year they will need blanching and peeling. But be warned; in all cases unless they have been recently picked, i.e. the same day, I really do think you are better using frozen baby broad beans. They are second only to peas in their suitability to freezing. If I'm using frozen then I just put them in a large bowl and cover with boiling water straight from the kettle for a minute. Drain them and they're done. You can then skin them or not as you choose. As with all things in the kitchen, taste a couple; then decide. Next thing to do is start chopping the vegetables—just toss them straight into the serving bowl as you go. Deseed the peppers and cut into little squares or thin strips, as you prefer. I like the combination of red and yellow peppers in this. Don't use green peppers though—they are truly horrible when eaten raw. Cut the cucumber in half and deseed it by running the bowl of a teaspoon along its length. Discard the seeds. Cut the cucumber into little chunks, batons, or thin slices, as you please.

Slice the radishes as thinly as you possibly can. If you have a choice, use the sort that are round and that wonderful purple-red all over, as opposed to the elongated French Breakfast variety, one end of which is white.

Remove any mankey-looking outer leaves from the spring onions. Cut the roots off and discard those. Now cut the spring onions straight across into thinnish rings all the way from the white root end until the green bit becomes a bit too leafy (don't fart around doing silly angled cheffy chiffonades).

I never used to like black olives. I'm coming around to them, but I still don't fancy them as a bar-snack. Still, they have a proper role to play in this. Try to get some good olives from a deli or the deli-counter. The ones that come loose packed in olive oil are immeasurably better than the ones that are sold in jars or tins of brine. If you can't get stoned ones then just lean on the olive with the side of your kitchen knife and squeeze the stone out. The olives will look a bit messy after that, but I quite like that scruffy, just been in a fight, look. You may have in your kitchen gadget draw an olive stoner—I have no idea how these work, so don't ask me. Add as many as you like, just don't overdo it.

Anchovies come packed in brine or salt or oil. The best brands will be expensive—use them if you like. I get mine salted, out of little tall thin jars into which they pack more of them than seems humanly possible. Simply pry a few out and rinse them under the cold tap before using. I like to split them lengthways before adding them semi-whole to the salad. You could chop them quite finely or even mush them into the dressing if you are entertaining some anchovy-hostile guests. That's the last of the ingredients to be tossed, so as you prepare the rest keep them to one side.

Traditionally the eggs come hard boiled and quartered. That's fine and dandy. The egg looks great mounted atop the salad, with just a little extra dressing spooned over, a twist of black pepper, and pinch of sea salt to finish it off. I suggest that the egg is served cool, maybe slightly warm, a hot egg straight out of the pan would not feel at home here.

Get the best tuna you can, preferably in olive oil. Whatever it's canned in, drain as much of the canning juice off as possible. Flake the tuna into big chunks and scatter over the top of the salad.

Taste the olive oil—it may be good enough to use in the salad dressing, but I wouldn't bet on it.

Tear up a decent amount of basil leaves—each leaf into just two or three. Tuck them into the salad and scatter on top only once it has been dressed. The leaves will wilt, almost immediately, if added to the salad before the dressing.

To make the dressing combine the mashed garlic, a little sugar, a splash of good red wine vinegar (not balsamic on this occasion) and three to four times that quantity of your best olive oil. Whisk together, taste, adjust and season if necessary. Dress the salad at the last minute, using just enough to coat everything and *no* more. Get the quantity right and there will be no puddle of dressing at the bottom of the bowl.

Then finally, hum the Marseillaise as you carry it to the table.

BARBECUED CHICKEN WITH OPEN-SECRET BARBECUE SAUCE

It is a universally given fact that any restaurant serving any food that drips with sticky barbecue sauce always does it to "our very own special *secret* recipe." It therefore follows that, when a barbecue sauce recipe is published, as the first book rolls of the press at that precise moment it has become an *open-secret*. Indeed, one of the occupational hazards of being a food writer is that you must reveal your sauces.

Every house in which I've ever lived has had a rosemary bush. It's the first thing I buy at the garden centre when we move. They don't need to be huge but buy the biggest bush you can find—then it will be all the quicker to supply all the rosemary you'll ever need in the kitchen, sometimes in extravagant quantities. And, what, exactly, is an extravagant quantity of rosemary, you may well ask? First extravagant use I can think of is using the branches as skewers; this is very wasteful. Take a length about ten inches long, strip off the leaves from the bottom eight inches. Whittle the bottom end into a spike and thread meat or fish onto the improvised skewers. Pork, chicken, and especially scallops are well suited to this. Extravagant use number two, when barbecuing, is to go and cut (or tear) off a large branch, maybe two to make a basting brush. Tie a little bundle together with some butcher's string and then trim the bouquet into a brush shape; just like doing mini kitchen topiary. I then dip this into the warm barbecue sauce to infuse the sauce; so no need to add chopped rosemary to the sauce. I think the best barbecue sauces are as sticky as Vaseline and just as smooth. No chopped onions, herbs, or any modish affectations (I'd single out lemon grass and lime leaves for particular recent overuse in this area). If you can't get hold of that much rosemary, then chop a sprig or two very finely and add that to the sauce. (If you want a smooth sauce, just sieve the sauce before marinating.)

I have never before done any sort of measuring for this sauce. I'd just wing it as I went along. The measurements I've given, even more so than anywhere else in this book, are really only a guide. I implore you to try a bit more of your favorite ingredient and a bit less of what you don't like—but keep the sugar content up. Barbecuing is not the time to start counting calories. This is one recipe where men (I'm guessing it will mainly be men making this sauce) feel comfortable with a little culinary adlibbing. If I say, "add more chili" most men would say, "yerr—no problem—that Tim's a big girl's blouse if he thinks that's all the heat I can take! What-a-wuss." But if I'm free and easy with quantities for the rosemary, vinegar, or ginger, then the chili-cheerleader cook will freeze mid sentence—staring at this book like a rabbit caught in headlights. Please just calm down. Start breathing. There's no need to worry.

Although this sauce is also the basis for buffalo wings, I don't generally put in the vast quantities of butter which the buffalo wings require. It's because the butter will drip onto the coals and flare up, burning the chicken. The sauce is perfectly fine without the extra fat.

Pimenton picante is a Spanish ground red pepper (similar-ish to cayenne) and it's becoming quite widely available. A little goes a long way. The picante bit means hot—as in chili hot. If all you can find is a mild one, then use more chili.

For extra flavor get the chicken into the marinade for twenty-four hours before cooking. Don't despair if that's not going to happen. I've made this on the spur of the moment and it was still excellent.

INGREDIENTS

MAKES ENOUGH TO SAUCE AN ENTIRE JOINTED CHICKEN, WITH SOME LEFT OVER

- One big chicken cut into the usual eight pieces, with the breasts possibly cut into two if especially large. Alternatively buy pre-jointed chicken for four people

FOR THE OPEN-SECRET SAUCE

- A really, very big squeeze of tomato ketchup—at least a cupful (Heinz for preference)
- One tablespoon of dark brown muscovado sugar, Demerara will do at a pinch
- One teaspoon of pimenton picante
- Three tablespoons of red wine vinegar
- Three tablespoons of Worcestershire sauce
- 2.5 cm/one inch of fresh ginger root, peeled, smashed, then finely chopped
- Four cloves of garlic, peeled, then smashed to a paste with a little salt
- One rosemary bush brush (see above)

In a small non-stick pan add all the ingredients (along with some salt and pepper) except the rosemary brush. Bring to a gentle simmer, and then turn down, so that it whispers the merest blip for a further five minutes. Stir occasionally. Be very careful tasting the sauce: it'll be *very hot*. You may want to adjust it slightly—go ahead—add anything, except the pimenton. That really tastes better if cooked a little first. Lemon juice can be quite handy at this point. Turn off the heat and dip in the rosemary branch. Leave it to cool completely.

Using a sharp knife make some slashes in the surface of the chicken, where appropriate, down to the bone. This will make the chicken look a little scruffier but gets more marinade into contact with the chicken and helps to prevent that burnt-outside raw-next-to-the-bone infamous barbecue look.

If you want to serve a little extra barbecue sauce with the cooked chicken, spoon some out now and put it to one side. Obviously, you can't serve the left-over sauce once it's been marinating the raw chicken; it will have raw chicken juices in it.

Mix the marinade and chicken together in a large bowl, or Tupperware box. Cover with plastic wrap, or the lid, and refrigerate—ideally for up to twenty-four hours. It's easiest to put the rosemary brush on top of the chicken, just for safekeeping.

Fire up the barbie and wait until all the flames have died down. Cook the chicken over the glowing embers until done. Baste from time to time with the rosemary brush—remembering to stop sometime before the chicken is ready, to avoid that raw chicken juice problem mentioned above.

It can be a real problem trying to tell when chicken is done on the barbie. People worry about it. I simply cut a piece open and have a look. It's the easiest way to do it. When ready remove it all to a big plate and serve directly.

VARIATIONS

For the quickest barbecued chicken ever, tip a jar of hoisin sauce (Chinese barbecue sauce that can be, it seems, addictive) over the chicken, along with a splash of soy sauce and a little sunflower oil. Cook on the barbecue and garnish with a sprinkling of very finely chopped spring onion and some toasted sesame seeds. Try adding a few drops of sesame oil, just before serving, to really big-up the Chinese taste.

SPATCHCOOCKED POUSSIN

Poussin are just little chickens, only a few

weeks old. Most of the full-grown chickens for sale will be, at most, twelve to fourteen weeks old—so please don't start writing letters of complaint; "poor little chickens," "full and proper lives for farm animals," "veal is cruel." Besides, you probably eat lamb rather than mutton, and that's exactly the same set up as veal and beef. So why not eat little chickens?

It's also a happy coincidence for the garden breeder that the time taken to grow chicks to poussin size coincides with the time when you can reliably tell which of your brood are cockerels, and therefore destined for the pot. I have to admit I've never slaughtered any cockerels at this age, always preferring to let them grow on to a full roasting size (that's the theory, anyway). You can easily buy poussin from the supermarket; some butchers may have them too.

The beauty of these little chickens is portion control: it's one bird per person. Sometimes I roast them whole, sometimes with simple stuffings, but what I like them best for is the barbecue. Not so much with a thick barbecue sauce, but mostly with simple Italian marinade seasonings of good olive oil, lemon juice, garlic, and herbs. If you're buying them from a butcher, why not ask him to do the donkey work. Many supermarkets will sell them ready spatchcocked and skewered. The trouble is that they will normally have been seasoned or marinated as a way of maximizing the value-added mark-up. If you're going to dress them yourself, read on ...

To spatchcock a bird: You will need a good, sharp heavy knife or, ideally, a pair of poultry scissors. It's definitely easier with scissors, but if you're only likely to do this once a year, it's hardly worth the expense of getting a pair. Your domestic scissors certainly *won't* do it—so don't even try. It's worth mentioning that most people will spatchcock the bird from the other side, i.e. through the breast bone, but that's just sloppy butchery—it leaves the backbone in. It also makes it all look, to my eyes, a bit like road-kill.

If using poultry scissors, lay the bird breast side down on a chopping board, with the leg end towards you. You need to remove the backbone. Do this by snipping either side of the parson's nose all the way down to the wings. Repeat on the other side.

If you are using a knife, opt for a large heavy chef's knife rather than a boning knife. Put the bird breast side up (as it sits on the shop shelf), with the legs towards you. Put the knife into the cavity either side of the backbone and, holding the knife handle with your usual hand, clasp your other hand on top and push down with sufficient force to cut out the backbone. It may take a couple of hefty shoves and you'll probably need to repeat the operation two or three times along the length of the backbone.

With the backbone successfully removed, turn the bird over. Splay the bird out slightly and, using the palm of your hand, lean on the breasts until the bird is flattened. There will be a slight crunching noise when you have been successful. Some people like to skewer the birds before barbecuing or grilling, but I fail to see the point of this. If you are barbecuing the birds (there is no benefit in roasting them like this, and a domestic grill probably won't get hot enough) then using a marinade to impart some flavors is a pretty sound idea.

Of course they can be seasoned with salt and pepper, and rubbed with just a little plain oil; always oil the meat, not the barbecue. But a couple of hours (or even just as long as the barbie needs to get going) marinating with some rosemary, garlic, a little lemon juice and extra virgin olive oil will make a world of difference.

Other possibilities are my Open-Secret Barbecue Sauce or a little dry rub with some fennel seeds, chilli flakes, salt and pepper. People seem happier to experiment on a barbie than when in the kitchen.

When the barbecue is ready—no flames, just glowing embers—put the poussin skin side down and leave it as long as you dare before turning it over or faffing around with it in any way. If flames shoot up as a result of dripping fats, immediately move the meat to another area of the grill. Then extinguish the flames by dousing them with a squirt from a garden spray bottle ideally kept just for the job. A little sprinkle of cold beer works just a well—in an emergency.

The little bird is ready to eat when the juices run clear. More likely is that you'll cut into a leg and have a look. If it needs a little more cooking, do so. Let it rest a few minutes after cooking, that helps the juices settle and the temperature of the flesh equalize, just like when cooking a roast.

SPANISH OMELET

Why is there a certain type of person who takes a stupid arrogant pride in being more "cultured" than others when holidaying in Spain? This sort of person looks down with disdain and contempt on people enjoying egg and chips (fries) and a pint of lager at some "tacky restaurant" on the seafront for lunch (you know the sort—big umbrellas, plastic chairs, photographs of the food). They will then, with puffy-chested pride and booming stage whispers about "local culture" head off, out of the touristy areas, to find a little tapas bar that "only the locals know about." More than likely, once there, they'll order the mainstay of the tapas bar: the Tortilla Espanola (probably with a nice cold glass of *cerveza* to drink) ... but isn't this basically the same thing—Egg and Chips with a glass of beer?

This omelet is (like egg and chips) one of my favorite things to eat, especially in the summer. It makes an ideal "help yourself to a slice" sort of starter. I often find I'll have cooked a large one if friends are coming round for a barbecue; it's ideal to help sate their hunger as people, inevitably, have to stand around waiting for the barbie to get going with a drink in their hand and another one or two already inside them.

If it's just Annie and me at home for lunch, then a small one is a great lunch for two with a fresh salad or some crusty bread.

Sometimes it's made with the addition of garlic and parsley; personally, I prefer the simplicity of it like this.

One last piece of advice: don't even consider using red onions. When the first *River Cafe Cookbook* had just come out, like many people I guess, I started using red onions in almost everything. I once used them in this—a complete disaster! The onions turn grey and their color leeches into the egg as it cools. It still tastes fine, but looks wickedly unappetizing.

INGREDIENTS
MAKES ONE LARGE OMELET
- 750 g/1½ lb potatoes (something old like Maris Piper, definitely not new potatoes)
- About half a Spanish onion, the large mild ones work best
- Six or seven eggs
- Olive oil

Finely slice some of the onion. You won't need the whole thing, so maybe make a tomato and onion salad with basil out of the leftover bit. Peel and either slice the potatoes quite thinly or cut them into chunky chip sizes. It's unlikely that you'll be using your favorite omelet pan for this, as you'll need something a little bigger. So choose a larger 25 cm/10–12 inch non-stick frying pan. First fry the onion, then the potatoes in plenty of olive oil until the potatoes have softened but have not quite taken on the look and color of a chip.

Now put the potatoes and onion into a sieve, either in a clean sink or over a bowl, to let the excess oil drain away.

Tip any remaining oil out of the pan. Wipe the pan spotlessly clean with a folded wodge of kitchen paper—cleaning it so thoroughly helps reduce the chance of the omelet sticking. Lightly beat the eggs in a large bowl and season them, be really quite generous with the salt—the potatoes will need it. Pour the potato and onions into the large bowl with the eggs and quickly mix it all together. Add a good splash of fresh olive oil to the pan. Pour the sloppy potato mix into the pan. Now turn the heat down to about medium or the bottom will burn before the middle is cooked. It doesn't need to be forked about—so just leave it well alone.

Make sure you're happy that it's as cooked as you like it underneath (check by lifting the edges with a spatula and have a little peek at it). Place a large plate over the pan using oven gloves or a tea towel to prevent burnt fingers. Hold the pan and plate together using both hands (just as you would a really big drippy doner kebab) and turn it all upside down so that the omelet ends up on the plate. Check the pan for any remnants that may have stuck, again removing any offending bits with a paper cloth. The pan must be clean. You should also add another splash of oil to the pan before cooking the top. Simply slide the omelet off the plate and back into the cleaned and re-oiled pan. Continue cooking what was, previously, the top. When you're also happy with that side's progress, preferably before the middle is cooked firm, slide the omelet onto a serving plate.

The omelet is best served once it has cooled a little, even down to room temperature. My first choice is a nice big wedge on my plate—nothing else. But it also works well cut into little cubes and passed around as nibbles. You could even shove a cocktail stick in the top if it takes your fancy!

DEAD-POSH EGG & CRESS SANDWICHES

One of my pathetically slight ambitions in life is to one day visit some fancy London hotel for the whole English afternoon tea experience. But I've always been put off, certain as I am, that the doorman would not let some unkempt, shorts-wearing, raggedy-shirted, sandal-shod, scruff like me into their nice hotel without wearing a bloody tie. That and the fact that it's, well, in London.

Fortunately for me, over in Suffolk, in every medieval-beamy town and village, there are tea rooms. Lots of them. They are here like cities have Starbucks and McDonald's. These places will serve you a pot of Darjeeling, a dainty selection of elegant sandwiches, maybe scones, and a frivolous little cake or two for about the same price as a Skinny Three-Shot Grande Latte and an oversized blueberry muffin to go.

If you've decided to lay on an afternoon tea party at home, then sandwiches must always come first. You are never, ever, allowed to go straight to the scones with jam and cream, or worse still, move directly onto the cakes. Firstly, what little hunger you might have at 4.00 p.m. must be sated with a sandwich or two. As with the cakes, I like to see a selection of sandwiches being offered. There is a simple trinity that go perfectly together: First, the absolute classic, the Edwardian daddy of them all—the cucumber sandwich. The thinnest possible brown bread with gossamer slices of lightly salted cucumber layered between them. Next, a white bread sandwich, filled with a good slice of Suffolk-cured ham, and perhaps, a little scraping of mustard—Norfolk or Dijon as you prefer. Last, but not least, the egg and cress sandwich, white or brown bread (opinions differ). Within, simply some hard-boiled egg, mashed with some mayonnaise, and a generous layer of mustard cress.

Perhaps you're feeling generous, or hungry, and want even greater variety. A simple grated cheese sandwich, made with some mildish cheddar. Perhaps cream cheese spread in a miserly fashion with a few finely chopped chives mixed in. Or even smoked salmon sandwiches—either wafer thin pieces of it or the simplest mousse—maybe even both. They are actually my least favorite—I find all but the lightest of smoked fish can taint everything that follows.

Follow with some plain scones and stiffly whipped cream, or West Country clotted cream, either way they will need some strawberry jam. Never serve sultana scones with cream—they are for jam alone. You can either put the cream on the jam or the jam on the cream—supposedly one is the Devon way and the other is the Cornish way. Just don't ask me which is which! Scones are the simplest of all home baking. I urge you to try making them—look them up in Delia. Leave toasted crumpets and buttered fruit loaves for high teas.

Finish off with some cakes. They should always be painfully small, preferably some little fancy, pointless thing (think TV-celebrity-fluff-girl on a doyley): eclairs, millefeuille, fairy cakes and the best possible jam tarts. Slices of fruitcake, rock buns, Eccles cakes, flapjack and the like, are all, I think, too substantial for this occasion—again, high tea fayre. French fancies aren't nice, neither are they amusing, even in a post-modern kitsch retro way.

When making these egg and cress sandwiches, I can seldom be bothered with preparing mayonnaise from scratch. I cheat by dressing up plain Hellmann's in the following manner.

INGREDIENTS
MAKES TWO HEARTY ROUNDS OF SANDWICHES, OR EIGHT DAINTY TEATIME AFFAIRS
- Four slices of thin white or brown bread
- Soft butter
- Three medium-sized hard-boiled eggs, cooled and shelled
- One punnet of mustard cress
- Either: One quantity of home-made mayonnaise
- Or: Two tablespoons of Hellmann's mayonnaise and a little squirt of Heinz salad cream
- A tiny squeeze of lemon
- In either case a dash of Tabasco or a ½ teaspoon of mild mustard is an optional extra

Make sure the butter is soft. Ideally it will be at the room temperature of an overcast summer's day. If it's not easily spreadable, warm it up in an airing cupboard, on a windowsill, next to the Aga, or wherever is suitable. If that's not possible, put it on a clean board and repeatedly squash it with the side of a knife.

Spread the butter thinly and evenly over the four slices of bread. Put to one side.

Take the eggs; place them in a bowl and mash to a fine-ish consistency using the back of a fork. I prefer this texture to that obtained by hand chopping—and a food processor would quickly produce a paste. Add sufficient mayonnaise (or mayo/salad cream combo) to just bind the eggs together—without them becoming at all sloppy. You may not need all of it. Add a little squeeze of lemon to sharpen things up a little, being mindful of the pips.

Add a pinch of salt and a grind of black pepper. Mix together and taste. Adjust the seasoning if necessary.

Spread the mixed egg evenly over two slices of the bread. Using scissors cut the cress from the punnet. Lay this over the egg, like a bouncy green duvet. Gently press the remaining slices of bread on top. Cut off the crusts (if serving for afternoon tea) and cut into triangles, long fingers, or square-ish rectangles, as you prefer.

NOTE I personally prefer white bread to brown for these sandwiches. I've found it increasingly difficult, impossible actually, to buy thin sliced white bread. Plenty of thin brown around—but no white. That may affect your decision. Thin brown or medium white, I honestly don't know which I'd choose.

TEENY TINY TEA-TIME MERINGUES

I remember that, on those childhood occasions when friends came for tea (mum's and dad's friends, not mine), mum would invariably make up some tea-time meringues. These are little meringues (although they seemed HUGE to a hungry six-year-old) that are simply glued together with a big dollop of whipped cream. Mum served them in little frilly paper cups and decorated the cream with a good covering of hundreds and thousands. The fancy-schmansy school of thought goes that they should be piped into elongated shapes, much like an eclair, glued with cream, and topped with little slices of fresh fruit. All far too particular for my tastes. Even further over-the-top is the practice of dying the meringues Barbie doll pink or peppermint green. Do me a favor!

I've recently discovered that meringue is much easier to make than I'd thought. It is nothing more than whisked egg white and lots of sugar baked in a very slow oven. The oven must be gentle; all it does is dry the meringue mix. It doesn't really cook at all. I've heard that you can do this in the airing cupboard for a really crisp, brittle finish, but I haven't tried it yet.

When I asked her, mum claimed that she never measured the amounts. I guess that makes sense; egg whites (like eggs) vary enormously in size. So here are some thoughts on quantities. On a couple of occasions I've tried to make the meringues with less sugar (pretty pointless, I realize). They didn't work at all; the meringue is just sugar that's held in place by the aerated egg white. Not enough sugar—no meringue.

INGREDIENTS

FOR THE MERINGUE
- Three egg whites
- 150 g/6 oz caster sugar

FOR THE FILLING
- 150 ml/¼ pint whipping cream
- Just one of the following to decorate the cream filling: hundreds and thousands, chocolate sprinkles, silver balls, glacé cherries and angelica, strawberries (if they're in season), fresh black cherries (ditto)

Preheat the oven to 100°C/225°F/gas ¼, probably its lowest setting. Put the egg whites in a really spotlessly clean bowl. Break them separately into cups to avoid any possible broken-yolk contamination. Any foreign objects and they won't become light and fluffy— no matter how much you whisk. Using an electric hand whisk—or an old fashioned big balloon whisk and your forearm—beat the eggs until they have risen to form peaks; more than soft peaks, but not quite yet fully firm. At this stage (or thereabouts) sprinkle half the caster sugar all over the surface of the whites. Continue to whisk. (If you have a fancy food processor with whisk attachment, just add the sugar slowly in a gentle, steady stream.) Once the egg whites have reached a state of excited stiffness, sprinkle over some more sugar and gently fold it in. I do this using my hand whisk. If you're electric it would be better to use a big metal spoon. Repeat this sprinkle/gentle folding until all the sugar is incorporated.

Next they need to go on a baking tray. There was a time when buttering and flouring the tray was the only option. Then along came greaseproof paper. Now in the 21st century (whilst I don't yet wear a Bacofoil jumpsuit and travel about in my personal hovercraft) technology has come a long way. I suggest you invest in one or two of those super-dooper-non-stick-reusable baking sheets. They are quite beloved by professional bakers these days. Failing that, quality greaseproof paper will do.

Gently spoon generous teaspoons (or small dessertspoons) of the meringue onto your chosen baking sheet. The ideal size is about the same as a halved small lime. Space them a little way apart; the meringues will swell a little, but they won't rise like a souffle—if they do, your oven is too hot. Put them on the middle or lower middle shelf in the oven. I've found most domestic oven thermostats are pretty untrustworthy at these low temperatures so cooking times will vary. Some may take two hours, some three or four. Any less than two and you'll have problems with them going brown. If that happens open the door just a little bit. The other reason your meringues may go brown is that the inside of your oven is *filthy*. It happened to me once! Some people swear by turning off the oven once the meringues have been put in—but, in some ovens it would cool down too quickly.

They are done when the meringue has completely dried out: it will sound hollow if you flick it gently with your fingernail. Take them out and let them cool completely.

For the filling, I prefer to use whipping cream. Double cream can be used, but I find that, once it has been whisked to stiffen it sufficiently, it becomes rather too heavy for this. Whipping cream, conversely, retains a pleasant lightness. Whip up some cream (no need to add anything at all to it) until stiff. Spoon a generous blob onto the flat bottom of one of the little meringues and then glue another one to it. The effect is like two halves of a lemon pulled apart by about a finger's width, the space in the middle being filled with cream. My favorite way of decorating this creamy filling is to cover it with dozens and dozens of hundreds and thousands. But feel free to use any of those listed above. Serve them on their sides, preferably inside one of those little frou-frou cupcake paper cups.

PRAIRIE OYSTER
June and July are the traditional months for a proper English summer wedding: *Four Weddings* and ... all that. Where there is a wedding there is also a stag do. I'm aware that the stag do is getting a bit out of hand these days. Given that many weddings need a Saturday night away in a B&B somewhere, then, for the pre-nuptial jollies, it's another weekend away for the boys (Dublin, Amsterdam, Barcelona, Prague, Acapulco!) and another one for the girls. Honestly, three weekends taken out of the summer for each wedding. And then the cost of it all—ouch!

Now, I know it may make me unpopular but I say "do it the old fashioned way," go to the pub and drink too much; then, when you're asked to leave, do it all again in the next pub. You should then either find yourself handcuffed to the night-train to Carlisle or in a police cell until you sober up.

Either way, you'll have a hangover. Bigtime. If, and I know it is unlikely, I were to be suffering a monumental hangover in a really good hotel (the sort with room service and a proper old fashioned barman who knows how to make an Old Fashioned properly) then I'd order one of these. Or perhaps, I'd just sidle down to the bar at midday—an hour or so after waking up. If, and I know it is *very* unlikely, you find yourself waking up in your own bed, I recommend making one of these drinks. Best to leave the fry up for an hour or two. You can, of course, mix a little vodka into the ketchup—will we ever learn?

Although the list of ingredients may appear quite revolting, to my mind the overall taste is similar to the lovely goo left on a plate after a full English breakfast, those little smears that are mopped up with a bit of bread; some ketchup, some egg yolk and a little greasy fat.

INGREDIENTS
MAKES ONE GLASS
- A slug of extra virgin olive oil
- A couple of big squirts of tomato ketchup
- One egg yolk
- Salt and pepper
- Tabasco
- Worcestershire sauce
- A squeeze of lemon or lime

You'll need an old fashioned, wide and shallow, Champagne glass (incidentally, I think it's almost impossible for well-dressed people to look inelegant when holding one of these). A martini glass will do at a pinch. Rinse the inside with the olive oil and don't worry if there's a little pool of it left in the bottom. Now squirt in the ketchup, then very carefully place the egg yolk on top of the ketchup, bang in the centre of the glass. Finally add all the trimmings on top in the sort of quantities you like in a Bloody Mary.

Serve with an egg spoon and a tall glass of iced water.

CLASSIC SHERRY TRIFLE MADE WITH CUSTARD

I utterly adore trifles. I could write a whole book on trifles—*With a Cherry on Top*—or something like that. Most people must surely think of the sort of thing that gets put onto a farmhouse table in an Enid Blyton novel when you mention classic trifle: sherry-soaked sponge, fruit, custard, cream, and lots of fancy utterly naff decorations. But no jelly for me—save that for children's birthday parties. For maximum retro-points, serve it in a silver-rimmed, cut-glass bowl.

It doesn't matter whether you use a thin Victoria sponge cake, Madeira cake, those special trifle sponges, or boudoir finger biscuits. Any one of them will do. What matters is that there is plenty of jam spread all over the pieces of cake, either strawberry or raspberry, don't be coy with it. There should be enough

cake/biscuit to cover completely the bottom of the bowl and be
at least an inch thick. Then the sherry: something sweet, Amon-
tillado, Oloroso, even (and most authentically) Harvey's Bristol
Cream. "Three fork-fulls," we always said as children. Certainly
use enough to soak the cakes really thoroughly. Then some fruit:
tinned pears are surprisingly good here. Poach some fresh pears if
you can be bothered, fresh strawberries, more raspberries, plums
or greengages in season—as you like. Again, it needs a full solid
layer. Next, a good 2.5 cm/1 inch of custard. Then, a little less
than that, of whipped cream. The cream must be fairly loosely
whipped—still thinner than the custard—otherwise it will bob
around sort of raft-like on top of the custard. Decorations are entirely down to you: The big bits normally go around the edge, like
a clock face, with the nuts or sprinkly things as a filling. For the
numerals I suggest bright red glacé cherries (I've no time for those
PC un-dyed ones), slivers of crystallised angelica, and/or quite a
few ratafia biscuits. Then in the middle, lots of little chopped nuts
or very many hundreds and thousands. A particular favorite of
mine is what I use on the English tiramisu, just crushed amaretti
biscuits and roast, flaked almonds mixed together. Whatever you
feel like doing is okay—decorating a trifle is definitely a case of
Less is Less. Throw restraint out of the window. Have a ball.

Peas and Eggs Jewish Style
Thai "Son-in-Law" Eggs
Chicken Waldorf Salad
Ten Great Summer Omelets
Buffalo Wings
Grilled Satay Skewers

JULY

Quick Chicken, Cucumber, and Satay
Salad
Poached Chicken with Horseradish
Cream
English High-Tea Salad
Proper Pavlova
English Tiramisu

J uly has been a big month this year. We moved house *and* threw a big party for Annie's fortieth birthday just days beforehand. (Don't worry—Annie is a wonderful, secure and confident woman, who won't mind me sharing her age with the world.)

Moving house gets harder as you get older—no question. When you're a teenager you just throw all your clothes into a couple of black bags and find two big boxes. One big enough for your hi-fi system, the other for all your LPs. Now there's so much clobber—it beggars belief. Why do children need so much stuff? Where did they get all these books? And, how come I've got so many? I'd decided to limit myself to taking just one box of cookbooks—the rest are in storage. But, do you take Delia and pack Nigella—or vice versa? There's no room for both. Hugh came with me—Rick's in a box somewhere. Jamie had to go, Sophie stayed.

I decided to keep the ones I'd most recently used and pack all the others. The ones you most often use, the ones with torn covers, the ones that are filthy dirty, the ones that are smudged with grease stains, they are the books you need to keep with you. Now, without any premeditation or planning, I've realized that I've packed all my cheffy cookbooks—the River Cafe cookbooks excepted, but then, they are exceptionally good cook books—and kept hold of (nearly) all the food-writer's books. I did however slip up with Delia, I stupidly packed her *Complete Cookery Course* and have very quickly come to regret it. Sorry Delia—never again.

Annie's big Four-O was great. I went and brought some of those lights that can be strung up in trees (the sort normally kept for Christmas) and lit up the old plum tree in the back garden. The weather was perfect. The neighbours lent us their garden tables and chairs. I laid on too much wine and got the balance of lager to bitter woefully wrong; it seems, like me, my friends all gave up drinking lager around the same time they gave up smoking.

It was mostly barbecue food. Of course there were endless trays of nibbles too—mainly some sort of crostini. Some came with my home-made air-dried ham, dressed rocket leaves, and a nugget or two of Parmesan. Others had little merguez sausages cut in half, served as plainly as that. Yet more with just tomato and mozza-rella. Of the salads that I'd made the most popular, by far, was an Italianesque combination of sliced roast red and yellow peppers, onions, and celery sticks. This is mixed up with lots of roast garlic, toasted pine kernels, soaked raisins, oregano, and parsley. I dressed it with red wine vinegar, Dijon mustard, and most of the olive oil leftover from the roasting. More authentic versions may also have roast aubergine in them but I find cold, oily, aubergine to have the precise consistency of snot. So I always leave that out.

From the barbecue came some long strings of big coiled rings of chipolatas—I asked the butcher to make half a dozen sausages three foot long. I wound these into coils and skewered them with sticks to form a cross; these big wheels were interwoven with fresh bay leaves and rosemary. Also homemade burgers; nothing more than several pounds of best ground beef a little cooked and cooled shallot and garlic, and plenty of salt and pepper. Form it into patties and refrigerate for about half a day—no more. The salt will provide all the stiffness needed—absolutely no need to add an egg! I also did what amounted to about a bucketful of wings and drumsticks in my favorite barbecue sauce.

Finally, and mainly because we had to empty the freezer, I roast a whole leg of mutton. This was studded with the now fa-miliar rosemary, anchovy, and garlic combo, then slowly cooked through to a uniform greyness (pink mutton is not at all pleasant). This got sliced up and stuffed into halved pitta breads and covered in a dollop of herby salsa verde (a sort of Italian mint sauce).

I blame it on the alcohol: Around about midnight at parties all nonsmokers (including me) forget that they don't smoke any more. A few of us ended up sitting under the plum tree, merrily drinking anything to hand and smoking anyone's cigarettes. In desperation we finished off a stale old packet of B&H that had languished at the back of a kitchen drawer for at least a year. At three in the morning the neighbor's babysitter stuck her head over the fence and said "I'd like to go to bed now please." We all realized our children would be up in three or four hours time, so we also went to bed. I suppose that's the reality of turning forty.

JULY'S DIARY

SUNDAY 6 JULY

4.00 p.m. —Candled the eggs again in the airing cupboard. Saw all five moving about. Some went cheep.

9.30—Went to lock up the chickens at dusk. Looked in on Angelica and one Araucana had hatched.

MONDAY 7 JULY

Another three chicks by tea-time. Final Welsummer arrived by dusk. Removed all the shells from the nest.

TUESDAY 8 JULY

I was a bit worried about a couple of the newborn chicks—trouble getting to their feet. Angelica agreed with me and had rejected them—she pushed them into a corner. I found one chick nearly dead from cold and the other one shivering. I put them out of their misery.

WEDNESDAY 9 JULY

With Angelica off laying, Anastasia gone, and all the January hatching and recent swapsie chicks not yet old enough to lay, we are down to 1-2 eggs a day max. I seriously considered buying a couple more laying hens ... then came to my senses.

FRIDAY 11 JULY

Moved to Suffolk today. I had to take the chickens in boxes over in my car—removal firms don't have livestock licenses. Chicken coops needed to be lifted over garage roof—very inconvenient.

MONDAY 14 JULY

Down to just one laying hen—Princess Amidala. The two Welsummers have almost completely stopped laying. Expect it's to do with the move.

WEDNESDAY 30 JULY

No Welsummer eggs for over a week now. The youngest hens keep on flying over the three-foot high hurdles. It's very annoying having chicken poo on the grass again.

PEAS & EGGS JEWISH STYLE

There are few things I'd rather put in my mouth than fresh peas. If you're really lucky you'll grow some in your garden; the slightly less fortunate may have a friend who grows them. At the bottom of the food chain you can buy fresh peas in their pods from the supermarkets, but, in all honesty, if that's your best opportunity for fresh peas—you're better off with frozen. Peas are meant to be sweet and fresh, once they've been sitting around in the inert atmosphere of sealed plastic boxes they will have lost almost all their sweetness.

I'm planning to grow some peas next year—fingers crossed. This year I've been generally irritating the good folk at the nearest farm shop—I even asked them to go and pick them whilst I waited. This did not endear me to them. No matter, I still most frequently make this dish with frozen peas. They can give me a quick hit of English summer in the middle of February, when it's too cold to go outdoors without three coats on. If you're cooking this in the middle of winter, then the lettuce and spring onion can be easily left out.

INGREDIENTS
SERVES TWO FOR A BIG SNACK AT LUNCHTIME
- A big quantity of peas, if frozen-thawed, if fresh, podded and blanched for one minute in boiling water, if super-fresh just pod them
- One little gem lettuce, shredded
- A couple of spring onions, finely chopped, including greenbits
- A small slug of cream
- Two best quality eggs

The easiest way to thaw frozen peas is put them in a dish or bowl and pour over plenty of boiling water. Leave them for a minute or so and they will be ready.

In a small frying pan melt a little butter. Add the spring onion and then, after a couple of minutes, the lettuce. Add a mere splash of water and then the peas. Season at this point. Pour over just enough cream to coat the peas. Mix it all together and then cook for just a minute—or until all the peas are warm.

Using the back of a spoon, make two little wells in the surface of the peas. Crack an egg into each of these divots. Continue to cook until the whites are set and the yolk remains runny. The white will partly disperse amongst the peas and hold them together; the yolk will sit perfectly in its little hole. This is exactly what is wanted.

Serve using a large spoon by scooping out the eggs, with attendant peas, and place on a plate. Spoon any loose peas all around. Serve with a big chunk of bread.

THAI "SON-IN-LAW" EGGS

This is a well-known dish from Thailand. Traditionally it is made with duck eggs, which can be difficult but not impossible to get hold of. Duck eggs are unpopular with retailers because their shells are considerably more porous than a hen's egg. They don't keep as well and therefore have a much shorter shelf life—about a week. Large hens' eggs are absolutely fine for this.

They need some sort of dipping sauce. It's easiest to buy some sauce in a bottle but, if you're a bit obsessional, it's easy enough to make some up. The supermarkets are now so good at providing these types of international sauces it seems churlish not to use them . . . imagine some Asian food-writer explaining how to make a tomato ketchup from scratch to go with a "British Bangers and Mash." Pointless.

I normally serve them with some thinned-down Lingham's Chili, Garlic, and Ginger sauce, which is always in my cupboard—not authentically Thai but, then, it doesn't need to be, does it? Add a nearly equal quantity of water and don't worry if the sauce splits.

I generally serve these at summer parties. They are a good starter before Thai-curried drumsticks and other spicy-sauced chicken fresh from the barbie. Somehow, they don't seem to taste quite right when eaten indoors.

INGREDIENTS, PER PERSON
- One whole egg, "softly" hard-boiled
- Half a shallot
- Half a clove of garlic
- Vegetable oil, for frying
- Some sort of dipping sauce

Boil the eggs for just five minutes for this recipe—they'll be getting cooked again, in the hot oil, later. Once the eggs have had five minutes at a rolling simmer, run them under the cold tap for a minute or so. Let them cool and then peel them. Tap the rounded end (as opposed to the pointy one) to start peeling them. If you start in the middle, because the yolk is firm but not hard, the white may crack.

Use a small, high-sided pan to deep-fry them. If you have a deep fryer, I suppose you could use that. I wouldn't really know—I've never used one.

Heat the oil and add the whole eggs. Make sure that they are getting properly browned all over, turning them if necessary. Once they have a nice crunchy outside to them, remove them and drain on a piece of kitchen paper.

Very finely slice the shallots and garlic and add them to the oil. They will take very little time to cook—mere seconds. Don't let them burn or they will taste utterly rank.

Now cut the eggs in half down their length and arrange on a plate, cut side uppermost. Place the crisp, crunchy shallots and garlic on top. Serve when cooled to room temperature (don't refrigerate) with at least one dipping sauce.

CHICKEN WALDORF SALAD

Basil: May I take your order, Sir?

American guest: I'll just have a Waldorf salad—please.

Basil (confused): A Waldorf salad?

American: Yes—a Waldorf salad!

Basil: Errm, I'm afraid we're all out of Waldorfs today.

My sister recently visited from France, where she and her boyfriend live. They have an old walnut tree in their garden—walnuts are a big deal down there in the Lot Valley. The locals eat plenty of them as plain nuts, of course, but they also make a sweet dessert wine from them, and a particularly fearsome home-distilled "brandy." She kindly brought all of the above with her. This was the first thing I made with a tiny portion of the nuts.

INGREDIENTS
- Cold, cooked, de-skinned, chicken—torn or cut into bite-sized pieces
- Walnut halves
- Chopped celery, use the pale pieces from the centre
- Sliced green apple (Granny Smiths most likely)
- Mayonnaise, slackened slightly with some lemon juice

You will need roughly equal quantities, by volume, of the first four ingredients. Break the walnut halves up by hand; don't chop them or you'll end up with some powdery bits in the salad. Peel the stringy ribs off the celery using a potato peeler, or snap the end and draw the strings out. The apple needs to be quickly dipped into some cold water with a little lemon juice added to prevent it browning. I like to leave the skin on, but it's your call.

Place the chicken, walnuts pieces, chopped celery, and sliced apple into a large bowl. Add enough mayonnaise to just coat everything. Mix it all up. Season and serve promptly.

VARIATIONS
Strictly speaking, adding the chicken is a variation on the classic—but it suits my purpose to simply let that one slide! Some may prefer a lighter dressing made from half mayonnaise, half natural yoghurt—very modish. I've seen halved seedless black grapes added with great effect, and/or a little raw mashed garlic put into the dressing. It can also be served on a bed of lettuce leaves to bulk it out a bit, making it the main course of a lightweight dinner.

TEN GREAT SUMMER OMELETS

Once you have mastered the, pretty simple, art of making a filled omelet they can be enjoyed in a myriad different ways. Just follow the basic concept outlined and try these different fillings.

PLAIN CRESS   This is the stuff that goes into egg and cress sandwiches—so of course it works brilliantly in an omelet. Buy some from the grocers, grow a packet of seeds on your windowsill, or wait for the kids to bring home some that they've grown at school.

SORREL   Again this is available (especially early summer) from good grocers/supermarkets. It's also a cinch to grow from a packet of seeds from the garden center. It will need to be roughly chopped and then sautéed very briefly in a little butter before being added to the eggs. Mix into the eggs or place in the middle as you prefer.

TOMATO   You can simply slice good ripe tomatoes and put them in the omelet, which tastes good. Given a little more time I prefer to skin them, quarter them and deseed them, which tastes better. Or, (and, trust me, it's worth all the effort) skin, deseed, chop them, and then sauté them in a little olive oil, perhaps adding a tiny amount of finely chopped garlic and a few thyme leaves. This then gets reduced, slowly-slowly-slowly, down to a thick pulp—nearly a paste. Once that's done and it has cooled down a bit, mix it into the raw beaten eggs to make a tomatoey eggy mix. Use that to make the omelet. It takes a lot of top quality tomatoes to do this properly (four or five large ones per person) but, if you're growing them yourself, you will probably have a considerable glut of them at some point in the summer. It is my favorite tomato omelet of all time.

BROAD BEANS AND BACON   Pod and boil the beans until tender (or defrost some). Remove the leathery jackets if they are at all woody. Fry some little scraps of bacon, combine the two and fill an omelet. It's a bit of a palaver just for one omelet. I tend to make this if I've got some beans/bacon left over from dinner the night before. The combo is fabulous on some pasta (just dress with olive oil and a little grated Parmesan or, better still, use some nicely aged pecorino). It also works brilliantly as a vegetable side dish to accompany a bit of roast or grilled chicken.

PEAS   Fresh is best. However, unless they've been picked no more than a few hours previously then, I think, you're better going for frozen. Choose petit pois, plain peas—even minted—as you prefer. Just bring them up to the boil, drain, and put them inside the omelet. Perhaps add a little chopped spring onion or a grating of cheese. The French go to the trouble when serving this omelet of tucking it into a neat roll, cutting a slit in the top and spooning a few more peas into that open gash. If you ask me it's gilding the lily—for a bit of simple home cooking.

WILD LEAVES   It's most likely that dandelions will be the mainstay of your wild leaf collection. That's fine, everyone (even my three-year-old daughter) can recognise them—thus there's zero risk of eating anything bad for you. Only use small, young, tender leaves—once the plants flower the leaves will be too bitter to eat. Add a mix of borage, sorrel, cultivated and wild rocket, and young beet tops. Swiss chard and/or spinach can make an appearance but are a bit too commonplace, aren't they? Add some fresh mint and/or marjoram leaves if you have them. Just blanch the leaves in boiling water, all together, for just 30–40 seconds. No more. Drain them, squeeze them dry in your hands, and finely chop them. Add them to your omelet, either in with the raw eggs or sprinkle over the top as the eggs are cooking.

COURGETTES   Nothing to this really. Get some courgettes (the smaller the better) chop them into little cubes and sauté them in butter. Remove them from the pan, add the eggs and then sprinkle the cooked courgettes over the top. Possibly a tiny squeeze of lemon juice onto the courgettes if you like.

ASPARAGUS   Allow three or four spears of English asparagus per person. Snap off their woody bottom end, and boil or (preferably) steam until tender. Refresh in very cold water. Only then do you cut them, at an angle, into little pieces, suitable for fork-only consumption. Add these to the omelet.

LEFTOVERS   Look in your fridge or cook a few extra vegetables for dinner tonight. With some common sense, most things can be quite happily warmed up and added to an omelet. But, quite obviously, I think not baked beans or pizza.

FRUIT   Sweet dessert omelets are deeply unfashionable but gorgeous. They are due a comeback. To make the sweet omelet simply add a heaped teaspoon of caster sugar to the raw eggs before cooking in the normal way. Think of it simply as a very eggy pancake if it helps. Fresh summer berries are good, but most of them will benefit from a little heat and sugar first. Also, try filling sweet omelets with some simple fruit compote. Try spreading some raspberry jam on the omelet and add a scoop of vanilla ice cream (at the last minute before folding—assemble it on the plate for ease) for an "Omelet Alaska." Or maybe fried bananas and toffee sauce may be more your thing.

BUFFALO WINGS   In 1977, Buffalo Mayor Stan Makowski, proclaimed July 29th as official Chicken Wing Day. That's one for the diary.

"The best wings in the world," or so say the people who claim to have invented them.

Although there are bound to be people who doubt any major claim, such as who first used the chicken wing as a bar snack, it is generally accepted that the Buffalo wing was invented on a

Friday night in 1964. Dominic Bellissimo was pouring drinks at the Anchor Bar, Buffalo, New York, when, late that evening, a few of his friends came in. They were hungry, so Dominic asked his mother Teressa Bellissimo if there was anything to eat. A short while later she produced a plateful of deep-fried chicken wings. They were coated in "her very own *secret* sauce" and served with blue cheese dip and fresh sticks of celery.

I'm always intrigued by the inevitable "*secret* sauce," and wanted to find out more. One thing you can safely put money on, is that, if the Americans like something, they will write endlessly on the internet about it. I Googled "Buffalo Wings": Three hundred and ninety-five thousand hits. Thorough though my research is, I can't say that I looked at every last one of them. However, the consensus is that, whilst many different off-the-shelf barbecue sauces will do the job, the real trick for Buffalo Wings is to heat about half a pack of butter in a saucepan and then add half a pint of barbecue sauce. This needs to be gently heated to let the butter and sauce infuse. The deep-fried wings should then be smothered in this buttery-barbecue sauce and served without delay.

If you visit the Anchor Bar's official website at www.anchor-bar.com (there are also, inevitably, an awful lot of fans' own sites) you'll find that not only can you buy an Anchor Bar T-shirt, baseball cap, or shot glass, but you can order food too. They will ship their Buffalo wings and special *secret* sauce to you, next day delivery (mainland USA only). You can buy the *secret* sauce by the gallon (only in the USA), and the wings in multiples of either 50, 100 or 150. Americans did, after all, invent the phrase "Do you want to GO LARGE with that?" (I can't help but wonder: is that a simple question—or a subliminal warning?)

All you need to do to get hold of a bottle of the Anchor Bar *secret* sauce, is head down to your nearest supermarket. Inevitably it's gone global. I, however, ended up using my favorite homebrew barbecue sauce—previously also a guarded *secret*—but now I've gone and published it. The secret's out.

INGREDIENTS
MAKES TWO DOZEN BUFFALO WINGS
- One dozen whole wings
- 150 ml/quarter of a pint of open-secret barbecue sauce
- About 50 g/2 oz of butter—conveniently, most manufacturers put little marks on the wrapper to indicate how much 25 g is Americans will want to at least double this quantity
- Plain sunflower oil or shortening for deep-frying

Heat the oil to 375°F/190°C. Or use the quickly crisping bread trick. Normally I just dip the end of a wing in: if it sizzles—it's hot enough; if not—then it isn't.

Whilst that's warming up cut the wings into their separate joints. Keep the pointy wing tips for chicken soup or gravy—they are of no use in this recipe. The useful two joints from each wing should be seasoned with salt and pepper. Deep-fry them until golden in color and crisp to the touch (please mind your fingers—they will be hot). It should take no more than ten minutes. Remember not to overcrowd the pan.

To make up your own *secret* sauce, melt the butter in a small pan, add my barbecue sauce, and let it all warm through, gently. The sauce will look like a bit of a mess—but will taste great.

Serve the cooked wings immediately on a big plate and pour the warm *secret* barbecue sauce all over the top. Let people dive in and help themselves. Traditionally you should offer some blue cheese dressing and fresh celery sticks on the side. These are especially good served with very cold, fizzy American beer. If you can find it, watch some Nascar racing on satellite TV whilst eating these. Nylon baseball hats and double-barreled first names are not absolutely necessary.

BLUE CHEESE DRESSING

INGREDIENTS
- 250 g/8 oz blue cheese, see note below regarding what particular type
- 225 ml/8 fl oz mayonnaise
- 100 ml/4 fl oz sour cream
- A splash of white wine vinegar, optional
- A squeeze of lemon juice, optional

Most blue cheeses will work with this, though I tend not to go with the big hitters like Stilton or Roquefort—a bit too flavorsome, I feel. My current favorite for this—and these things *do* change with the wind—is gorgonzola. Try your own particular favorite first of all; chances are that, if you like the cheese, you will like the dip it makes.

Simply mix all the ingredients together, taste and season with a little salt and pepper. Add the vinegar and lemon juice if you think the dip needs sharpening up—it will depend on the cheese that you have used. Various recipes also suggest adding finely chopped onion, a little finely chopped garlic, a little heap of chopped parsley, and various other goodies from beer to chili. I always prefer to keep things simple, and would much rather drink the beer!

Traditionally this dish is served with sticks of fresh celery to shovel into the dip. I'm not personally that fond of fresh celery but I suggest that you only use the inner stalks, and peel the horrid stringy bits off first, using a potato peeler. It seems a bit of an effort but is well worth it.

GRILLED SATAY SKEWERS (DOES CONTAIN NUTS)

Take it from me—everybody likes satay chicken. If there is somebody out there who doesn't like the combination of moist chicken, grilled over hot coals, that has been smothered in a sweet, hot, nutty sauce, I've yet to meet them.

If you're hoping to find a recipe to make the satay sauce from scratch, I'm sorry; you're going to be disappointed. Frankly, it is a laborious task, and I think that your efforts will be better invested elsewhere. Use the time to make a dipping sauce. I much prefer the peanut sauce to have been used as a marinade and then left on the chicken as it cooks. I don't think it makes a great dipping sauce for the cooked chicken. I like to serve the chicken cooked in the peanut sauce with one of those sweet, sour, hot, and salty dipping sauces on the side.

I suggest you simply buy a jar of satay sauce, but try to get one that is of proper oriental origin; it will be thicker and more pungent than a westernised cook-in-sauce type of thing.

INGREDIENTS
SERVES FOUR AS A MAIN COURSE, EIGHT AS A PICKY BAR-BECUE STARTER
- Four skinless, boneless, chicken breasts
- Many wooden or bamboo skewers
- A jar of good quality satay sauce

FOR THE DIPPING SAUCE
- One small shallot, peeled and coarsely chopped
- Three or four medium red chilies, deseeded
- Half a cupful of white wine vinegar
- One tablespoon of caster sugar
- A good pinch of salt or, better, a big shake of Thai fish sauce

Cut the chicken breasts into 2.5 cm/1 inch (or thereabouts) cubes. Toss these into enough satay sauce as you need to coat everything thoroughly. Cover with plastic wrap, and refrigerate for a few hours; better still a whole day. Soak the wooden skewers in water.

To make the dipping sauce, whiz the shallot and chillies in a blender, with some of the vinegar, until smooth. Dissolve the sugar and salt in the sauce and taste. Add the rest of the vinegar, more salt or sugar to taste. It should be a pleasant balance of chili, sweet, sour, and salt. Pour it into a ramekin or some other little dish to be dipped into.

Fire up the barbie, or put the grill on to maximum. Thread the chicken pieces onto the skewers. It's almost impossible to give cooking times for barbecues, but at a sensible heat about eight-ten minutes should do it. Cut a piece open to see if it's done.

NOTE There will be a lot of marinade left behind in the bowl. I brush this liberally over the skewers whilst they are cooking. But please remember—it will have raw chicken juices in it. So you must stop basting a good five minutes before they are ready. Don't pack the stuff onto the skewers too tightly. They'll cook quicker and be more succulent if the heat can get all around the little cubes.

Serve the skewers nestled into a crisp lettuce leaf, with the bowl of dipping sauce at their side.

QUICK CHICKEN, CUCUMBER, AND SATAY SALAD

In order for this to be called quick, you'll need a part-used jar of satay sauce lurking at the back of the fridge. That's how this came about. Inevitably, one day, I was staring into a near empty fridge—a bit of left-over chicken, half a cucumber, and about a tablespoon of satay sauce left in a jar. I put it all on a plate and bingo—it was great.

Using your fingers, tear up whatever cold chicken you have until it is really very finely shredded. Season it and place in one little heap on a plate. Cut a cucumber in half and deseed it, but leave the skin on. Cut this into the finest possible strips you can (I have, on occasion, and with great success, used a potato peeler). Place in another little pile on the plate. Thin the satay sauce down with a little sunflower (or other plain) oil and lemon juice. Add a good dollop of this as a third pile. You should aim for roughly equal quantities in each pile. And that's it. Mix together with your fork as you eat it.

POACHED CHICKEN WITH HORSERADISH CREAM

This is one of those really fresh-tasting dishes. You feel, instinctively, that it is good for you. Maybe it's the lack of starchy carbohydrate in it that makes it feel so light or maybe it's the near complete absence of fat. As I write this, low-carb diets are in the news. When will people realize that diets don't work? If there was one, just one, diet that actually did work then the world would never need another diet book. They're a scam, a rip-off. People pay their money in the false hope that this new "diet" will let them keep eating more food than they actually need to live on—and still lose weight. Underneath all the smoke and mirrors, the fads and weird eating regimes, they all quietly collude to sell the same solution: Eat 1500 calories per day and you'll lose weight. Eat less, move around more—that's all there is to it. Now, I've no idea about the low-carb or weight-loss credentials of this dish—I eat it only because it tastes wonderful.

It covers the transition nicely between summer and autumn food. Normally it is the first slightly "stewey" thing that I cook, just as the first wee leeks of the season are starting to show up.

The horseradish is a superb accompaniment to this. I've also tried it with mustard. That was okay. When we lived in Cambridge I used to buy horseradish sauce ready-made in pots. When I knew that we were moving to Suffolk, I bought a horseradish plant in the garden center (along with a plethora of herbs) and potted it up to help it get started. My father-in-law came round one day and was kind enough to point out that horseradish is a weed that grows all over the verges and along the hedgerows in the countryside. Sure enough, the potted plant quickly withered in its very shallow pot, unable to send down its vast taproots into the ground (that's the bit you eat—just like a carrot). I now simply take my spade in hand and nip out to the rough ground just behind the bowling-green to dig up a root whenever I need one.

INGREDIENTS
THIS QUANTITY WILL SERVE TWO, LEAVING YOU WITH
TWO LEFTOVER COLD CHICKEN LEGS

FOR THE CHICKEN
- One good chicken, about 1.4–1.6 kg
- One leek
- Two or three sticks of celery, taken from the inside
- Two or three big carrots or a similar weight of smaller ones
- One whole clove (I mean the spice—not garlic)
- Half a dozen whole black peppercorns
- A bay leaf
- A few parsley stalks
- A chicken stock cube

FOR THE HORSERADISH SAUCE
- About equal amounts of horseradish and double cream
- A splash of white wine vinegar

This is an utter doddle to make. All you need to cook this, is a pot that has a lid and is big enough to take the chicken and vegetables without too much room to spare. Rinse the chicken under the cold tap, inside and out. Put it in the pot with sufficient cold water to cover it. Put that on the hob and bring it slowly to a boil. The moment it starts to boil, turn it down to a simmer. In the meantime you can be prepping the vegetables.

If the outside of the leek is a bit woody, peel a layer off. Cut the leek straight across to make little "log" shapes. You mustn't cut the leek pieces too short or they will fall apart while poaching. Don't use any of the dark green top or the actual root. I normally get three, maybe four if they're big, pieces from each leek. Use the celery from the centre of the plant. Peel it carefully using a potato peeler—I detest the stringy little bits in the rib—the other way to de-string them is to snap each end, carefully. Do it just right and the string will stay attached and you can simply pull them out, as you would the string from a big old runner bean. Cut them into three or four pieces each. Peel the carrots and cut through their length into halves or quarters, depending on their diameter. If they are very long, cut them in half. Smaller carrots, with an inch or so of the green bit left on, are also nice earlier in the year. I prefer all the vegetables cut straight across for this—none of those jaunty angles and lozenge-shaped pieces of baby vegetables here.

Once you have established a simmer and skimmed the top to remove any fat and scum (ideally you should do this every ten minutes or so throughout the cooking time), add all the other ingredients. Leave it alone (save for the skimming) to simmer very gently with the lid on, but ajar, for about forty-five minutes, until the chicken is cooked through.

Take the chicken out of the broth and put it on a chopping board (or whatever you normally use to carve on). I like to take the breasts off whole, de-skin them, and then cut them in half. Place these in the middle of a wide, deep soup plate—the sort modern bistros so adore using. Arrange the vegetables around them and spoon over a reasonable quantity of broth. Taste it to see if it needs any salt; it probably won't if you have used a stock-cube. If it does, rub a pinch of flaky sea salt through your fingers all over the top. This is one of the rare occasions when I prefer the breast to the legs. Use the legs up as leftovers.

To make the horseradish cream, peel and wash the horseradish root. Be certain not to put any of the root on the compost heap. Each piece will grow a new plant if it finds its way into your garden, and once there you will never get rid of it. Grate the root on a medium grater—it'll clear your nose out for you! Mix the cream and vinegar together; the vinegar will suddenly, and considerably, thicken the cream—that's okay. Add the grated root little by little; you may not want all of it. As the year progresses and the roots get a little older, their strength grows considerably. Add a little salt and pepper to taste.

Put a generous spoonful of horseradish sauce on the rim of the plate and eat it with the aid of a knife, fork, and soup spoon.

VARIATIONS I have successfully used créme fraîche instead of cream, and even a mix of both. A little dab of hot English mustard also helps (particularly if you have a mild early season root). Avoid using red wine vinegar unless you want a pink-tinged sauce. Balsamic is a hideous mistake for this.

A friend of mine told me she tried this with a star-anise in the broth. She is super-fond of aniseed, so adored it—I'm not, so probably wouldn't. Although you could play around with the vegetables, don't stray too far. Potatoes are hopeless in it; it instantly becomes a stew. Peeled and quartered turnips worked well on one occasion, but, again, it became a bit stew like. Other than that, I leave it well alone

ENGLISH HIGH-TEA SALAD

Scene inside a typical American diner: George Clooney's sidekick: *"Do you have a green salad?"*
Waitress: *"What the f*** color would it be?"*

Joel and Ethan Coen, *Intolerable Cruelty*

High tea is not to be confused with afternoon tea. They are held at different times of the day, not that you could possibly eat both on the same day. Afternoon tea is at four o'clock *sharp*. High tea is at five or six—it doesn't really matter so much, but it is still tea and definitely not an early dinner. It is a proper, substantial meal (quite unlike afternoon tea) and might include some good ham carved off the bone at the table and served with chutneys or sinus searingly strong mustard, perhaps a cold savoury pie of some sort, many rounds of thick doorstep sandwiches, or plain bread and butter with an array of jams. And cake (there must always be cake) probably the sort that is stuffed full of dried fruits. What there will almost certainly be is some simple main dish—such as scrambled eggs, beans on toast, or a traditionally assembled English salad.

By English salad, I mean the simple throw together of lettuce, cucumber, tomato, and hard-boiled eggs. It must be served naked, unadorned by anything so European as olive oil or fancy vinegars.

No, the sharp vinegary kick comes from pickled beetroot—which should always be served in its jar, placed straight onto the table.

These were the teas of my youth, Saturday and Sunday, regular as clockwork. Mum had given us big lunches, so we needed less than weekdays—when the school cooks obviously couldn't be trusted with filling us up properly. Best of all though were the teas we had on holiday in Devon. Granny, my sister, and I would go into Tavistock and buy a great big tub of clotted cream and eight scones from Crebers. These didn't replace any of the usual items—but were held back 'til last, as an incentive to help us finish up everything else placed before us.

INGREDIENTS
SERVES FOUR
- One big old-fashioned English lettuce
- Half a cucumber, washed and finely sliced—leave the skin on and the pips in
- Four ripe tomatoes, simply quartered
- Four properly hard-boiled eggs, cut into halves

The type of lettuce is really important for this. It's generally called English lettuce; any greengrocer and certainly all supermarkets will sell it year round. It is always sold whole and never cut and pre-washed in plastic bags. It costs just pence. If the lettuce looks even remotely earthy, wash it under a running cold tap.

Tear the leaves off but leave them whole. Arrange around a large shallow glass bowl or serving plate, completely covering the bottom. When you have reached the heart of the lettuce, cut this into four sections. Place those in the center of the serving dish. Lay the sliced cucumber evenly out over the lettuce. Then lay alternate halves of egg and quarters of tomato around the edge of the serving plate—just like a clock face.

Serve with a bottle of Heinz salad cream. And—I'm fanatical about this point—plastic squeezey bottles won't do; it must be a glass bottle that you can smack the bottom of. I actually keep the smallest glass bottle you can buy for taking to the table. When it's empty, I refill it from a giant squeezey—it's considerably cheaper to do it that way. Whatta cheapskate.

PROPER PAVLOVA

I really like the satellite channel UKTV Food. It has some great repeats of my old favorite cooking programs, and a good live program. But—and I know this makes me sound like both a food snob *and* a grumpy old man rolled into one—sometimes the chefs do cook the most ridiculous things. The other day someone made a Peach Melba Pavlova. What was he thinking of? I've since seen pineapple Tarte Tartin. What on earth is next? Sticky toffee pancakes anyone? Or how about rhubarb crumble granita (... actually, you know what, that one might just work—rhubarb granita with a light crumbly biscuit-like topping made from crushed amaretti and flaked almonds ... No!—get a grip Tim!). Pavlova is a classic and, if you ask me, it should stay that way.

There are just two legitimate things with which to top a Pavlova. Raspberries when they're in season, and preferably fresh off the night train from Scotland—and passion fruit for all other occasions.

A good Pav, unlike other meringues, should be a bit chewy in the middle. If you don't agree, just follow the recipe but forget about the cornflour and vinegar. That's what makes this meringue chewy.

The last big decision is whether to make one big one or individual ones. This, I think, is all down to the occasion. If you're having supper with a couple of friends: one big one will accommodate greedy appetites and second helpings. If it's a wedding breakfast: I'd go for individual ones, just for ease of service. Picnic: big one. Smart dinner party with all the finery for your boss/publisher: individuals.

INGREDIENTS
FOR FOUR
- Three egg whites
- 175 g/6 oz (one and a half heaped tablespoons) caster sugar

- One teaspoon cornflour
- A little splash (½ teaspoon, if you must measure it) white wine vinegar
- 300 ml/½ pint whipping or double cream
- Plenty of raspberries or passion fruit (one per person, of the latter) to serve

Separate the egg whites into a large clean bowl. Whisk them into nearly stiff peaks. Then sprinkle half the caster sugar over the surface of the eggs, gently beat that in. Add the rest of the sugar and beat that, even more gently, into the fluffy egg whites. Now add the vinegar and cornflour and very, very gently beat those into the meringue.

Ideally you'll have a non-stick lifetime-guarantee baking sheet, the black-Teflon-floppy kind; if not, use some good-quality non-stick greaseproof paper. Either way, get the baking trays ready with the non-stick stuff on.

If you are making a large one, spoon the whole mixture onto a baking sheet and smooth out with the back of a spoon. If you've opted for four little ones, divide the meringue into four roughly equal blobs on the baking sheet. Using two sheets is a better idea than cooking them in batches. It is important that meringues will fit onto the plates on which they will be served. If you're at all worried about this, cut out a sheet of paper that will fit on those plates, allowing a little tolerance for expansion. These aren't to go underneath the meringue but to have handy as a reference. If you want, draw around them on the greaseproof. It is really irritating, making up a batch of meringues that won't fit on your favorite dessert plates.

These now need to be cooked in the middle or bottom middle of the warm oven (preheated to just 100°C/225°F/gas ¼) for anything between an hour or two or three, depending on the size of the meringues and the accuracy of your oven.

When they're done, some people turn off the oven and leave the door ajar. I'm invariably too busy and need to put something else in to cook. I've found that as long as you don't leave them near an open window or in some other draft, no harm will come to them. Just take them out, put them to one side and get on with things.

To serve, whip the cream until thickened but not stiff. Spoon it onto the centre of the cold meringues. Either tumble some raspberries (possibly seasoned with a little sugar and lemon juice) over the top, or cut the passion fruits in half and scrape the pulp and pips out with a small spoon and dribble over the Pav. Serve promptly or the fruit colors will stain the cream.

VARIATIONS If you're using the passion fruits, spread just a little lemon curd over the meringue before covering with cream.

ENGLISH TIRAMISU

Yerr, right. I know, I know. Not very authentic. But we're all in the EU now. I've nothing against the authentically Italian "Italian Job." I just happen to like this, too.

As with the little trifles and a couple of the other desserts in the book, these can be made up in large, plain, straight-sided glass tumblers.

Break up a few boudoir finger biscuits (one and a bit per person) and place these in the bottom of the glasses. Pour over a few dashes of very strong coffee—ideally espresso—barely enough to wet the biscuits. Next, add a couple of crunched-up amaretti biscuits, then splash in a little amaretto liqueur. Pour on about 2.5 cm/an inch of custard. The glass should now be about half full (I'm an optimist, you see). Refrigerate until needed. Just before serving, pour on just a little double cream and dust a layer of cocoa powder (or grate some plain chocolate) over the top. An alternative topping, and an extra little English twist, is to crunch up yet more amaretti biscuits, mix them with some toasted flaked almonds and sprinkle them over the top. Forget about the cocoa powder. However you choose to finish them, simply place on a side plate and eat with a teaspoon.

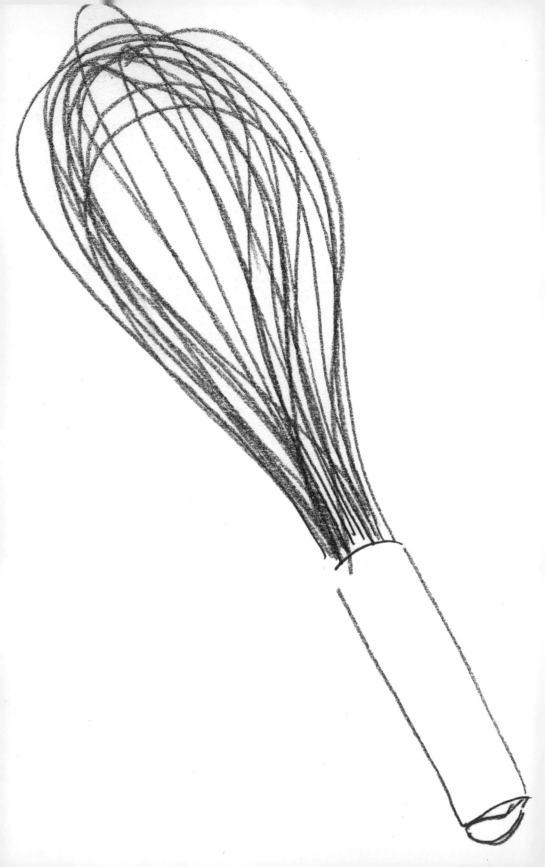

Omelet with Fine Herbs
Piperade
Plain Ordinary Hard-Boiled Eggs
Scotch Eggs
Pea Risotto

AUGUST

Summer's Leftover Chicken
Pasta Dinner
Chicken and Rice Salads
Summer Fruits Sabayon
Floating Islands

A ugust was amazing. It was the height of the hottest summer ever recorded—except for '76. We were sleeping with the windows wide open until 4 a.m., when I would have to close them after being deafened by the dawn chorus. When the nights are, to us, so newly dark (they have no effective street lighting here in the countryside) and silent you really notice when the sun and the birds get up in the morning. In fact, if there is a new moon on a cloudy night, you can't see the person you're lying next to—it's that dark.

The food genuinely seems so much fresher, so much tastier here in the country. I think that's simply because it is. I've been revelling in the brilliance of the produce from my new suppliers since the day we moved here. We've been very lucky with the new butchers. Ruse & Son are one of the handful of butchers who continue to run their own small abattoir out the back. (Initially this just heightened my disappointment at not finding anywhere remote enough, or big enough, to raise a couple of pigs every year.) They tell me that the fact so few places now operate their own abattoir is what makes theirs commercially viable (apparently there are only two butchers who still do this in Suffolk). There are plenty of people within a reasonable distance who *do* fatten a couple of pigs annually, keep a few cows, or keep the grass down in the orchard with a few small sheep. Of what they sell in the shop, their pork is fantastic. It all comes from a small local farmer, who occasionally slips in a particularly fat pig. If you ask them nicely, they will cut you a pork chop which is an inch and a half thick with a decent bit of fat on it. Their beef is excellent, although with only three or four weeks hanging. I like mine "aged" a little longer. If I'm planning a big Sunday roast, I'll ask them, a couple of weeks in advance, to put one aside for me—giving it two extra weeks of maturing helps enormously with the flavor. The lamb is good—but, as before, it's my least favorite of the three main meats we eat.

Unsurprisingly there is no fishmonger for miles around here. It means supermarkets or nothing. I think I'd rather take my chances with frozen—unless all you're after are endless bags of mussels and farmed salmon fillet steaks.

There is a small farm shop, Willow Tree Farm, on the road between Cavendish and Long Melford, that fronts a quite considerable market gardening operation. Their tomatoes are astounding. Picked when ripe, they have a depth of flavor which no supermarket purchase has ever matched. Broad beans, green beans, runner beans; I've come to experience their seasonality, properly, first hand. In Cambridge it was all theory and some careful checking of the labels in the supermarket to see when plastic-wrapped British beans silently changed to Spanish or Kenyan beans. Here, at the farm shop, they tell you, with a sigh of genuine sadness, that there will only be broad beans for another week, if that. If they've not got what you want, I've found it's worth asking. They may even go and pick some for you there and then.

There's also Stumpy's honesty box. Stumpy has a sizeable vegetable patch and single poly-tunnel—up the road—just on the edge of the village as it turns into farmland. On his little sheltered table, if you're lucky, you'll find for sale his tomatoes, broad and runner beans, cucumbers, beetroots, potatoes, onions, lettuces and courgettes. Everything goes very quickly, except for the marrows—you'll always find a couple of those for sale.

The food I've been cooking in August, indeed ever since the day we moved here, reflects these locally-grown superb ingredients. Unlike Annie, I'd never previously been very fond of tomatoes but, the other night she actually asked if we could have a night off from tomatoes—I'd been serving them that often. My father-in-law has agreed that, next year, he will let me fill his greenhouse with tomato plants. Cherry, plum and big-beefy-boy ones I think. My one (very minor) grumble is that the local producers grow too limited a variety. I plan to plug this gap by growing my own, less hum-drum, vegetables. I'll be growing chards, squashes, fennels, interesting beans, bitter salad leaves—at least. It strikes me as pointless to use the little space I'll have available to grow runner and broad beans, onions and potatoes, when I can buy these all for pennies. Besides, they'll have grown either a few hundred yards or half a mile from where I live. Food yards—not food miles.

My distinct shortage of cookbooks on hand has forced me back into the bookshops (happily running, actually). So far it's been a poor year for new cookbooks, *River Cafe Easy* being the notable exception. I am also amazed that I hadn't previously owned Marcella Hazan's *Essentials of Classic Italian Cookery.* Her recipes are brilliant. I've worked my way quickly through all the summer vegetable recipes and many of the salads. Every kitchen should have a copy.

With the exception of making some salads, I hardly cooked in the kitchen for the whole month. When I have done, it's because I'm bored with eating barbecue food. Now how fickle is that, huh?

AUGUST'S DIARY

WEDNESDAY 6 AUGUST
Angelica has started laying again.

FRIDAY 15 AUGUST
I thought the fact that Angelica was laying again meant that she was ready to return to the main coop. She seemed happy enough to be back with the grown-ups—but the chicks cried and didn't seem to realize they had to go in at night. I put mother and chicks back together again.

TUESDAY 19 AUGUST
Little Bo (the smaller of the Blue Andalusians) is clearly not a hen. She's started to crow. Annie insists that I take her back to the chicken lady. Reluctantly I agreed—she's too small to eat.

SUNDAY 24 AUGUST
Ate a delightful lunch in the garden—marred only by all the chicken poo. Will find a man to come and put up a six foot fence.

FRIDAY 29 AUGUST
Quote arrived for £368—just 20feet of chicken wire and a gate. Bugger that—I'll do it myself.

OMELET WITH FINE HERBS

The French would pronounce this as "omelet avec feen 'errbz," and spell it with an extra e at the end of herb (like Concorde). I prefer to Anglicise it.

This is the omelet that announces that summer is here in all its absolute glory. There really is no better reason in summer to have a few herbs growing in your garden or even on your windowsill. Although the herbs started to grow again some months earlier and some newly planted ones have taken hold, in order to go and gather a really large harvest of them has meant waiting until about now. Whilst taking one little sprig or a couple of leaves from each plant won't do them any harm, it won't make much of an omelet either. It is exactly that abundance of herbs from many different plants that makes this so good to eat. One or two herbs will provide you with a nice omelet, but it won't reach the dizzying complex heights that half a dozen, generously-chosen, different ones will.

Herb-wise I try and go for at least five of the following but, at a pinch, four would do: marjoram, thyme, parsley, chervil, chives (or a little very finely chopped spring onion) and *either* tarragon or basil (oddly, they don't really work together). Avoid the woodier rosemary. Use that in the winter with a little melted chopped onion for a more wintery omelet.

It really doesn't make any sense to cook this omelet if you have to buy your herbs in little packets from the shops. It would be absurdly expensive to do it that way. The only way that you might get lucky, is if you can find a *bouquet garni* selection. This should provide you with the bare essentials of parsley, thyme, and perhaps a little basil. Use any others for something else.

INGREDIENTS FOR ONE

- Two large eggs
- At least a dessertspoon of finely chopped mixed herbs (see above) the more heaped the better
- Butter

Proceed as you would for a basic omelet and as it is about to set, sprinkle the herbs over the top. I like to serve this one folded in half, with perhaps just a final pinch of those herbs sprinkled on top. Others prefer to add the mixed herbs to the raw eggs so that they are evenly distributed through the whole omelet.

Serve immediately with a cold, crisp glass of wine and, what else but a simple green salad—packed with summer herbs!

PIPERADE   It now seems impossible to believe but there was a time (and it wasn't that long ago either) that Keith Floyd was, virtually, the only chef on the telly. Naturally he's rerunning all over the satellite channels now; I had no idea he'd made *so many* programmes. Compared to some of the other TV chefs, he almost warrants his own channel: KFTV. Don't think I'm kidding: the way things are going there's sure to be DeliaTV and, of course, the JamieChannel before long.

Anyhow, I have two favorite moments from his vast number of broadcast hours. My first favorite is when he is high up on a hillside in Catalan, Spain.

"I think I must be one of the luckiest chaps in the world!" he says, "I get away from the hurly burly of it all and come up here for a little old barbecue and a slurp ... and, round here they're *meat* eaters." Clive then tilts down to a little makeshift barbecue which has a little leg of kid goat, a big chorizo sausage, a whole Spanish black pudding (the sort with rice in, called a morcilla—pronounced *mor-chee-ya),* and a few quails, all gently cooking away. Floyd then adds some perfect skinny little cutlets of lamb. "Back up to me please, Clive." He pours himself a—glass of red Rioja, looks straight down the camera lens—and toasts us all. What I wouldn't give to have been there, in his place, eating that meaty feast with my family and friends. My favorite sort of food—in one of my favorite places.

Second best Floyd moment (and it's nearly joint first) is when he's cooking piperade in some French madame's kitchen. And this particular cooking sketch isn't going at all well (worse, even, than the "fish baked in a salt-crust" sketch). Madame is pulling faces in the background, tutting and shaking her head. As always, at the end he shows us the bloody mess he's knocked up—scrambled eggs with great lumps of peppers and tomatoes in it. Madame looks offended and, naturally, refuses to eat it. She then soundly trumps him by cooking a perfect piperade herself. In fairness Floyd takes it with very good grace indeed.

In *The Big Red Book of Tomatoes* Lindsey Bareham points out that there is a coarser, less well-cooked, version of piperade (which she prefers—I don't) called Menemen from Turkey. That's pretty much what Floyd, albeit inadvertently, cooked. The difference being that Menemen has just peppers and tomatoes in it and they are still very much identifiable, but not crunchy-raw.

Furthermore, most books seem to agree that, for maximum authenticity, piperade should be served with some dry-cured ham that's been fried to a crisp—then, with no sense of their own stupidity or ineptitude, they suggest using ordinary bacon instead. I think either addition wholly unnecessary and never bother with it.

INGREDIENTS
FOR TWO
- One red and one yellow pepper
- Four big, very ripe, preferably plum, tomatoes—tinned absolutely cannot be substituted here
- One smallish clove of garlic
- Four of the best quality eggs you can get
- A little heap of chopped parsley and/or chives

Roast or grill the peppers in a very hot oven until blackened on the outside. Seal them in a plastic bag to steam the skin loose. Once cool remove them from the bag and peel off most of the, now black, skin. It doesn't matter if you leave a little on them. Deseed them and chop them into pieces about 2.5 cm/an inch square. Skin, deseed, and roughly chop the tomatoes.

Heat a little olive oil in a medium-sized saucepan (I prefer not to use a frying pan for this—though many people do). Finely chop—don't crush—the garlic. Cook the peppers, tomatoes, and garlic until the peppers have almost completely collapsed. If the tomatoes are properly ripe they will, by then, have long since lost their shape. Quickly beat the eggs, then pour them into the saucepan on top of the peppers and tomatoes. Cook them gently, exactly as you would scrambled eggs. Just before they're ready, add salt, pepper, and the herbs. Remember that, just like scrambled eggs, they will continue to cook after you've taken them off the heat.

Serve immediately with, I think, a big chunk of country bread and red wine in a stumpy little Duralex glass. So nouveau-peasant of you.

PLAIN ORDINARY HARD-BOILED EGGS

When I was a child, I ate like a child. I did not like hard-boiled eggs—no, no, no, not one little bit. If I were absolutely forced to, I would simply throw a fit. Now I've grown up and have children of my own, I utterly despair of trying to get them to eat plain ordinary hard-boiled eggs. Unsurprisingly, they don't like them much either.

There are however occasions that call for hard-boiled eggs. My favorite is the Beach Picnic. Those, inevitably sand-covered, eggs were always forced upon me then, so now I, too, pack them in the lunch boxes next to the cheese and pickle sandwiches and bananas. It's traditional—like traffic jams on the A30, windbreaks, 99 ice creams, and grannies paddling in the sea.

Quartered eggs are an integral part of the High-Tea Salad, and you'll be hard pressed to make egg and cress sandwiches if you can't first hard-boil an egg. The main thing to remember is not to use eggs that are spanking fresh—they'll be the devil's own job to peel. Use some that are at least a few days old and you'll be fine.

INGREDIENTS
PER EGG
- One egg
- Boiling water

Place the egg into already-boiling water for just five minutes. Time it accurately. After five minutes, take the pan over to the sink and place it under the cold tap. Run the cold tap into the pan, with the eggs still in it, for a minute or two. This will gently slow down—then stop—the eggs from cooking any further. I've found this the best way to prevent the yolks getting that hideous grey ring around them, and it keeps the yolks *just* on the soft side of solid. Cook them for six or seven minutes if you want solid yolks.

SCOTCH EGGS Fairly obviously, these come from Scotland. What other nation could have come up with deep-frying hard-boiled eggs *and* have the genius idea of wrapping them up in sausagemeat? I think they're great. I've recently rediscovered them, having been put off, for years and years, by their appearance alongside wilting salad at school. They were utterly, stomach-numbingly, no-thanks-I'd-rather-go-hungry, nearly-as-bad-as-gammon-and-pineapple: disgusting. The cheap sausage meat tasted of nothing to do with a pig. And those eggs—how long must you boil an egg for it to achieve that uniform greyness of yolk? I was not, knowingly, any sort of a foodie at the age of eleven but I could recognise utter filth when I was expected to eat it.

Make them yourself—with properly cooked eggs and your favorite sausagemeat—they are a revelation.

INGREDIENTS
MAKES FOUR
- Four "softly" hard-boiled eggs, peeled (see previous recipe)
- Five or six of your favorite bangers, more if you've bought chipolatas, or about 250 g/8 oz if you are getting loose sausagemeat

- A good pinch of salt
- One egg, for coating
- Plenty of breadcrumbs (see below)
- Sunflower oil for frying

If you are using your favorite sort of sausages (and that is a sensible place to start, isn't it?), slit the skins and remove the meat. I always seem to need slightly more than one sausage per egg; about one and a half seem to do it. Mix in a good pinch of salt per egg. This will help the meat to firm up and contribute a little extra seasoning, necessary for the eggs.

The tricky bit is getting the meat around the egg or, indeed, the egg inside the meat—depending on your point of view. I do it with the aid of some plastic wrap. Stretch a large piece, at least a foot long, out on a work surface. Take a quarter of the sausage-meat (i.e. one and a half de-skinned sausages) and form it into a ball. Place it on the plastic wrap. Put another piece of plastic wrap on top of the meat. Using, initially, the palm of your hand and then, perhaps, a rolling pin, flatten it out. It must reach a diameter where you can roll the egg across it without running out of meat.

Take the top piece of plastic wrap off and place an egg in the middle. Pick the whole thing up, with your hand under the bottom piece of plastic wrap and wrap the meat around the egg— obviously making sure you keep the plastic wrap on the outside! Once the egg has disappeared within its sausagey jacket, discard the plastic wrap. Wet your hands, and finish shaping the Scotch egg into an egg shape. Take a bit of time to get them egg shaped, rather than rugby or football shaped. Set this to one side and do the other three in the same way. You will get a lot quicker and more confident as you go along.

If you want to, you can muck around with the sausagemeat before you start. Add some extra herbs—especially sage—or some very finely chopped, gently-sweated onions, mace, nutmeg, even lemon zest—all are good. However, I tend not to. At most, I may add some fennel. I'm very happy with the quality and flavor of the plain sausagemeat that I get from my butcher. It is also why I recommend that you use your favorite sausages in the first place. If you want to have a go at trying things out, then add something different to each handful of sausagemeat. They don't all need to taste the same, do they?

Before frying them, they need to be coated. I prefer not to use those ghastly little orange breadcrumbs, so beloved of Cap'n Birdseye, but I still buy my breadcrumbs. Freshly made ones will burn too quickly and will not do at all for this. The brand I buy is Goldenfry Natural Breadcrumbs. They have the same texture and taste as the orange ones but look a little more appetizing. I also use them for coating chicken croquettes.

Beat the raw egg (for coating) in a small dish. Put the breadcrumbs in another dish. There is no way *not* to get sticky fingers now. Have a plate ready and waiting to put them on. Dip each Scotch egg into the beaten egg and roll it around to make sure it's fully coated. Then put it in the breadcrumbs and smother it until completely covered in crumbs. If you want an extra crisp coating (yes you do) do that all over again for a second time.

Put them in the fridge for at least an hour to let it all set and firm up a bit before deep-frying. When you want to cook them, heat the oil to 180°C or, if you don't have a thermometer, drop a little bread into the oil to test its temperature—it should bubble and turn slowly into fried bread. Too hot and it will quickly burn; not hot enough and it won't brown. Cook them one or two at a time; don't overcrowd the pan or the heat will drop and they will get very greasy. Yuk!

When you're happy with their color—after about five or six minutes—remove the eggs and sit them on a piece of kitchen paper to soak up any excess oil. Leave them a minute or two, if you want to eat them hot, or let them cool to room temperature. They taste horrid when cold from the fridge. I like to eat them tepid with homemade salad cream.

VARIATIONS Welsh Eggs. It was news to me when I recently discovered that the Welsh also have a national way with the hard-boiled egg. Simply wrap the hard-boiled egg up in mashed potato (instead of sausagemeat) and then egg and breadcrumb as above. The mash should be well-seasoned and quite stiff—very little butter and no milk. If you want to glam it up a bit, add some grated cheese to the mash. Try anything hard from cheddar to Parmesan and everything in between, except, I think, blue cheeses.

CHEFFY TIP   This really is a great trick with the plastic wrap. I often use it to hammer out an onglet steak or to thin down a veal escalope. It works well for flattening a chicken breast (as for Piri-Piri Chicken). For a chicken escalope, cut a chicken breast in half through its thinnest side (to give you two "thin" chicken breasts). Then flatten each piece between the plastic wrap and egg and breadcrumb it, just like the Scotch eggs above; but shallow fry it in a little butter and good plain olive oil. Put a thin slither of mozzarella on the top as soon as you take it out of the pan—it will melt perfectly from the heat in the chicken. I used to buy these in a sandwich—chicken escalope, roast red and yellow peppers, and onions, all stuffed into a huge piece of ciabatta from an Italian deli/ sandwich bar just off Tottenham Court Road. I forget the deli's name, sorry about that. It has probably closed now anyway—too many McPrets stealing the little man's business.

PEA RISOTTO   I find that making risotto is therapeutic for my soul.

There is real pleasure to be derived from having to spend about twenty-five minutes in the kitchen—at the end of a long day in the office or with the children—just stirring your dinner until it's ready. Sounds crazy, I know. You'd think you'd just want to sit down and "veg out," but I find it works wonders for me.

I make lots of different risottos but they must all start with a good chicken stock, either dark brown or pale in color. Which one you make will depend upon whether you have made the stock with the roasted carcass (dark) or with the raw carcass (light).

If you've got a dark chicken stock then, undoubtedly, mushrooms are top of my list and I always have dried ceps in the kitchen for just such an occasion. If you've made a light chicken stock, then you have many more options open to you. Chicken stock is all I use in my kitchen. If a recipe I want to try says "combine 250 ml of game stock, 250 ml of chicken stock and 250 ml of veal stock..." then 750 ml of chicken stock will do just fine. A light chicken stock can even be used in place of fish stock, as long as you remain light handed with it

It's currently in vogue for trendy restaurants to use a collection of different, inevitably baby, vegetables to make a chi-chi little risotto and name it Risotto Primavera. Vegetable infanticide risotto would be nearer the mark! I've nothing against little vegetables, but can we please start eating the grown-ups again? Big vegetable equals big flavor. Whatever vegetable you choose, the rice is always the base carbohydrate and you can experiment with what you add, almost endlessly.

A particular favorite of mine—and I list it partly because it can be entirely free of any form of seasonal snobbery—is pea risotto. It's a variation of *Risi e Bisi,* which is *the* classic Venetian soupy risotto. It varies from the classic in that I normally use frozen peas—not fresh—and there are no pods in mine. If you grow your own peas, then you'll need to shell them and add the finely sliced pods (minus the internal membrane) about half way through the cooking. I personally wouldn't bother with buying those packets of podded fresh peas to try and make the *Risi e Bisi.* I find they have always lost their essential sweetness by the time you can get them home.

INGREDIENTS
TWO PEOPLE
- 150 g/6 oz good risotto rice such as Calasparra, Carnaroli or Arborio
- Plenty of defrosted frozen peas, about a cupful
- One medium onion, very finely chopped

- Two sticks of celery (not the tough outer ones), very finely
    chopped
- Two cloves of garlic
- Freshly grated Parmesan
- Butter
- Olive oil
- Pale chicken stock, made from one carcass

Boil the kettle. Put the chicken stock into a pan and bring it up to the merest blip; it needn't boil. I haven't given any quantity for the stock because it's going to be the stock from one carcass. If you run out before the rice is ready, then just finish off with water from the kettle.

Melt a big knob of butter in a deep-sided roomy pan. Add a little good olive oil. Now gently sweat the finely chopped onion and celery until they become soft. Add the garlic. Don't let these vegetable catch. There will now need to be some butter and oil visible in the bottom of the pan. If there isn't any, then add some more. Add the rice and stir it around in the buttery oil until you can hear the rice start to make a weird screeching sort of sound. It will be quite quiet. Keep stirring. A visual clue is that the edges of the rice grains will start to become translucent. Either way you measure it, a minute or two at the most will do. Now add the first ladle or two of stock. There will be an almighty hissing sound. Keep stirring the rice and add more stock as the rice absorbs the liquid and swells up. Keep stirring the rice and adding more ladles of the stock. Don't add too much seasoning as you go but you'll need to check it again at the end. I like the rice *al dente* (with bite), this does not *ever* mean "a bit chalky." My wife prefers the rice cooked soft the whole way through—you choose. At this stage, add the defrosted peas (they were cooked briefly before freezing so need nothing more than reheating). Stir them into the rice. Now add the handful of freshly grated Parmesan, a little splash of dry vermouth, perhaps a little chopped basil and/ or mint if you have it to hand. Stir it once more. Taste and adjust the seasoning. Sometimes I find a tiny squeeze of lemon helps.

Leave the risotto to relax for a minute or two (you should do the same) with the lid on, then serve immediately. Risotto will not be kept warm.

Yes, it's labor intensive, but deeply rewarding.

SUMMER'S LEFTOVER CHICKEN PASTA DINNER

Cook some pasta (penne, farfale, rigatoni); season and toss it in a little butter to stop it sticking. Whilst it's cooking tear the leftover chicken into little pieces. Halve some seedless green grapes and roughly chop some tarragon leaves. Add these three ingredients to the cooling pasta and squeeze over a little lemon juice. Stir in sufficient double cream to enrobe everything. No need for cheese. Serve dinner in the garden tonight.

VARIATIONS

Add a little finely chopped spring onion or shredded lettuce (something crisp, like Little Gem) to make more of it if the leftover chicken is a bit sparse.

CHICKEN AND RICE SALADS

This salad can—just about—be made from leftover bits of plain roast chicken. But I think the secret of a good chicken and rice salad is, simply, good chicken. Lots of it too—roughly equal volumes. Far too often this sort of salad is a "throw-together" with mean little scraps of chicken to add just a little interest to what is, otherwise, a mountain of cold rice. There are many much better things to be made given just half a handful of cold chicken.

Having said that I do, quite often, make this with leftovers, just as long as there's lots of it. When I've simply roast a whole chicken, and eaten half of it—then I might make the other half into this dish. That's two main meals for two people. As always, make stock from the carcass for the basis of a third. I suggest tearing the chicken into little pieces, rather than chopping it.

It looks nicer and (I theorize, at least) the coarsely torn ends hold the dressing a little more eagerly.

I always, only ever, use plain basmati rice for this salad. I've tried making it with Calasparra, Arborio, American Easy Cook and, on one terrible occasion, Thai sticky rice. If I have some left-over rice in the fridge then so much the better. I always cook more rice than I need at the time—it's so useful for thickening soup or eating cold like this. And there's always egg-fried rice. Cook it exactly as per the instructions on the packet. Do this allowing plenty of time for the rice to cool down.

Now, the man from the Environmental Health Office will tell you that cold rice is a problem. There is a bacterium associated with it that in adverse conditions produces spores, which when cooked rice is left for a few hours, or overnight, can be released allowing the bacteria to multiply. The best advice is to refrigerate the rice rather than leaving it out in the kitchen, so significantly reducing the risk. I read the advice of one EH officer who thought it was safer to throw away leftover rice rather than reheat it, such as with fried rice. But then he would say that.

I've not supplied a recipe to make this whole dish—just a basic dressing, which really is fantastic—and then a list of combinations of things that work together as additions. I can't remember ever making two salads the same. Wouldn't that be boring? What's important is to balance sweet with sharp, and the soft textures of the chicken and rice with something a little crunchy. Beyond that, make it up as you go along.

BASIC DRESSING
- One fully laden teaspoon of French mustard
- About three teaspoons of good red wine vinegar
- A big slug of extra virgin olive oil, use the good stuff

Simply whisk all these three thoroughly together in a little bowl. Mix the dressing into the rice salad at the last minute. The other dry ingredients can be added to the rice beforehand. Once the salad has been fully assembled taste it, adding some more seasoning and vinegar or oil as needed.

My favorite additions: A few coarsely chopped capers, plenty of diced cornichons, pine nuts and lots of raisins.

Annie's favorite additions: coarsely chopped pitted black olives, finely chopped spring onions, diced red pepper, and a few dried chili flakes thrown in for good measure.

OTHER COMBINATIONS ARE:
- Finely diced hard cheese, such as Beaufort or Gruyere
- Roughly chopped parsley and flaked almonds.
- Broken up walnuts and pomegranate seeds—very pretty indeed

Asparagus is the only vegetable that makes a starring appearance in my rice salads, but then, when it's in season, I'll (almost) eat it for breakfast, such is my passion for it. For this, choose the thinner spears, snap off the woody ends, and quickly blanch. When cooled down, slice diagonally into little pieces. Reduce the quantity, or forgo completely, the vinegar.

A lovely summer version needs nothing more than a really generous selection of freshly chopped herbs from the garden: Parsley, chervil, thyme, chives, and *lots* of mint.

In the depths of winter, chopped apple (leave the skin on, and drop the diced apple into lemon acidulated water until the last moment), raisins, maybe some chopped dates or dried apricots, and a pinch of cinnamon.

The store-cupboard-standby. A jar of pesto. Use just enough to make the whole thing turn a delicious shade of pale green.

SUMMER FRUITS SABAYON

I remember exactly the occasion I first ate a sabayon, and it was spread over a tumbled mass of summer fruits just as I describe here. A simple sabayon is undeniably similar in execution to the Italian zabaglione. It's egg yolks and alcohol beaten to a froth over a low heat. The Italians always use marsala wine and serve the froth, as it is, in a glass with a biscuit or two on the side. The French use their native sweet dessert wines, then might spoon it over fruits and place it under the grill to give it a little color. Two very different results from two very similar beginnings. I couldn't pick a favorite between them. What I can say is that I tend to cook the sabayon in the warmer months and the zabaglione as the evenings draw in a bit.

You will need to be able get your grill blisteringly hot or have a blowtorch to get the top brown.

INGREDIENTS
SERVES FOUR
- 150 ml/¼ pint good dessert wine—ideally a French muscat variety
- Four egg yolks
- 40 g/1½ oz caster sugar
- A big pile of your favorite summer berries: raspberries, strawberries, blackcurrants, redcurrants
- A little extra caster sugar
- A generous squeeze of lemon

First of all, pick over the berries, discarding any less than perfect ones. Hull the strawberries. Place them in a bowl and sprinkle over a little caster sugar and squeeze over some lemon juice. Fruits generally, but especially berries, benefit from a little seasoning with sugar and lemon, just as a piece of beef needs the salt. Don't do this too far in advance though; leave it 'til you're getting started.

Place the egg yolks in a Pyrex or stainless steel bowl that you know will fit comfortably over a small pan of simmering water (or use a double boiler if you have one). Whisk the yolks until smooth. Add the wine and whisk again. Add the sugar and whisk again. Get a little pan of water (about half full—the bowl mustn't touch the water) up to a very gentle simmer. Put the bowl containing the egg mix on top of the simmering pan and whisk it over the heat for about five minutes until it is a voluminous froth. Remove from the heat and set aside.

By now the grill should be hot—or have your blowtorch ready.

Arrange a mixture of the berries onto individual plates. Spoon the sabayon all over the berries. Either place each plate in turn under the grill—in which case it will take only 20-30 seconds for the sabayon to turn a tasty looking shade of brown—or set to it with the blow torch. The trick with this is not to get the heat too close. It's not a creme brulée that you are trying to caramelize. The sauce will quickly scorch, so start gently and see how it goes.

Serve it straight away, with some delicate little almond biscuits and the rest of the bottle of wine, which should be served very well chilled.

FLOATING ISLANDS

Assuming that you've made real custard and not opened a carton, you'll have some egg whites sitting around in a little bowl. This is a great way of using them up. It's an easy thing to cook since the custard will have been made in advance, leaving you just the whisking, poaching, and plating up to do at the last minute.

Have the custard chilling in the fridge. Whisk two egg whites until they form stiff peaks, then whisk in 125 g/4 oz of caster sugar—just a little at a time. Keep whisking until the frothy meringue holds its shape. Have a wide pan of water, with a snug fitting lid, already holding a gentle simmer. You will need about 5-7.5 cm/ two to three inches of water in the bottom. Add spoonfuls of the meringue to the water (if you want to make quenelles—just little cheffy rugby ball shapes—go ahead. I'm happy making puffy blobs). Don't overcrowd the pan. They will only take a couple of minutes to puff up slightly and stiffen, so there's no pressure. When ready, remove them from the water with a slotted spoon. Serve by placing one or two islands on a plate that is covered with cold custard.

VARIATIONS

The French bourgeois classic has the islands dressed with a little drizzle of toffee-colored caramel.

Just heat a couple of tablespoons of caster sugar and a tablespoon of water to the point where the sugar turns brown. Use a teaspoon to flick little strands of this hot caramel over the meringue. Be careful though, melted sugar gets incredibly hot.

Hugh Fearnley-Whittingstall *(River Cottage Cookbook)* suggests a drizzle of his blackcurrant sauce and a scattering of fresh berries.

A Belgian restaurant once served me this dish with little flakes of pistachios on top of the meringues.

Eggy Bread
Potted Chicken Livers
Summer Herby Roast Chicken
Pigeon Breast and Chicken
Liver Salad

SEPTEMBER

Roast Chicken with Fennel
Chicken with Lots of Garlic
Classic Crème Brûlée
(and three variations on a theme)
Fresh Fruits Fools

September is the month when the Cavendish and District Horticultural Society hold their annual show. It's thrown in a big marquee at the top of the village green. Naturally, it's always on the same day as the Cavendish Village Fete. Christopher Biggins' face was on all the posters—he was to be our big celebrity opening. The marquee was at the top of the green, in front of the little village school. Further down the green were the tombolas, coconut shies, WI cake stalls, and dainty old-fashioned merry-go-rounds that you would expect. The children loved sitting in the vintage fire engine that rolled up for the afternoon. My daughter had a ride around the green on a little Shetland pony courtesy of the local riding school.

I obviously didn't have any vegetables in my garden to exhibit, and I didn't trust my new (utterly rubbish) oven to bake a cake. So I decided to enter my home craft just in the chutney and crab apple jelly categories. From the garden I was able to enter "a selection of four herbs in a vase," "five culinary apples" and "five dessert apples." Our garden is blessed with a fine old Bramley tree (much older than the house) and an established dessert apple tree. Brogdale—the home of the National Fruit Collection—have since identified it as an Ellison's Orange. Its apples are superb.

On the day, I couldn't find the chutney (still in some unmarked box somewhere). After four separate attempts, I finally managed to make a crab apple jelly, that whilst not really cloudy, was certainly not gin-clear. I opted for interest with the herbs: Blue hyssop, purple sage, flowering chives, and fennel (in seed). The judges apparently prefer to see a selection of predictable rosemary, sage, basil, and mint (most looked like they'd come from the supermarket to me). Sadly, everyone else has a good selection of apple trees too. It was a fiercely contested category—unlike some of the other more obscure fruits, like quinces, in which the sole entrant was assured First Prize (I've since ordered a quince tree for the garden!).

I was devastated at not even scraping third prize in anything. To make it worse, my father-in-law romped home with "best exhibit in show" for (... drumroll please ...) a pot plant! A bloody pot plant! All he'd had to do was buy it and water it! Life's not fair, is it?

On top of all this, there was further upset when Biggins cancelled at the last moment. Last time I'd seen him in person was in Harry's bar, Venice, one cold January cocktail hour. The first and only other time I've ever seen him was just three days beforehand buying a sandwich in M&S in Cambridge when he was at the end of a panto run.

I'm still smarting about that pot plant.

SEPTEMBER'S DIARY

TUESDAY 2 SEPTEMBER
Only three hens laying at present —Angelica, Princess Amidala, and Beatrice (sole remaining Light Sussex from the January hatch). Two old Welsummers are now in moult —two younger ones are still too young. Big Bo has an enormous wattle and comb — worried she might be a cockerel like her sister. Of Angelica's three chicks— two are cockerels. Fattening them up for the table — Annie's agreed not to get attached to them or give them names. The Araucana is quite small but may be laying by Christmas.

SATURDAY 6 SEPTEMBER
Big Bo is doing the shuffle (chicken foreplay —I suppose). This is a good sign.

MONDAY 8 SEPTEMBER
Big Bo has just laid her first egg — very white, quite small— perfectly formed.

SATURDAY 13 SEPTEMBER
Went to buy some posts and chicken wire from a local fencing supplier. They gave me the phone number of a bloke who could install it—much better idea!

MONDAY 15 SEPTEMBER
New fencing bloke came around today. He will do the job for £100 —all in. I reckon that the materials alone are about £50. Done deal. Getting about two eggs a day now —four hens laying.

FRIDAY 19 SEPTEMBER
Fencing bloke has finished the fence. Chickens still running around the garden. Rather than trying to round them up —I left the gate to their run open. Come dusk, they all trotted in to their coop —I closed the gate after them. Easy.

EGGY BREAD
Great comfort food, and our children adore this too. It is not to be confused with pain perdu—this is the down-at-heel cousin—quicker to make and rough at the edges.

Sometimes I make up a slice of this to go with either bacon or black pudding for a late-morning weekend breakfast. If there are some excellent local berries at the farm shop or in the hedgerows, I'll buy them or pick them and make a quick compote. It takes no time to gently heat through these blackcurrants, raspberries, strawberries, or blackberries with a little sugar. Spoon the warm mixture (quite unlike jam) over the finished bread and you have a delightful summer's lunch—best eaten outside. When it gets colder, I might have a slice with my favorite sweet chili sauce (Lingham's chili, garlic and ginger) for lunch or a quiet supper after a big lunch out.

This seems to work best with slightly stale bread of most sorts. I've used sliced white, crusty white, wholemeal, French bread, and even brioche. They were all pretty good, with the baguette being the biggest surprise—the edges were a fabulous textural mix of crunchy and chewy and the centre the softest of them all. The brioche was a bit rich and prone to sogginess. Avoid that just by dipping the brioche quickly in and out of the egg before frying.

Stay away from granary completely—the grainy texture is really quite unpleasant. One other type of bread that didn't really work was pain Poilâne. It is distinctively heavy, naturally-leavened bread, so the finished slice didn't get that puffy soufflé-esque finish that the other more open textured breads achieve. Still, as it makes such good toast, why bother with this at all; just remember that the staler Poilâne gets, the thinner you cut it for toasting.

I've been deliberately vague about the quantity of bread you'll need. If I say one slice per person and you have a dirty great big doorstep of a loaf—you'll not thank me. Neither will you if you have only cooked a single slice of skinny little baguette.

INGREDIENTS
- Enough slices of bread to feed however many people there are
- One egg per person

Beat the eggs in a shallow plate, one that is large enough to allow the bread to lie completely flat on it without the edges being forced to curl up over the rim. Season lightly and don't add any milk. Allow the bread to soak for as long as you like. Impatience and hunger normally means it is likely to be no more than five to ten minutes. Turn it once or twice during this time. If you're making up a big batch, then use more than one plate to soak the bread in. Stacking the bread up with a little egg mixture spooned into the middle doesn't do the job at all.

Get a frying pan nice and hot. Add a knob of butter and whoosh it around the pan. When the butter has stopped sizzling, only then is it as hot as it will get without burning. Now is the time to slip the bread into the pan. Cook until a lovely deep-golden brown and then turn it over. You may find that you want to add a little more butter to cook the second side; if so, go ahead. When it's ready, serve immediately.

POTTED CHICKEN LIVERS

"You know what everybody likes? Parfait. Have you ever met a person and you say—hey, let's go get some parfait, and they say—hell no, I don't like no parfait. Parfaits are delicious! Parfaits may be the most delicious thing on the whole damned planet. Do you have a tissue or something, 'cos I'm making a mess? Just the word parfait's made me start slobbering."
—Donkey (in *Shrek The Movie*)

You see, parfait is good, but I don't particularly care for liver pâté; coarsely-ground over-cooked dried-out liver, clumsy seasoning, and with much too much booze (people always add too much booze don't they)? In fact, liver pâté aside, I think just about any sort of thing with chicken livers is good. I like them in omelets, spiced up and served with rice, or simply fried until just done; spread on a piece of decent toast that's been rubbed with garlic and drizzled with a splash of good olive oil (a bruschetta, in fewer words). That alone is good but you can make it brilliant without the oil and garlic;

just butter the toast and add a generous dob of mango chutney. I know it sounds weird but trust me (and thank Lindsey Bareham, in whose book *A Wolf in the Kitchen* I read about it). It is stupendous.

But that greying chicken liver pâté will never ever tempt me. It's neither heavenly ambrosia smooth, as in a parfait, nor is it properly country pub chunky "hold the ploughman's, landlord—I'm in the mood for liver." It's just a lazy, in limbo, doesn't know what it wants to be when it grows up, thrown together, livery mush. And I don't want it.

This recipe will give you little chunks of liver, flushed with pink, yet cooked through, set in lovely scented butter. Try and use fresh livers if you can. Some supermarkets stock them and most butchers will get them for you, given a little notice. You are unlikely to find certified organic or even free-range ones. If you do, you are indeed blessed—eat a lot of them.

INGREDIENTS
MAKES ⅝–¾ RAMEKINS FULL
- 340 g/12 oz fresh chicken livers, this is the amount Waitrose sell them in, a little more or less will do

FOR THE BUTTER
- One Spanish onion, or a few shallots
- Half a cup of white wine vinegar
- One cup of white wine
- 125 g/4 oz of unsalted butter

First make the butter. Finely chop the onion or shallot, and place it in a saucepan with the vinegar and white wine. Bring it to a rapid boil and reduce until there is just the onion in a rather sticky syrup. Add the butter a little at a time, stirring it in. Once all the butter has melted, pour it through the finest sieve you have. Keep to one side.

Heat up a big, heavy-bottomed frying pan. Pick over the livers, cutting away and discarding any slightly greenish looking bits.

Cut the livers into their two main parts. Cut each piece into three or four—the idea is that the final pieces will be just the right size to scoop out of the ramekin and press onto a piece of toast with a knife.

Put some butter, and just a little sunflower oil, into the hot pan. Add the livers and season with salt and pepper. Cook until nearly done but definitely still pink in the middle. Remove them from the pan and leave to dry and cool down on some kitchen paper. If they went straight into the ramekins and got covered with warm butter, they would overcook. Once they are quite cool, spoon them into the ramekins, positioning them so they are fairly tightly packed, but don't push them down too hard. Pour the cool, but not yet set, butter over them to cover. Traditionalists would now want to set a small bay leaf into the surface. I prefer to leave them half an hour in the fridge, then place three bruised juniper berries in a little triangle in the centre of each ramekin.

Serve this with a couple of slices of dry toast. Unsurprisingly it won't need buttering!

SUMMER HERBY ROAST CHICKEN

This is my all-time favorite "last meal before I face the firing squad" way of roasting a chicken. My way certainly won't be unique but it is delicious.

I had originally intended to call this recipe Sinatra Roast Chicken (Frank Sinatra—"My Way"—Geddit?), but it turns out there is already a recipe called "Chicken-Sinatra Style." I was leafing through the *Sopranos Family Cookbook* the other day, trying to find a recipe for cannoli (I had, some days beforehand, had one of those stupid, over-heated, slightly-drunk, nerdy, obsessive, discussions in the pub, over whether the line "Leave the gun. Bring the cannoli" was from *The Sopranos*, or *The Godfather*. Turns out, I was right—it's in *The Godfather*). I found the recipe for the Gangster Cannoli, and Chicken—Sinatra Style. Not wanting to upset these goodfellas, I changed the name.

This recipe doesn't do the traditional trimmings—whatsoever. I also use a small chicken—an ordinary one-and-a-third to one-and-a-half kilogram supermarket-size bird. It will, at a pinch, just feed four (with no leftovers, at all). I like to cook this most in the summer, with the freshness and lightness of the herby gravy (it may be more appropriate—but *unthinkable*—to call it a "jus"). Conveniently there are often six people around to feed, so I cook two birds. Who could complain about leftovers?

This is a particularly good recipe to have up your sleeve for those Sunday lunches when the weatherman is being no help whatsoever and you can't decide whether you dare stoke up the barbie or should just turn the oven on. A barbecue for four or six is easy enough to cater for—six of us can sit comfortably around the table in the garden. A barbecue for eight or more brings a whole different level of commitment: rugs have to be laid on the lawn, massive salads dressed, a Spanish omelet produced, spare ribs and chicken legs marinated, and sausages purchased.

As long as I have two of these little chickens in the fridge, I can decide, as late as an hour before friends arrive, whether to barbecue or roast (assuming there are no more than six of us). I have served these roast chickens when eating al fresco and no-one missed the barbecue. There is, in fact, something indecently decadent about sitting at a properly laid table in the shade of a fruit tree and bringing warm food out from the kitchen. They also seem to improve if kept in a very, very low oven for half an hour, maybe more. The skins gets crisper, the flesh becomes almost sticky at the extremities and falls more easily from the bone. Perfect for when you finally abandon your fork and want to pick up a wing or leg to gnaw on.

Simon Hopkinson was the first person to introduce me to the affinity of tarragon and chicken through his, now sadly departed, column in the *Independent on Saturday*. (Note to commissioning editors everywhere; when he left, circulation dropped by, at least, one—so always pay the food writer whatever his agent demands!)

Tarragon is strong stuff and a little goes a long way. Two or three sprigs per chicken are plenty. If you don't like tarragon, or haven't got any, replace it with a selection of herbs. Parsley, sage, rosemary, and thyme always form a pretty good basis. Chervil, chives, fennel (leaves and seeds) are good too. Sage and rosemary on their own in the middle of winter are fantastic. Don't even think of roasting basil leaves. Use what herbs you have available to you. Experiment.

INGREDIENTS

SERVES FOUR, JUST
- One good quality chicken (free-range, or organic for preference)
- One lemon halved
- Half a smallish onion, very roughly chopped
- Two cloves of garlic, skinned but left whole
- A few sprigs of tarragon—leaves removed from the stalks (or some other fresh herby combination)
- A great big knob of butter
- A glass of dry vermouth or dry white wine

Start by checking that there is no bag of giblets inside the bird's body cavity (if there is, remove it). Then rinse the bird inside and out. Remove any fatty bits inside the vent flap. Pat the bird's skin dry. Season the inside of the bird with salt and pepper. Push the tarragon stalks (having stripped off the leaves for later) and the onion inside the bird. Squeeze one half of the lemon into the cavity. Then push that in too.

Smear all of the butter all over the chicken's skin and then season generously with salt and pepper. Roast the chicken in the oven, preheated to 200°C/400°F/gas 6, for about one hour or until it is fully cooked. Baste it occasionally.

To make the gravy, scrape the bits of onion, lemon, and herb stalk that are inside the chicken into the roasting tin. Remove the chicken to a warm place and give it a tinfoil blanket. Add the vermouth or wine to the roasting tin and place on a hob. Get it really hot and scrape all the bits off the bottom. Pour this buttery, winey sauce through a sieve into a clean pan. If you feel there is too much butter/chicken fat spoon a little off the top. Similarly add more vermouth/wine if you wish. Finely chop and then add the herbs to the pan. Bring it up to a simmer and let the herbs infuse with the gravy/sauce.

I prefer to joint the chicken roughly, then take it to the table for people to help themselves. Put the herby sauce in to a warmed jug or gravy boat. Serve with simple roast potatoes and a seasonal vegetable.

NOTE If you're using a selection of herbs, mix half of these into the butter before rubbing that into the chicken skin. Add the other half to the little saucepan instead of the chopped tarragon leaves.

PIGEON BREAST & CHICKEN LIVER SALAD

I first ate a pigeon breast and duck liver salad, probably about fifteen years ago, in The Crown in Southwold. Something (can't remember what) recently jogged my memory of it, so here is my version. Duck livers are a tad tricky to get hold of, unless you're a restaurant—so I use chicken livers instead.

There are two distinct ways of serving this salad. Either cut the livers and breast into little mouth-sized pieces before scattering over the salad or serve them whole, just as they come out of the pan. Both have their merits. I'm not really fussed either way. I think it's better as a "pile it up high" salad, rather than some sort of deconstructed group of little piles on a restaurant-sized plate that's as big as a coffee table.

Pigeon breasts can be bought from some supermarkets already off the bone. If you've got whole pigeons, just whip the breasts off with a boning knife. If you want to make some stock from the carcasses, roast them first and you'll find it tastes closer to beef stock than to chicken stock. Add to that some peas and a few bits of broken spaghetti, maybe some chopped parsley and chives, and you've got a classy little soup.

One pigeon breast and two or three livers will make a substantial starter—or use a few more leaves and double up on the protein. Then you have a substantial lunch or supper-time salad.

INGREDIENTS
FOR TWO STARTER-SIZED SALADS

- Two plump pigeon breasts, try to choose ones without any shot in them
- Four chicken livers, if frozen—completely defrosted
- Sufficient bitter salad leaves, such as frisee, endive, watercress to satisfy
- One quantity of mustard salad dressing, see below

Start by checking the livers for any green-tinged bile spots or little bits of fat. Trim off any that you find. Rinse the livers under cold water and pat them dry with some kitchen paper.

Put a little frying pan on maximum heat. Make the salad dressing, and prepare the leaves. Don't pour the dressing on just yet—salad leaves wilt very quickly.

Season the skinless pigeon breasts with a little salt and pepper and then rub them all over with a little sunflower oil. Slip them into the searingly-hot frying pan. After about two minutes, they should be ready to flip over—it's impossible to be exact, no two pans will be the same temperature, just as no two pigeons are the same size. What you're looking for is a little browning and evidence that the heat has started to work its way up the sides. Four minutes total cooking time should ensure a nice rare, pink breast. Place the breasts to one side to rest. Season and oil the livers. Fry them until a little crisp at the edges. The livers are ready when still just pink. If you're inexperienced at cooking these, the easiest thing is just to cut one open and have a look.

Dress the salad leaves and arrange them on a plate. Place the breast on top of the leaves and the livers around. Alternatively slice the pigeon breast into five or six pieces, then cut the livers into quarters and scatter these over and around the salad leaves.

MUSTARD DRESSING

This is a little punchier than an ordinary oil and vinegar emulsion. It goes well with the richness of the meat and the bitterness of the autumnal leaves.

INGREDIENTS
- Four tablespoons extra virgin olive oil
- One tablespoon red wine vinegar
- One teaspoon Dijon mustard, either with or without grains
- Half a clove of mashed garlic
- Dashes of Tabasco
- A pinch of sugar
- Salt and pepper

I'm not really a fan of the jam jar approach to making salad dressings—but it has its uses: Place all the ingredients in a clean jam jar. Shake until completely emulsified. This is particularly useful if you want to make up extra dressing to keep in the fridge. The downside is, if you're at all like me, that you'll end up with half a dozen jam jars festering at the back of the fridge. I always make up dressings as I need them.

The other method, the one I use, is to put all the ingredients into a large bowl and use a little hand whisk to emulsify them. It takes mere moments.

ROAST CHICKEN WITH FENNEL

You might just see some native bulb fennel in the shops by the end of July; it will certainly be available all through August, September, and October. Then it's all over by Bonfire Night. Then, back to the imports.

Although this is definitely roast chicken it isn't "roast whole." It goes into the oven jointed, like the Easy Chicken with Lemon and the Chicken with Parsnips and Pears. I'm a huge fan of cooking chicken in this way—no carving, so less bother. Everything is in one dish.

Either buy some chicken joints, or ask the butcher to joint it for you. You'll get eight pieces from each bird.

The size of bulb fennel varies enormously. What is important is to have roughly twice the quantity of fennel to onions. Beyond that it's up to you how much you want.

INGREDIENTS
SERVES TWO
- One chicken, about 1.3 kg, jointed into eight—breasts kept aside for another meal
- Two fennel bulbs
- One onion, see above
- Four cloves of garlic
- One teaspoon fennel seeds
- A glass of dry white wine

If there are just two people, then the legs and wings from a 1.3 kg bird will be plenty. Keep the breasts in the fridge for something else. If there are four people to feed, then a whole 1.6–1.7kg bird will do the job.

Remove a sliver from the bottom of the fennel bulb as this can be quite grubby and unattractive. Slice the fennel, fairly thinly, down its entire length. The few center pieces will illustrate perfectly the bulb's construction. Peel and then cut the onion through its length into eighths, trying to keep a piece of the root on each section.

Place the fennel and onion across the bottom of a large roasting pan. Peel and roughly chop the garlic. Scatter this over the vegetables. Place the chicken joints evenly on top of all of this. Sprinkle with the fennel seeds and some salt and pepper. Drizzle generously with olive oil and roast for 30 minutes in a preheated oven at 200°C/400°F/gas 6. Then add the wine and roast for a further fifteen to twenty minutes. Should the chicken look a bit anemic towards the end of this, just whack the heat up to max for five or ten minutes until it's all nicely browned.

Serve hot with roast or new potatoes.

CHICKEN WITH LOTS OF GARLIC

When I say lots, I mean thirty or forty cloves! Don't panic. When garlic gets cooked long and slow, as it does here, it becomes wonderfully mellow—losing all its raw coarseness. If you can get some new season's garlic (July-October), so much the better. As garlic stays in storage, it will, inevitably, get more pungent. If I were cooking this in May, then I'd cut back to, maybe, twenty cloves. Since it's more likely your local supermarket will be selling imported garlic, rather than stored British product, at this time of the year, don't fret about it. Don't be tempted to use the very wet green garlic for this dish.

Having said all that, this is, inevitably, going to taste very garlicky. So, if garlic is not quite your scene, turn over the next few pages.

Versions of this recipe seem to be popping up all over the place, but they all insist that you make up a simple dough to seal the lid on the cooking pot—completely airtight. What a load of phooey! I've tried it both with and without and I honestly couldn't tell the difference. Admittedly you will need a good tight-fitting lid so don't use earthenware. My Pyrex casserole does the job just fine.

There's no escaping the fact that legs take longer to cook than the breasts. In this dish, I think it's especially important to have the flesh just falling of the bones. Succulent is too small a word. To achieve that, with or without the dough seal, the breasts will be hopelessly overdone. For that reason, I choose just to cook legs and wings and save the breasts for another dish entirely. It would be easier, but more costly, to buy only legs. Go for thighs in preference to drumsticks.

The garlic cloves will become soft as butter inside their little skins. I normally serve four or five of the best looking ones per person. That's plenty. To eat these little wonder-nuggets, just press them with the flat side of a knife, the garlic will squeeze out of the root end. All a bit similar to, but much tastier than, toothpaste.

INGREDIENTS
SERVES FOUR
- Four whole chicken legs, or eight thighs, plus a few wings if easily obtainable
- Aforementioned lots of garlic
- A little olive oil or butter
- A small glass of dry white wine

Rub the inside of the dish with a little oil or butter. Place the chicken in the dish, season with salt and pepper. Break the garlic bulbs up into separate cloves, but don't peel them. Count out thirty or forty cloves and fling them straight into the pot. Pour over the white wine.

Place the dish in the oven, preheated to 150°C/300°F/gas 2, for at least 2 hours.

Serve with plain rice, or boiled or roast potatoes. I suggest a separate vegetable course beforehand.

VARIATION A little coarsely chopped rosemary in the pot can be pleasant, but I think, goes against the minimal purity of the dish.

CLASIC CRÈME BRULEE (and three variations on a theme)

I utterly adore crème brûlée. It's my all-time favorite pud. Annie's favorite is a traditional summer pudding. So, unable to agree, we served both at our wedding reception, obviously.

Crème brûlée/burnt cream, call it what you like. Don't let the Frenchified name fool you—they did not invent it. The chef at Trinity College, Cambridge did, a few hundred years ago. No argument—end of story.

I prefer to make mine a bit thinner than many might think proper. I don't add cornflour to stabilise it and I don't bake it in the oven. I've made these so many times now that I don't even bother to measure out the sugar. I simply cream the egg yolks with some sugar, taste it and if it needs more, it gets more. In order for you to get a bench mark, I suggest you follow the recipe and decide whether, next time, you'd like it a little sweeter or less so. You may, of course, be happy with it exactly as it is.

For years and years, I used to get all huffy about people who changed the basic concept of the crème brûlée, adding exotic fruits and the like. Then, on one occasion, I had no option but to invent the Crème avec Broken Brûlée (my gas gun had run out). Next time I added the hazelnuts to the caramel and, hey presto, Crème avec Broken Brûlée et les Hazelnuts. Raspberries have been lurking around in crème brûlée recipes for years now. The version below is the best, on this theme, that I've tasted. It is my approximation of the one that Jonathan Nicholson cooks at my local foodie-pub, The George in Cavendish (since writing this he's sold the place and moved on).

If you're overly worried about exactly how many you will get from the quantity—it obviously varies according to ramekin size and fullness—try making one big bowl. It looks great when you take it to the table and have to crack the top with a serving spoon. Alternatively just make a couple of extras—someone's bound to be grateful for seconds.

I've suggested that you use a gas gun. Supermarkets sell them now, so there's no need to visit the local plumber's supplies shop to get kitted out with a big blowtorch—although they are *much* quicker than the tiny gas guns. I've tried using an ordinary domestic grill—they just don't get hot enough. It will melt the crème long before you've brûléed.

CLASSIC CRÈME BRÛLÉE

INGREDIENTS

MAKES ENOUGH TO FILL FOUR OR FIVE RAMEKINS
- 600 ml/one pint double cream
- Four egg yolks
- About 1½ tablespoons of caster sugar (depending on taste)
- One vanilla pod (or simply use vanilla sugar)
- Extra caster sugar for the top

Have the clean ramekins ready within arm's reach of the cooker. Pour the cream into a heavy-bottomed pan. Split the vanilla pod (if using) down its length with a sharp knife. Scrape the insides of the vanilla pod into the cream. Place the spent bean into a jam jar and cover with caster sugar. This is all you need do to make vanilla sugar—leave it alone for a few weeks and you will have vanilla-perfumed sugar (keep stuffing additional future pods in on top).

Place the egg yolks in a bowl and whisk in the sugar. Keep whisking until the yolks turn a pale creamy color and increase in volume. All this effort helps to lighten the final crème. Taste it for sweetness (remembering the brûlée topping is nothing but sugar).

Now scald the cream. Put it on a burner and bring it quickly up to just sub-boiling point—you will see the surface start to tremble. Stir the whole pan (not just a circle in the middle) frequently. Pour a little of the hot cream (about a ladleful) onto the egg yolks. Stir that in. Add a little more. Stir. Then add more. Now that the yolks have become accustomed to a little heat, tip the whole lot back into the pan, stirring vigorously as you do so. Place the pan back on a *very* gentle heat.

This is the critical bit. If the phone rings, let it ring. Leave the Jehovah's on your doorstep. As the crème starts to heat up, it needs constant stirring. I've found one of those plastic spatulas to be the best thing for the job. No part of the pan can remain untouched as you stir. The custard can catch and burn on the bottom if you're in any way slack with the stirring. It's a game of dare; dare you cook it any longer and risk scrambling the custard; dare you take it off now and have it a bit runny. (When I started making this, I used to have the sink three-quarters full of very cold water to dip the pan in to cool it down instantly, a handy trick for those of a nervous disposition.) Not more than a few moments after you first notice the custard thickening, take it off the heat. Quickly ladle the crème into the ramekins. Remember to stir the crème in between each ladling. It will, even now, catch on the bottom of the pan if you let it. Another option is to pour the whole lot into a big jug and from there pour it into the ramekins.

Leave the crème ramekins to cool down, then plastic wrap them and refrigerate until needed.

To finish off, remove from the fridge, bin the plastic wrap and sprinkle about a level teaspoon of sugar over the top of each one. Add just enough to give it a thin coating. Turn on the gas gun and point the flame at the sugar. It will melt into little clear balls and then turn a light brown before reaching the required nut brown. Leave them alone for about ten minutes to let the top cool and get a crunch. Don't do this ahead of time because the caramel will turn syrupy with the moisture from the crème and ruin your efforts.

CRÈME AVEC BROKEN BRÛLÉE ET LES HAZELNUTS

This is an option for those without a gas gun. I try to avoid innovation just for innovation's sake but this is good enough to warrant sharing with you. The brûlée is nothing more than a pounded caramel spooned over the top of the ramekins just before the custard/crème is served. The normally "crunchy as seaside-rock" topping will be a coarsely-pounded carmelized sugar—still much coarser than granular sugar. The hazelnuts make it all a bit praline-esque.

ADDITIONAL INGREDIENTS
FOR FOUR OR FIVE RAMEKINS
- Two or three tablespoons caster sugar, you may not need all the caramel
- A dash of water
- About one heaped teaspoon of roast chopped hazelnuts—you can often buy them pre-roast and already chopped
- Make the crèmes as given above

To make the caramel, put the sugar and a splash of cold water into a heavy-bottomed pan. Place on a fairly high heat. Do not stir it; if it needs a little help shake the pan from side to side. As soon as the caramel reaches a nut brown stage (I never bother with a thermometer for such tiny amounts) remove from the heat and pour immediately onto a lightly greased, clean baking tray—if you're lucky you may have a lightly bendable one, that's handy later down the line. Don't, under any circumstances, touch the caramel—it is unbelievably hot and will stick to your skin.

Sprinkle the hazelnuts over the caramel. They should sink in a little. Allow it to cool completely before you break it up using a toffee hammer, rolling pin, whatever you have to hand.

Remove the crèmes from the fridge ten to fifteen minutes before you want to eat them; sprinkle with the broken toffee and hazelnut mix just before serving.

CRÈME CATALAN

This is the Spaniards' version of burnt cream. It seems to appear on virtually every restaurant menu there. Traditionally it is served in a much wider, shallower terracotta dish. I've seen many places stick a big flat iron, like a culinary branding fork, into the burning embers of their solid-fuel stoves to let it get really hot. They then press this onto the sugar topping to get their brûlée-ing done. There is also an electric version—basically a big kettle element attached to a round piece of metal. I keep meaning to try and find a blacksmith who can make me a simple version to shove in the barbecue—it is quite spectacular to watch, and smells wonderful too. In the meantime I continue to look like a plumber that's stumbled onto Ready-Steady-Cook.

ADDITIONAL INGREDIENTS
- Thinly-pared peel of one orange
- Thinly-pared peel of one lemon
- One stick of cinnamon, about 7.5 cm/three inches long, broken in half

These are made in exactly the same way as the Classic Crème Brûlée, except for the additional ingredients which are added to the cream to infuse it with their flavour. To do this, place the rinds and cinnamon stick into the cream, bring up to a near simmer, then turn the heat off and leave it alone for ten or twenty minutes. After which time, remove the rinds and cinnamon. Reheat the cream and continue as above.

CRÈME BRÛLÉE WITH RASPBERRIES AND AMARETTI

I've passed up the opportunity to eat "Raspberry Surprise Crème Brûlée" more times than I care to remember. These, though, are brilliant. The soaked amaretti biscuits turn it, almost, into a little slushy trifle. Inspired.

Because of the added bulk of the biscuits and raspberries you may get as many as six, or even seven, ramekins from the quantity given above. Choose raspberries that are in season (obviously) and, crucially, ones that aren't too ripe.

ADDITIONAL INGREDIENTS
- One punnet of raspberries
- Two little amaretti biscuits per ramekin
- A few good splashes of amaretto liqueur

Start by soaking the amaretti biscuits in the liquor for five minutes. Pour on just enough to soften the biscuits a little—too much and they will simply disintegrate. Divide these and the raspberries equally between six or seven ramekins. Make the crème exactly as given above. Then pour over the berries and biscuits. Some may rise to the surface, others won't—it doesn't matter a jot. Should there be more than enough to fill all the ramekins, quickly scoff the leftovers while nobody's looking!

FRESH FRUIT FOOLS

All the world loves a fool! Convention has it that they're made from puréed fruit mixed with fresh cream. I can tell you that they are much better when made with custard (maybe a 50/50 custard/ cream mix). Stew whatever fresh seasonal fruit you have, with a little sugar. Taste, and season with a squeeze of lemon juice and perhaps a little more caster sugar. If it needs sieving, pass it through a nylon sieve (you'll thank me when doing the washing up afterwards). Let it cool completely. Stir in sufficient custard to make an agreeable consistency. Pour into a serving bowl or individual glasses. Serve these delights with little almond biscuits, fine macaroons, Langue du Chat, boudoir biscuits or even good shortbread.

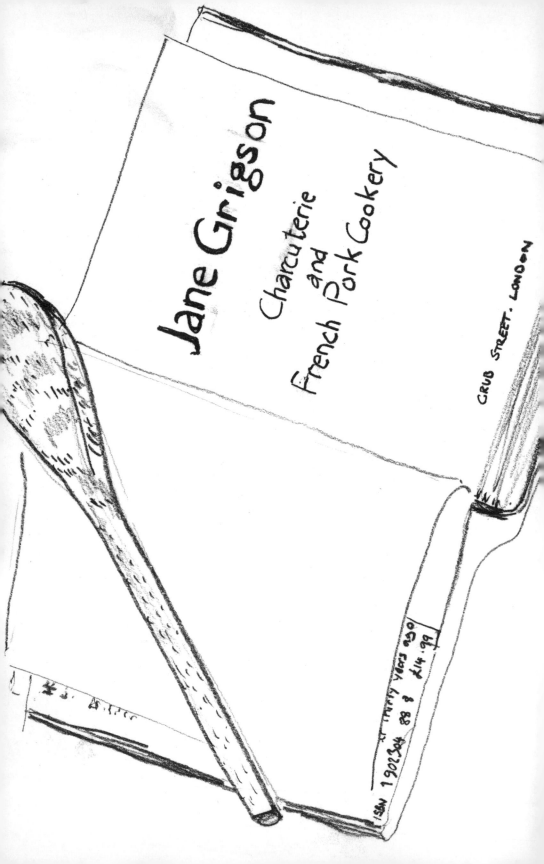

Raw Cabbage with Raisins,
Walnuts and Salad Cream
Kedgeree
Oriental Omelet
Chicken Chasseur

OCTOBER

Chicken in a Basket
Burmese Dry Chicken Curry
Winter's Leftover Chicken Pasta
Dinner
Proper Vanilla Ice Cream
(and others)

October is one of my favorite months of the year. The weather is often clear and it frequently remains, at its worst, somewhat crisp. At its best it can be warm enough to walk around in shirtsleeves. Everyone's back from their summer holidays, no-one is really thinking about Christmas (except a few shopkeepers)! There is a very tangible feeling that now is the time to really get on and do something—yet there was remarkably little chicken activity this month. The Welsummers are still not laying; so I'm getting very few eggs for my trouble.

The saddest thing about October is that by the end of the month, the heating will be on, and I will have completely stopped wearing shorts.

This year's hatch of spring chickens are fully grown and some have started laying eggs. I've found it important to get the hatching done as early as possible to allow the chickens to start laying before the winter gets cold and wet. If they are born too late into the summer, then chances are they won't start laying until the following spring. With the older hens going off lay, those young birds can represent your only chance of fresh eggs through the winter.

Now, I'll bet all the change in my pockets that, like me, you didn't know that beetroot is the top selling vegetable seed sold in Britain. A good fresh beetroot is a revelation. The early ones arrive as quickly as July and are fabulous as a salad ingredient. At that young age the tops can be eaten raw—just like any other salad leaf. By October the leaves have become a vegetable in need of some cooking; just blanch them quickly in salted water and serve nestled into the side of a grilled pork chop. I think the roots are best baked in the oven—leave the skin on. My favorite way with the young beet is to roast them in the oven, wrapped in foil, with a little scrunched foil nest underneath to prevent direct contact with the roasting tin. Once they have cooled a little, peel, slice, or quarter, and simply dress with the best olive oil and red wine vinegar that you can buy. With a pinch of salt and a twist of pepper you'll be eating the best warm summer vegetable course available, it really is that good. To make a more substantial lunch-sort-of-a-dish, add fresh marjoram or rocket and some crumbled salty feta cheese.

I'm delighted to say that my new butcher is turning out just fine. The pork is fabulous, the lamb reliably good, and the beef—well, for my taste, frankly, it could be a little longer hung. Don't misunderstand me; by any supermarket standard it is astoundingly good, but I can't taste the age in it. Also, almost inevitably these days, the beef is from dairy cross bullocks. I asked them about pure breed suckler herd beef and they said they'd love to stock it but it would be prohibitively expensive. So I'm at an impasse: Do I search out some mail order meat herd that will arrive maybe via a freezer, probably barely hung, and certainly "vac-packed," or stay with the locally raised cross-breeds that after a very short journey, have been walked into the back of the butcher and been swiftly dispatched? I think, on balance, I'll stick with the butcher. I can always start pestering them for a bit of pure-bred meat. Don't for a moment be thinking that the stuff you can buy at the supermarkets with a breed name on it will be pure-bred cattle either. Labeling laws currently allow an Angus or Hereford crossed with a Friesian (the black and white one that produces so much milk) to be sold as Angus or Hereford.

OCTOBER'S DIARY

WEDNESDAY 1 OCTOBER

Two cockerels growing nicely. Worried that we'll feel able to eat them. The Welsummer is a beautiful bird. Would love to be able to keep him. Phoned vet to enquire about caponising him or some way to surgically shut him up. They virtually laughed down the phone at me.

TUESDAY 7 OCTOBER

It's not even been a month and the chickens have reduced their run to bare earth. Fortunately the weather has been very dry —so no mud! I suspect the appalling quality of the grass —mostly moss —to blame. Am considering turfing the run in the spring.

FRIDAY 24 OCTOBER

So much rain in the last few days the chicken run is a quagmire. Went off to buy some straw bales — got there and realized that I could only fit one bale at a time in the car. Damn. Must be the reason why just about everyone drives Land Rovers in the countryside.

MONDAY 27 OCTOBER

Big Bo has stopped laying. Only getting eggs from Angelica (what a star chicken she is) and Beatrice.

RAW CABBAGE WITH RAISINS, WALNUTS, AND SALAD CREAM

You simply would not believe how difficult it was to find a recipe as a starting point for salad cream. Nobody it seems bothers to make this from scratch any more. You'd think Heinz would be laughing all the way to the bank, but then they announced, a few years ago, that they were going to stop making salad cream. Apparently, nobody was buying it. What a genius marketing scam. Instantly sales rocketed. The great British public single-handedly had saved salad cream from condiment oblivion. Now they are laughing all the way to the bank. The EU can keep their mayonnaises and vinaigrettes. Salad cream, after all, is as British as the bulldog, three-piece Tweeds, or a straight-six sports car.

There's a nice ritual to the salad cream bottle. Just like ketchup, it needs a bit of a slap on its arse to get it onto the plate. Heinz has completely ruined this with those awful plastic squeezable bottles. They offer instant gratification for people too impatient to wait for their salad cream, or ketchup, to roll slowly down the bottle. Everyone used to be familiar with the whole slap, shake and wait—and now that's gone. The only other way I've ever seen of getting it out was by Robert De Niro in *Goodfellas*. He sat at mama Scorsese's kitchen table and rolled the ketchup bottle between the palms of his hands, just as you would a stick to make fire in a primitive boy-scoutish kind of way. It worked—ketchup came out, of course, but I'm curious—was he acting, was that part of his character, or does De Niro always do it like that?

I like salad cream—no, I love it. It's the taste of my child-hood. We didn't have mayonnaise in the house, nor olive oil ... you must be kidding, you couldn't even buy it then. When the salad appeared at tea-time it was put on the table right next to a bottle of salad cream. Other salad cream opportunities from my childhood include a slice of pork pie, some corned beef fresh from the tin, or a Boxing Day sandwich: sliced white bread, cold turkey (durr—obviously), sage and onion stuffing, cranberry sauce (only post Delia's "Christmas") and salad cream. Marvelous.

If you want a genuine salad—something a tad more grown up than the tea-time salad—that *needs* salad cream and warrants the effort of making it yourself, try this: Pull all the outer leaves off a very freshly pulled Savoy cabbage, you need only that marvelous pale-yellow-crisp inner heart—ideally it will still be moist with dewy freshness inside. Remove and discard the core, then shred the cabbage as finely as you possibly can. Scatter this out over a plate. Dot the surface with plenty of good quality raisins and just as many pieces of broken walnuts. Finally drizzle, spoon, swish, pour, whatever it is that you do, but get the salad cream onto the top of all this in as cheffy a way as possible. That's all you need for a nice late autumn salad.

I'd love to see what a trendy chef would make of writing that up on his menu. You know the type of place: sausage and mash becomes *"Roasted Butcher's Pork Sausage with Crushed Potatoes and Jus of Caramelised Shallot."* Well, I call this Raw Cabbage with Raisins, Walnuts, and Salad Cream. But maybe it would sell more readily if it became *"Carpaccio of Shredded Savoy Greens with Sun-dried Grapes, Broken Walnuts, and Salad Creme d'Anglaise."* Okay I'm being a bit irreverent, obtuse even, but I hope you see my point about progress and fashion. It's not always necessary, is it?

The recipe that I found in the end was, almost inevitably, in the Jane Grigson book *English Food.* She admits to nicking it from Eliza Acton's *Modern Cookery for Private Families.* Now, here it is (almost) verbatim.

- Two hard-boiled egg yolks
- One raw egg yolk
- Salt, freshly ground white pepper
- Pinch cayenne pepper
- ¼ teaspoon sugar (use caster)
- One teaspoon water
- ¼ pint double cream
- Chili, shallot, or tarragon vinegar, or lemon juice

Sieve the hard-boiled egg yolks into a basin. Stir in the raw yolk, the seasonings, and water. Stir in the cream gradually. Finally flavor with vinegar or lemon juice.

Oh, how I wish I could write that concisely (although, we can argue about whether or not it would benefit from an Oxford comma). The trick is to use a really fine sieve for the egg yolks (a nylon sieve makes cleaning a lot easier) and remember that the cream will thicken automatically as soon as you put the vinegar in. Also the yolks must be properly hard-boiled—none of this modern "softly hard-boiled" malarkey—or they will simply turn to glue in the sieve.

KEDGEREE No matter what the currently most bankable British food writer tells you (amazingly it's *not* Delia), kedgeree *isn't* made with poached salmon, kaffir lime leaves, and Thai fish sauce—no matter how trendy everything Thai is these days. Mind you, she's not alone in getting it hopelessly wrong. Elizabeth David's recipe calls for just mace, and lots of it, as the only spice in the dish! I believe that kedgeree should be made with good, undyed, smoked haddock (Finnan if you can get it), top-quality hard-boiled eggs, and a familiarly gentle curry sauce:

it should be no more challenging than a Marks & Spencer's Coronation Chicken sandwich. This applies doubly so if you're having it for breakfast or brunch.

The amount of rice that I've specified may well give you more than you need but it's always handy to have some cooked rice in the fridge for a quick, egg-fried rice or as the basis for stuffing some little bird or vegetable. Use an easy-cook version of basmati if you're prone to rice anxiety.

I normally reach for an ordinary Madras curry powder for this, although one time, I'd run out and improvised an excellent substitute with crushed cardamom seeds, ground cumin, ground ginger, ground cinnamon, peppercorns, and crushed cloves. Quite clearly you'll either be a curry powder sort of person or one who maintains a fresh stock of all those spices in your kitchen in order to make up this sort of thing on a whim. Be comfortable with yourself and accept the person you are on this matter.

INGREDIENTS
SERVES TWO
- One onion
- A couple of cloves of garlic
- A teaspoon of Madras curry powder (see above)
- A handful or raisins and/or sultanas
- Two portions of undyed smoked haddock. Try and get pieces from the middle of the fish, rather than the tail end
- Two eggs, still in their shells
- 200 g/7 oz basmati rice (see above)
- A splash of double cream
- A squeeze of lemon juice
- A handful of chopped parsley or coriander, maybe a little of each

Start by finely chopping the onion and garlic and sweating them gently in a little sunflower oil. While that's happening, put a pan of water on for the rice. Poach the smoked haddock for about

3–4 minutes—I normally use one pot of water, first boil the eggs (5–6 minutes for hard boiled), then the fish, and finally the rice. When you take the eggs out run them under the cold tap for a minute or two. The fish needs to be left to one side to cool down a little. To the pan with the onions add the curry powder or spices and fry gently to release the aromas. Remove from the heat. Once the haddock has cooled a little, remove the skin and break into its natural flakes (keep an eye out for any stray bones). Add the flaked fish to the spiced onions. Add the cream and the raisins/sultanas. Peel and quarter the eggs.

Once the rice is cooked (follow the instructions on the packet), add most of it to the spiced onion and fish mixture. Stir gently to incorporate. Taste it. Add salt, pepper, lemon juice, and maybe a shake of Tabasco if you think it needs some.

You must decide whether you want the eggs and parsley/coriander mixed in to the kedgeree or put on top as decoration. Now is the time to mix it in, if that's how you want to do it. Use just enough herbs to get a nice speckled effect in the rice mix. Spoon onto plates and serve immediately. If you want the more trad garnish, spoon the mix onto plates and arrange the eggs at 12, 3, 6, and 9 o'clock, then sprinkle with the green herbs.

Eat without further delay.

ORIENTAL OMELET

Oriental omelet—it sounds a bit condescending, doesn't it, a bit arrogantly empiric. Imagine the Japanese referring to "British Stew" or the Chinese talking of "Italian Pasta." I know food writing (especially regarding food from the Far East) has come a long way from recipes for "Beef Curry" and "Chicken Chop Suey," but this is quite a generic sort of oriental omelet.

The only difficulty you'll find with this dish is getting a proper oriental omelet pan. It isn't that difficult, but you won't find one at the kitchenware section of your local Tesco. I bought mine, mail order, ages ago from some specialist oriental suppliers. I expect Google will help you out.

The pans are non-stick and rectangular in shape, about seven inches by five inches and about an inch deep. The principle behind this style of omelet is surprisingly simple—yet it produces a fantastically gorgeous-looking eggy roll. These are a great little pre-dinner nibble, if you're given to throwing that kind of dinner party. Alternatively serve them as a starter before some oriental-themed main course. They are great with a little pile of ordinary salad cress on the side of the plate. Add a little splash of plain vegetable oil and soy sauce with finely chopped ginger and chives as a dressing—just drip it around on the plate, just like the chefs do it on the telly.

INGREDIENTS
SHOULD MAKE FOUR LITTLE OMELETS
- Six good eggs
- One tablespoon light soy sauce
- One tablespoon toasted sesame oil
- One tablespoon sunflower oil
- One tablespoon rice wine (good, bone-dry sherry is an okay alternative)

Break the eggs into a pouring jug (Pyrex ones are always useful) and whisk to a smooth creaminess. Add the other ingredients and whisk again.

Warm the omelet pan over a medium heat. Pour in a little of the egg mix—just enough to cover the bottom. It will cook in about 20–30 seconds. You must now roll it up towards the far end of the pan. Traditionally this would be done with some chopsticks. As a ham-fisted westerner, I find it easier to use a fish slice. It is also necessary to tip the pan as you roll it. Like all these things there is a knack to doing it quickly, but it's really not difficult. Now pour in a little more of the mix; when that has cooked, roll the egg roll over the top of it to make a single, bigger roll. Then push it back to the far end of the pan. Repeat this, four or five times until you have a single roll about an inch thick. Take it out of the pan and if you are making a lot of them, keep it warm on a tray in a warm (not hot) oven. Now make a few more.

These look particularly nice if you take the trouble to trim the ends off square and cut them diagonally in the middle. If they're being served as a plate to pick at, cut them into quarters and stand them on end.

VARIATIONS   Being an omelet, they are particularly well suited to having things mixed in with them. Whilst most stuff works, the trick is not to Anglify (or Frenchify) them too much. My favorite variation is just to add some fresh crabmeat and maybe a little finely chopped red chili. About three or four generous tablespoons, mixed in to the eggs, makes a fabulous omelet. Buy dressed crabs for this—but not frozen; crab doesn't freeze well, it gets too mushy. Try to avoid using tinned crabmeat, and *never* use crabstix.

CHICKEN CHASSEUR   One of the things that I do, when starting to write down a recipe, especially for a classic such as coq au vin or chicken chasseur, is to try out several different recipes and methods—just to get the gist of the dish. I cook them for myself, see what works best, adapt it, change this, alter that, maybe make it all a little simpler—and only then do I invite friends or family round to taste the final version. In the middle of a fortnight of cooking various coq au vins, I found myself, in the supermarket, face to face with some packets of powdered just-add-water Colman's Chicken Chasseur Sauce Mix to cook with chickens, onions, and mushrooms. It had been a regular part of my childhood. Once a fortnight (I guess) mum had wheeled out chicken chasseur. I had no idea Colman's was even still making it.

My memories of childhood food, inevitably, have a rose-tinted focus: Sunday roasts, midweek steak and kidney with dumplings *and* jacket potatoes, shepherd's pies, home-made quiches, treacle tarts, chocolate cakes with preserved violets and silver balls on top, teatime meringues. They are as much a part of my childhood as Morecambe and Wise, Bruce Forsyth's Generation Game, and The Clangers just before bath-time. Of course, I also remember the stuff that I detested: Boiled ham and parsley sauce, and lunchtime leeks that had been boiling since just after breakfast. But, unbelievably, I had completely forgotten about that Colman's Chicken Chasseur. Is that not a truly terrible insult to food—that it was, eventually, quite simply forgotten?

I can't pretend that (most school food, and mum's boiled ham, excepted) I didn't eat very well as a child. Mum was a very good, competent cook—truly excellent on occasions—and a dab-hand at making a pound of ground beef feed six hungry people. Like all families, we had the familiar-family-regular sort of meals. I have this back catalogue in my mind of food, comfort food, food that I simply cannot shake my inveterate longing for. It wasn't just special occasion food and Sunday lunches—it was ordinary everyday well-cooked, tasty, nutritious, filling food— the sort of thing I now cook for my children. I wonder what my children's friends will be able to look back upon, with fond memories. It's unlikely to be a home-made cottage pie and peas on a Monday evening. Ping cuisine in front of the *Tellytubbies* is a piss-poor heritage.

I decided, there and then, that I would make my heritage-version of chicken chasseur. I looked at the shopping list on the back of the packet to make sure I had all the right ingredients. It said:

SHOPPING LIST
- One sachet Colman's Chicken Chasseur Mix
- Four chicken joints or pieces
- Two medium-sized onions, sliced
- 110 g/4 oz button mushrooms
- 425 ml/¾ pint cold water

Not much to it, so off I went to buy a couple of free-range chicken legs, and button mushrooms (I always have onions in the cupboard).

Common sense prevailed in the car park … I got the cookbooks out when I got home, to see how it's done. The consensus is that to make it properly, you need: Chicken, onions (or shallots), mushrooms, white wine, parsley, and some tomatoes. That is it. It is not difficult or complicated. Fortunately it was summertime so I had tomatoes and parsley in abundance. I had everything I needed.

The tomatoes are the only really contentious item on the list—what type should be used, if at all? Both *Larousse Gastronomique* and Simon Hopkinson *(The Prawn Cocktail Years,* Macmillan 1997, an excellent book), say "yes," but can't agree on the sort. Once I had simply to skip them, and used a teeny splash of passata instead. It worked okay.

Here's how I recommend that you cook it.

INGREDIENTS
SERVES FOUR

- Either a small whole chicken or enough chicken bits to feed four
- One large, strong, onion or equivalent quantity of shallots
- 225 g/8 oz plain ordinary mushrooms, button sized if you prefer
- Half a bottle of good dry white wine
- Four or five bouncingly fresh sprigs of flat-leaf parsley
- Four ripe tomatoes peeled, deseeded and chopped (or a little splash of passata from a bottle)
- Lemon juice to season
- Plain flour for dusting

You'll be either using a whole chicken or will have opted for the easier pre-jointed chicken. As always, it's swings and roundabouts over which to choose. If I am cooking this for a couple of friends for dinner, I'll use a whole chicken (girls, I have found—and, I freely admit, this is a scandalously sweeping generalisation—tend to prefer white meat). If it's just Annie and me for dinner, then I might chasseur a pair of legs. I never buy just breasts for this dish; I much prefer the extra flavor that you only ever get from the legs.

If you have a whole bird to butcher, first remove the legs. Slip a, definitely sharp, preferably "boning," knife (it should be pointy and not too flexible or small) between the legs and the main body of the chicken. Hold the leg of the chicken in one hand—with your knife in the other, cut through the skin down towards the hip joint. Move the legs around and get an idea of where the joint is, especially if you are unfamiliar with doing this. It is just simple anatomy. At the top of the chicken's leg (the bottom as it lies on the board) is the hip joint. You need to bend the leg outward to dislocate the joint—you'll hear, and feel, it click out. Push the point of your knife through the middle of the joint to detach the leg bone. Run the knife around the underside of the chicken, as necessary, to free the leg completely. Repeat on the other side.

Depending on the size of the leg you should now either leave it whole, or cut it into two. If you want to divide the leg, feel for the joint (pick it up and bend the leg with your hands), put it back down on the chopping board, skin side down, and cut straight through the middle of the joint—there is a soft cartilaginous bit, bang in the middle, between the thigh and leg bones— that's what you are aiming for. You'll notice there is a natural pale, thin line where the thigh muscle ends and the drumstick muscle starts, that's the place to cut through. It's as accurate as someone drawing on a dotted line, a pair of scissors, and the instruction "cut here." I admit it may take a little time to get it right first time, every time—but practice makes perfect.

If you're serving the breasts of the chicken, then remove them but, instead of dismembering the wings entirely, leave them on. I like to serve the first section of the wing still attached to the breast. Remove the middle and tip of the wing. I suggest you use these, along with the raw carcass, to make a stock for soup or risotto. The next day's soup or stew is, as always, an almost-free meal for you.

If this all sounds too gory or too difficult, then ask your butcher to separate the legs and remove the breasts, leaving the first wing joint on. Watch how he does it and, if you ask nicely (but I suggest you don't try this on a busy Saturday morning), he will probably be quite happy to show you how it is done. Try hard as I have to describe it, a good live demonstration is far easier to comprehend than four hundred and fifty-three words. But you may have to be specific with him. Butchers have an awful habit of just cleaving chickens into quarters. It's easy for them but difficult for you as you have to negotiate the irritating little bones.

The skin—and what to do with it? Generally, I like to leave it on, and this dish is no exception. There are the health conscious (think tanned Californians) who insist that chicken skin is the food of the devil and must be removed. Follow your heart on this; I'm not bothered either way. Leaving the skin on makes it taste better but means some more calories and a little extra fat—your choice.

Put a tablespoon, or so, of plain flour on a plate and add some salt and pepper. Quickly mix it up a bit with your fingertips, dibbling vigorously.

Get a large cooking pot, with a lid, nicely hot; I use my trusty Le Creuset. It should be big enough to take all the chicken pieces in a single, albeit tightly packed, layer. Add a little cooking oil and a good knob of butter.

Roll the chicken joints around in the flour and pat them with your hand to remove the excess. When the butter is frothing, add half of the chicken joints. Cook them gently until their skins are a pale golden color (think—Californians' tans). Remove them and similarly cook the other joints, adding more oil and butter if needed. Remove the second round of joints and keep them aside in a warm place.

While they're cooking, slice the onions and prepare the mushrooms. The onions are best finely sliced, not chopped, and the mushrooms should be bite-sized (large black gilled mushrooms are no good for this sauce—the color will seep from the mushrooms and turn the sauce grey). If they're too big, simply halve or quarter them as necessary. Don't wash the mushrooms. If they're a little grubby, brush the dirt off with a piece of dry kitchen paper.

Put the onions in the pan and slowly cook (sweat) them until translucent, then add the mushrooms. Let the mushrooms and onions cook for a further five minutes or so. The moisture that is cooked out of the mushrooms will prevent the onions from taking on any further color. Then pour in the wine. Don't let anything get too brown—the finished chasseur sauce should be a sort-of "dirty-blonde" color. If you brown the chicken and onions too much, it will look like gravy. Bring the wine to the boil whilst scraping at the bits in the bottom to dislodge them. It is important to boil the wine, for a minute or so, to drive off the alcohol.

Having done that, return the semi-cooked chicken to the pan. If you have a sprig of thyme and a bay leaf handy, add them now—but they're really not essential, just preferable. Jostle the chicken, mushrooms, and onions about to settle them into a single layer. The wine, when bubbling, should barely cover the chicken—it certainly shouldn't be boiling in the wine. Put the lid on but leave it slightly ajar, to let the sauce reduce. Cook at a gentle simmer for about twenty minutes for breasts, thirty-forty for legs. At that point you need to make a decision about the thickness of the sauce. If it's about right, put the lid back on tight and turn the heat off. If it still is too wet, take the lid off, and turn the wick up, to help it reduce a bit more. Either way, when the chicken is done, turn the heat off, add the tomato pieces, or passata (if using), and leave it alone for five minutes with the lid on. The heat of the dish will warm the tomatoes through without them turning to a mush.

Remove the thyme and bay, if they are in there. Add a little squeeze of lemon to sharpen things up a bit and check the seasoning, adding salt and pepper as needed. Dish it up onto warmed plates and scatter the parsley (finely chopped on this occasion) all over the top.

I like it best with just simple potatoes: boiled, mashed, jacket, or sautéed.

CHICKEN IN A BASKET

"Oh that's okay you can pick it up and eat it. Anything that flies —yeah it's okay, really—just as long as it flies. You can do that even in a fancy restaurant. Did you know that?"
—Holly Hunter in *Always*

Chicken in a basket is proper pub food. Like a ploughman's lunch or a pint of bitter with some real pork scratchings.

If I go to a pub, the chances are I want a drink. If it's a pub round here and they've got Nethergate's on, then I'll have that—support your local brewery, I say (it's about two miles from home). Failing that, if there's good cider available, I'll have that. Otherwise it will be ordinary beer, either lager or bitter—depending on the weather and my mood—a pint or two, at least. Wine in pubs doesn't really work for me—I drink wine in restaurants and at home. I enjoy drinking cocktails, although seldom get the chance these days (cocktail hour, in our house, having long since been replaced with kiddies' bathtime hour).

I like real pubs—not ones that get a makeover every three years by some floppy haired, French double-cuffed, designer type (who dresses with all the color of a Greek widow) from the Nationalized Brewery plc. This probably means it will be a freehouse. There were a couple of good ones in Cambridge; thankfully there are more out here in Suffolk. The gap between the two seems to be growing—as pubs get refurbished they seem to cater more and more for the kind of bloke who thinks it's okay to drink Bacardi and Coke in the company of other men. It simply isn't.

What I particularly don't want from pub food is Thai curries. Even worse is a blackboard menu that is so long, that you just know it has all come fresh from the freezer—via the microwave. It's easy to spot this rip-off food; it has that piping-hot but not warm feeling that only microwave food achieves, and, because the edges have been superheated, all the bubbly bits have welded themselves to the plate.

Pub food should be simple, filling and, most importantly, go very well with beer. One such thing that I hanker after, but am often disappointed by, is Chicken-in-the-Basket. A brilliantly simple concept: fried chicken and chips (fries), served—for everyone's convenience—in a basket; proper finger-food. Obviously the Environmental Health Officers won't let anyone use a real basket, lined with paper—any more than you can use a wooden chopping board or take your chips home wrapped in newspaper. No, a nice, injection-molded, brown plastic basket it has to be. (Do people from the EHO ever *dare* to eat out, and, if so, where on earth do they go?)

I changed the way I cook this dish after trying Nigella Lawson's recipe for Southern-fried Chicken published in *Nigella Bites* (Chatto and Windus, 2001). She'd picked up on the American habit of marinating the chicken pieces in milk (or, better still, buttermilk) to tenderize them before frying. But the thing that she does differently is to partially poach the chicken pieces in that milk before frying them. It's an enormous improvement on straightforward deep-frying. The downside to her recipe is that the milk the chicken is poached in, curdles and sticks to the chicken in messy clumps, like mutant cottage cheese. What I do, after the marination, is to rinse off the chicken pieces and then poach them in slightly-salted water. I've tried both side-by-side—I prefer it my way. I suspect it's because there aren't those deep-fried curds. The chicken is crisp on the outside and moist within. Perfect.

I theorise that the salt in the milky marinade/brine contributes at least as much, maybe more, to the tenderization of the chicken as does the milk.

It has to be winter food, although obviously entirely unseasonal, because of those long, long evenings that go on forever. Cuddle up on the sofa with a good movie, a pile of fried chicken, and a fistful of paper napkins.

A final word on quantity: there is something about fried chicken that enables you to eat twice as much of it as you might think possible. I can easily manage half a chicken, maybe more. John Belushi had it right.

INGREDIENTS
ENOUGH FOR TWO MODERATELY GREEDY PEOPLE
- Six pieces of chicken, drumsticks or thighs are good, wings also work well—but I prefer to "buffalo" them. Breasts are better used for something else—if you must use breast meat, see my note on nuggets at the bottom

- 600 ml–1 litre/a pint or two of milk, full-fat for preference
- One heaped tablespoon of salt
- Plain flour
- An egg or two, lightly beaten
- Cayenne pepper
- Sunflower oil for deep frying

Start the process the day before you want to eat. Put the chicken pieces, with skin still on, into a roomy bowl, add a tablespoon of salt and cover it all with milk. The milk and salt act as a tenderising brine on the chicken. Leave it in the fridge for twenty-four hours, turning once or twice (don't be obsessional about this— there's no need to get up in the middle of the night).

Scoop the chicken out from the milk (or simply strain it through a sieve) and throw away the milk; it's good for nothing now. Bring a pan of water to the boil and salt it as heavily as you would for pasta. Drop the chicken into the pan and bring back to the boil. Immediately reduce it to a simmer and cook for about fifteen minutes (assuming it's dark meat) or until the chicken is nearly cooked. Take the chicken out of the pan and pat it dry, taking the greatest possible care not to pull off the skin accidentally.

Once the chicken pieces have cooled enough to be handled comfortably, dip them into the flour, seasoned with plenty more salt, some pepper, and as much cayenne as you find comfortable. Then roll the floured chicken into the beaten egg, and then back into the flour for a final dusting. You may have to top up the flour or break another egg as you go along.

Leave this coating to set for ten minutes or so, coincidentally the same time that it takes to heat up the vegetable oil. Usual hot frying temperature for me will do; use the bread method or drop in a little blob of eggy flour goo to determine if it's hot enough. Add the chicken, maybe in batches. When the chicken is a rich golden-brown, it's done.

If you feel like making real chips (or "fries" as the Americans call them) then, apparently, the thing to do is part cook them first in cooler vegetable fat, remove the chips, then turn the heat up to do the chicken, then finish off by browning the chips. I'm no expert at making chips at home—I seldom think it worth bothering with—so seek others' advice. If I want something chip-like I'll roast some in the oven. I use exactly the same method as the wedgie chips but cut them into irregular chunky-chip shapes. However I normally serve this up with a bag of crisps (American "chips")—the handmade, extra thick, heavy crunchy type.

Although it isn't absolutely necessary, this chicken tastes at its best when you line a small basket with lots of kitchen paper and put the chicken and chips/crisps in that. We've got a few old baskets hanging around from Body Shop gift-pack days (a long, long time ago.)—they're perfect for the job. To go with all this I suggest you do the real bargain-bucket-blowout-bonanza and have some coleslaw or possibly a small corn on the cob on the side. Tommy ketchup or barbecue sauce, for a little judicious dipping is also called for.

VARIATIONS If you want to make chicken nuggets, suitable for children—of all ages—use a whole breast and cut it across the grain of the meat (somewhere between 60 mm-1.25 cm/a quarter to a half an inch thick) into familiar-sized nuggets. About two or three bites per piece, I think. Just marinate these—no need to poach them. They're fabulous for children's parties, but, since deep-frying with hot fat and children's birthday parties don't really mix, I suggest cooking them in advance and warming them through in the oven, or, indeed, simply serve them cold.

BURMESE DRY CHICKEN CURRY

I'm no expert on the matter of chicken curries. I've cooked Thai curries a few times—simple green curry for some hot and spicy exotica in the depths of winter. I'm certain that no Thai would recognise it as an example of their native cooking. The same probably goes for the Burmese and this curry. But that's how food evolves, so I can live with it.

This is currently my favorite curry. It, unsurprisingly, resembles both Indian and Thai curries—it takes the best from both its neighbors—marrying turmeric and cardamom with fish sauce and lemon grass. I personally think it is better than either of them.

It is absolutely at the cutting edge of the trend in curries right now. It doesn't slosh around in a creamy sauce; it is astoundingly light and fragrant; and I easily drink a glass of wine with it. Expect every pub in the country to be cooking Burmese curries within weeks. "Burmese is the new Thai." You heard it here first — except it isn't, because Myanmar is the new Burma.

This recipe comes from Sophie Grigson's book *Meat Course*. I've tweaked it a little bit (mainly to suit the fact I don't have a food processor) but it remains pretty faithful to her recipe.

INGREDIENTS
SERVES FOUR
- Two onions
- Six cloves of garlic
- 2.5 cm/one inch piece of root ginger
- Two sticks of lemon grass
- Two or three red chilies
- 1½ tablespoons of fish sauce (nam pla)
- ½ teaspoon of ground turmeric
- One big 3.5–3.7 lb (1.6–1.7 kg) or two little 2.4–2.6 lb (1.1–1.2 kg) chickens
- Six cardamom pods
- A small bunch of fresh coriander

Start by jointing the chicken or chickens. If you'd rather buy chicken pieces, always go for thighs and wings first, then drumsticks, and finally breasts. You may have a white meat preference—fine.

If you have a food processor, put the first seven ingredients into it and blitz into a smooth paste. If all you have is a knife and a whiz stick, then chop everything quite small and squeeze it into its associated blitzing cup. Add a tablespoon or two, no more, of water. Press down with the whiz stick switched on. It may take a little while, and probably require two batches but you will achieve a paste eventually. I read one authoritative book recently that suggests a blender is better than a food processor for making curry pastes. I haven't tried it, but pass that tip on to you anyway.

In a large pan, with a tight fitting lid (I use my favorite Le Creuset) lightly brown the chicken in a little sunflower oil. It will probably require cooking in a couple of batches. Remove the chicken from the pan and keep to one side. (This browning isn't very authentic and most of the color washes off in the sauce, but I like it.) Drain the oil and chicken fat from the pan. Add just a little more fresh oil and then fry the paste. The paste needs to lose most of its moisture, so cook it briskly and stir frequently until it starts to brown slightly and the flow of evaporating steam decreases.

Return the chicken to the pan and cover with a lid. The juices from the chicken will provide enough liquid for this curry—so don't add any water, however tempted you are. Stir it occasionally, and with greater frequency, towards the end of cooking.

While it cooks, split open the cardamom pods (lean on them with the side of a big heavy knife). Take out the seeds and crush them in a mortar and pestle. When the chicken is just cooked through, add the crushed cardamom and some finely chopped coriander. Leave it to rest, off the heat, lid slightly ajar, for a few minutes.

Whole chicken breasts will take about 20–25 minutes, cubed meat much less, all other joints 40–45 minutes. If you don't want to brown the joints, add another ten minutes to the cooking time. Obviously, if you're cooking both, hold the breasts back for 15–20 minutes—giving the legs and wings a head start.

When ready, taste for seasoning and serve immediately with plenty of plain basmati rice.

NOTE Unlike the creamy Indian and Thai curries this doesn't make a pleasant cold curry (I'm referring to the cold curry breakfast, perfect for the morning after). I think it's the absence of coconut milk. No matter—there won't be any leftovers anyway!

You wouldn't thank me if I did not warn you that turmeric stains are the devil's job to get out of expensive kitchen work-tops. They'll stain wooden surfaces quickly and even granite and marble if left overnight. Fair warning given.

VARIATIONS One of the more surreal cooking sketches I've seen on telly was Ken Hom, with wok, cooking a broadly similar curry for Terry Waite in the wisteria-softened courtyard of a Cambridge college. I can't remember the exact differences but the big change in method was that nothing got blitzed to a paste. Onions, garlic, etc. were simply added finely sliced, lemon grass bruised, and so on. I've tried this and found that the onions will cook down to a saucy paste after about an hour. So leave the chicken out for a little while.

WINTER'S LEFTOVER CHICKEN PASTA DINNER

Start by thinly slicing an onion. Melt a little butter or warm some oil in a pan. Add the onion and cook until brown, keep going until it's really caramelized—this requires long slow cooking. A pinch of sugar towards the end will help this color-up nicely. Add a splash of red wine vinegar to deglaze the pan. Throw in some scraps of chicken, and maybe a few raisins and pine nuts, salt and pepper, of course. Smother this sauce all over some pasta—tagliatelle for preference.

PROPER VANILLA ICE CREAM
(and others)

Real vanilla ice cream is nothing more than egg yolks, cream, sugar, and the best vanilla pod money can buy. I confess—there's always a tub of Cornish vanilla (the yellow, soft-scoop stuff) in my freezer—such is life with two small children in the house. But, if I'm doing a decent dinner for family or friends then I may just go to the effort of doing it properly. The difference between proper ice cream and children's favorite is chalk and cheese. Whilst it's not difficult to make, it is a bit of an effort—just as well, otherwise I'd be eating it every day.

You will need an ice cream machine to make this, though. Anyone who tells you that it can be made properly by forking over the custard as it freezes is, I'm afraid, quite wrong. You'll end up with big lumpy ice crystals. It will be oddly crunchy rather than velvety smooth. I'd rather have a nice granita (the lumpy sorbet, *not* New Labour's infamous restaurant of choice) any day.

INGREDENTS
MAKES ABOUT 750 ML/1¼ PINTS
- 568 ml double cream (a big pot)
- 100 ml/4 fl oz full fat milk
- One vanilla pod, split lengthwise
- Four egg yolks
- 150 g/5 oz caster sugar

Pour the milk and cream into a saucepan. Scrape the seeds from the inside of the vanilla pod; add the vanilla seeds and eviscerated pod, and bring to nearly simmering point. Remove from the heat. Meanwhile beat the egg yolks and caster sugar together (use an electric whisk—or you'll need a very strong forearm) until the yolks become quite pale and have increased in volume.

Pour a little of the hot cream/milk onto the eggs and stir vigorously, add a little more cream, then stir, until about half the cream is in the bowl with the eggs. Now pour the egg and cream mixture all back in with the rest of the cream. Bring this up to nearly simmering, stirring constantly; just as it starts to thicken, pour the whole lot into another clean bowl and leave to cool.

Once cool, pour into an ice cream machine and churn until frozen. Eat within a few days (never a problem!).

BLACKCURRANT ICE CREAM

My friend Mr. Cheese's all-time-favorite ice cream. He is a man of taste.

Make some vanilla ice cream mix, just as previous recipe, using the pod, or not, as you wish. Take a small punnet of blackcurrants and heat them up to simmering point with two tablespoons of caster sugar and a good squeeze of lemon juice. The berries are done when they have all burst. Strain the cooked berries through a nylon sieve, pushing the fruits to get everything out of them. Add the puree to the cooling cream and then proceed to churn when cool.

CHOCOLATE ICE CREAM

To turn your vanilla ice cream into chocolate ice cream, simply stir in 125 g/¼ lb of broken pieces of best quality dark chocolate (at least 70 percent cocoa solids) once the ice cream is made and has been set aside to cool. There is quite sufficient heat in the hot cream to melt the chocolate. On the off chance it doesn't—you'll have chocolate with chocolate chips! Stir thoroughly, though. Vanilla or not, is again up to you.

This will produce a fairly sweet, child-friendly, sort of a chocolate ice cream. Intensely bitter chocolate ice creams are very modish at the moment—this isn't one of them, I'm afraid.

A nice variation is to pour in a (biggish) tot of whisky once the mix has gone cold, just before churning.

CINNAMON ICE CREAM

One year some friends received an ice cream machine for Christmas. I asked what it was like, they said they hadn't used it yet (it was New Year's Eve). I offered to make some for them, but they hadn't a vanilla pod, or chocolate, or even any fruit in the house (the inside of their fridge is like a desert). I picked a couple of sticks of cinnamon out of their seasonal pot pourri and made some ice cream with that. I have been making it ever since.

All you need do is put 10 cm/4 inches of cinnamon stick into the cream instead of the vanilla (for heaven's sake don't use the powdered stuff for this). Repeat the process as for Vanilla Ice Cream, but remove the sticks and strain through a sieve (just to be sure) before churning.

Poached Egg and Bitter Leaf Salad
Baked Egg with Leeks
Mussel and Saffron Quiche
Three Offal Omelets

NOVEMBER

Leeks Vinaigrette
Chicken with Pears and Parsnips
Stewed Chicken with Quinces
Zabaglione
Stewed Apples and Custard

The funny thing is that, even up until the end of October, especially on a good day if the sun is really shining, I can convince myself that it's still summer—just. Maybe ... early autumn? Plainly it isn't, I know it's over but, then, my mind is a willing accomplice. There's no doubt that, when the clocks have gone back and it is getting dark far too early, winter (not just autumn) is tugging at my shirt tails.

All the summery British produce has gone from the shops and my appetite quickly changes from salads to hearty winter dishes. I find that I always put my wellies on to walk the dog and start making hot drinking chocolate again. The first steak and kidney of the season is made. Beef ceases to be quickly cooked steaks on the barbie and is, instead, ground and cooked in slow cooked ragus for pasta, lasagne, cannelloni, or cottage pies. Big chunks get braised to make un-thinkably thick daubes or stews with pickled walnuts.

Chicken, especially chicken, changes. It's now stewed with wine, put into pies, poached with winter roots. If it's a soup, it's a similarly thick one—or spicy and hot, like mulligatawny.

There's Bonfire Night at the beginning of the month—we watched the pretty bangs with a couple of pints on the village green. We used to watch the fireworks in Cambridge on Midsummer Common (they were a huge event) back when we lived near the river, just behind the boathouses. When we moved out to a nearby dormitory village, the thought of having to drive in and park—and all the hordes of people and with two little children—was just too much so we stayed at home. This was our first fireworks for three years and the best we'd seen. The intimate scale of the village green improved it immeasurably. There were a couple of blokes with an opened oil drum serving up some hot dogs and burgers, and a little tent selling toffee apples.

The next day, I noticed that some people had wisely moved the old wooden benches on the green down to sit by the glowing embers and (since there were, unusually, no bins provided) had chucked their empty bottles near the fire —presumably so the bottles wouldn't get trodden on in the dark. I was amazed to see the local press headlines of "attempted arson and yobbish behaviour in Cavendish." Police were reportedly looking for the culprits! I imagined what might be next month's big story "Children caught throwing snowballs."

Christmas, mercifully, doesn't start until the very end of November around here. The lights go up in the next village, Clare, ready to be turned on for the 1st December—they are the simplest and most beautiful Christmas lights I have ever seen. The turkey is ordered from the butcher (I'm cooking goose next year—no arguments!); apart from that I'll leave Christmas well alone for another couple of weeks.

NOVEMBER'S DIARY

SATURDAY 1 NOVEMBER
Was at the local farm shop this morning. Went round the back and saw all the turkeys and cockerels running around their field —waiting for Christmas. Have decided to cook the Light Sussex cockerel for Christmas lunch.

SUNDAY 2 NOVEMBER
Annie refuses to even consider eating the cockerel. She has named him Basil! Forced to put an ad in village shop window —paid 60p for a fortnight:

PUREBRED COCKERELS —FREE TO A GOOD HOME
WELSUMMER AND LIGHT SUSSEX
ONE OF EACH. HOME REARED, JUST ABOUT TO CROW —SO MUST GO.
CAN ALSO PROVIDE HENS. PHONE TIM ...
NO COQ AU VIN PLEASE.

FRIDAY 7 NOVEMBER
Still no sign of any eggs from the 4 Welsummers. Utterly fed up with them. Phoned the chicken lady —she will swap the four of them and Big Bo and the Araucana for four laying hybrids. I arranged to go on Tuesday.

SUNDAY 9 NOVEMBER
Annie returned from the chicken run, with a Welsummer egg. They must have my phone bugged —or something. Decide to give them one more chance.

SUNDAY 16 NOVEMBER
The phone hasn't rung. Clearly, nobody is interested in free cockerels.

TUESDAY 18 NOVEMBER
A distant neighbour knocked on the door 10 a.m. Asked if I kept hens, and was I missing one? Took the landing net —after chasing Big Bo through three gardens —finally caught her.

SUNDAY 23 NOVEMBER
Three days of non-stop rain. Three chickens missing —Welsummer cockerel, Big Bo, Araucana. Walked around the neighbourhood —no sign of them. Possible they will come home of their own accord.

MONDAY 24 NOVEMBER
No sign of AWOL threesome.

SUNDAY 30 NOVEMBER
It's been a week —no sign of AWOL three. Expect they've set up a commune or a fox has caught them. Seven hens seems a better number in the run. Possibly a little crowded before.

POACHED EGG & BITTER LEAF SALAD

The French, especially the French, are very keen on a poached egg and lardon salad. Bistro fayre typicale.

However, the best I have ever eaten was years ago, when Gary Rhodes had just started cooking at The Greenhouse in Mayfair. It must have been in the very early nineties—his hairstyle was quite commonplace then.

Being the reinventor of British food that he is (his faggots are certainly the benchmark by which all other faggots must be measured), he turned it into English Breakfast Salad. So, in addition to lots of simply dressed leaves, topped with a quivering, perfectly-poached egg, he added some crisp smoked bacon, some sauteed potatoes, and (according to the recipe in his book, *Rhodes Around Britain*, BBC, 1994), black pudding—although, I don't remember eating any such pudding.

Either with or without the black pud, this is a great plate of food. The egg makes this a more substantial salad than you might expect. If you add bacon, potatoes, and the mysteriously shy black pudding, it's a small meal in itself. I normally settle for making it with an egg, and some lardons cut from my home-cured bacon. If you're getting some pancetta from a deli, get it cut, either as a thick slice for the making of lardons, or wafer thin, so you can have it very brittle and crisp—either is fine. At some point, you should try it both ways—then you can make up your own mind.

A few thoughts on how to poach eggs successfully: The only reason mine have ever failed is because the eggs weren't fresh enough. As an egg loses its freshness, the white, basically speaking, becomes thinner. When you pour the egg into the poaching water, the yolk naturally will want to sit in the middle of the white. That's where it belongs; it's the natural order of things. If the egg is spanking fresh, then it will do that quite happily. If it is more than just a couple of days old, the white will be slightly, but significantly, thinner and will disperse in the water: A very horrid, nasty, stringy mess.

Freshness issues aside, poaching an egg is child's play. Bring a deep pan of (unsalted) water up to a very gentle simmer, barely a few bubbles breaking the surface. Crack the egg into a ramekin or something similar. I use a little Duralex glass (I am strangely nervous of breaking eggs straight into pans, except when scrambling). Poach it for about three minutes until the white has set. I can't be more specific about the timing because eggs come in different sizes.

The beauty of poaching an egg, over boiling, is that you can tell, with a little practice, the absolute moment the egg is ready. Put a slotted spoon under it and lift it out of the water, give it a little wiggle; if it wobbles too much, give it another ten or fifteen seconds.

Remove the poached egg with a slotted spoon and place it onto a small plate. Don't try to blot it dry with a piece of kitchen paper—you will, quite likely, damage it. You may need to use a very sharp knife, or a pair of kitchen scissors, just to tidy up any loose ends—the bits that are the scruffy tails coming off the main bulk of the egg. Blot up any water around the egg on the plate and slide the egg onto your finished dish. It might seem a bit of an effort, putting it on a plate and then onto the dish, but I have found this little ritual very effective at getting most of the water off the egg.

There are dozens of little "cheffy tips" that I've heard over the years. Most common are: adding some vinegar to the water, getting the water swirling in order to create a vortex in the middle, take the pan off the heat before you add the egg, and so on, and so on. I have found that the absolute freshness of the egg is all that matters.

INGREDIENTS
MAKES A STARTER FOR FOUR
- Four very fresh eggs
- Some good bacon or pancetta—equivalent to about two ordinary rashers per person
- One or two heads of lettuce—frisee is good at this time of the year. No lollo rosso or iceberg allowed
- A simple salad dressing made with four parts extra virgin olive oil and one part red wine vinegar. You may want to add a pinch of sugar or a dab of French mustard

Start by cooking the bacon or lardons. Whichever you choose to use, they must be cooked to a crisp. Next, poach the eggs as described above.

It is important to choose the right type of salad leaves. They need to be fairly bitter and physically quite strong leaves. Limp lettuces will not work at all well. Frisee is suitable but perhaps a little bitter for some. I've made this very successfully using heads of pale yellow chicory—very bitter. I would avoid bags of salad. They are a rip off—pure and simple. They also use strongly chlorinated water to wash the leaves, and the bags are filled with gases other than normal air. As if all that wasn't enough, they also cause more cases of food poisoning than you or I would believe possible. If you must buy salad in bags (it's about the only way to buy rocket) choose organic. Not just for the way it's grown but also the way it's been packaged—apparently they must use fewer chemicals. I suggest, whenever possible, you give them a miss and buy a whole lettuce with some earth on it.

If it's the summertime and a friend or neighbour has a glut of homegrown lettuces—suggest swapping some for a few eggs. Other leaves to look out for are mizuna, rocket (wild or otherwise), and watercress.

Try a few different leaves—decide which you like best. Obviously, if you have got "real" whole lettuces—then they will need gently washing. I like to let the leaves air-dry rather than using a salad spinner or tea towel.

To assemble the salad you will need a large roomy bowl. Add the oil and vinegar (and sugar if using), and whisk them together. Tip the leaves into the bowl and mix them together with your hands. Using big plates (I think it Scrooge-ishly mean to use little side plates for salads) heap up a smallish pile of leaves in the centre of each. Put a little of the bacon on top, add more salad, then bacon, then salad—until you have no more of either left. Place the egg on top of this little heap. If there is any dressing left in the bowl, then spoon it around the plate. But please *not* on the rim—it's another of my little foibles. It's like a painter choosing to paint the picture frame as well as the canvas; that only works if you are as talented as Howard Hodgkin.

VARIATIONS

The bacon can be changed for croutons—or, have both! You could, alternatively, forget the bacon and go with Gary's idea of sauteed potatoes to make this a vegetarian (but, obviously, not vegan) meal.

BAKED EGGS WITH LEEKS

Just as I like to make some simple baked eggs with tarragon to celebrate the first sprigs of fresh tarragon in the early summer, at the appropriate time I indulge myself by combining eggs and leeks. It's a weekend lunch or a supper starter.

INGREDIENTS

FOR TWO
- Two smaller than average young leeks
- Two spankingly fresh top quality eggs
- A splash of double cream
- A little grated Parmesan and Gruyere, just enough to sprinkle
  on top

Begin by splitting the leeks in half, lengthwise. Leeks don't seem to be the dirty little vegetables that they used to be but, just in case, fan the leaves open and have a look within. Rinse it under the cold tap if necessary. Probably just removing the outer leaf or two will suffice.

Finely slice the leeks, lengthwise, into little semi-circles 5 mm/ ¼ inch wide. Melt a little knob of butter in a saucepan and soften the leeks without browning them. It should take less than ten minutes, but they must be ready to eat—they'll receive no more significant cooking in the oven.

Meanwhile butter two ramekins, quite generously. Season the leeks with salt and pepper and add just enough cream to make them a bit sticky. They should not be at all runny. Spoon the leeks into the two ramekins, patting them down as you go. Break an egg into each ramekin, on top of the leeks, add a tablespoon more of cream on top of each egg, and sprinkle over the cheeses. Bake in the oven, preheated to 150°C/300°F/gas 2 until the whites have set but the yolk is still runny, about 7–10 minutes.

Good served with hot buttered toast on the side.

MUSSEL & SAFFRON QUICHE

This is not the perfidy act of a Judas upon the classic quiche, which, at first, it appears to be. Mussel quiche is a quite authentically French recipe—I *only* added the pinch of saffron.

Rope-grown mussels are available all year round now and quite safe to eat whether there's an "R" in the month or not, but are at their absolute best between early autumn and Christmas.

I know that this recipe sounds a bit odd, but I was keen to work at least one thing *fishy* into a book on chickens and eggs (other than anchovies in salad dressings) and this squeaked in on a technicality—that, and the fact that it's utterly delicious to eat. The custard filling has a bit of flour in it, to help lighten it up. A heavy eggs-and-cream-only custard would utterly dominate the deliciously light, almost moussey, mussels. I buy the mussels in a bag from the supermarket. They're unlikely to be the freshest you might find—but they're okay. If you live by the sea—lucky you—I suppose you could go and gather your own *for free* but be warned; they will need the barnacles scraping off them and some time in a bucket to purge them of any passing effluent. If you're blessed with a decent fishmonger nearby—use him.

INGREDIENTS

- One bag of mussels, about a liter, give or take a bit
- Half a packet of shortcrust pastry, or make your own (madness!)
- One whole egg
- Two egg yolks
- 150 ml/¼ pint of double cream
- 300 ml/½ pint of full-fat milk, to include any cooking liquor from the mussels
- One heaped tablespoon of plain flour
- One small pinch of real saffron stamens

Start by smearing a big knob of butter all over the inside of a quiche dish. Then put a small handful of plain flour in the centre of the dish. Holding the dish in one hand (over the sink, or outside the back door) at a forty-five degree angle, tap it sharply against the palm of your other hand. Rotate the tin a little after each tap. This will ensure that the flour is evenly distributed over the butter—there should be no bare patches.

Roll out the pastry, fairly thinly, and carefully place it in the tin. Leave a generous amount hanging over the edge. Put this, roughly trimmed, into the fridge for at least half an hour.

Remove the pastry case from the fridge, trim the edge, and prick the bottom with the tines of a fork, many times, all over. Bake in the oven, preheated to 200°C/400°F/gas 6 (using parchment paper and baking beans if you have them), for ten minutes, then remove and brush with a little egg white-milk mixture, return to the oven for another five minutes. Take the pastry case from the oven and let it cool before proceeding.

Warm up about a cupful of the milk in a little pan. Remove from the heat and put the saffron to soak in the milk turning it a pleasant shade of yellow.

De-beard the mussels, discarding any with broken shells. Get a roomy pan, with a tight-fitting lid, nice and hot on the cooker. Add a small splash of water, or perhaps white wine if you have some open. Immediately add the cleaned mussels and put the lid on. Shake the pan a few times. After a minute or two have a peek inside the pan; if the mussels are starting to open, then they are done; if not, leave them another thirty seconds before checking again. Take them off the heat and pour through a strainer—crucially—with a bowl below to catch all the cooking juices (there shouldn't be too much but what there is will be intensely sublimely flavorsome). If you think there's rather a lot of it, apply some heat to reduce it to a few tablespoons. Open the shells with your fingers and pick the mussels out; any that won't now open are dead mussels and should be thrown away.

Mix together the egg, egg yolks, cream, white and yellow milks, flour, a little salt and pepper, and any cooking liquor (don't use more than a tablespoon or two of the liquor, and beware of the gritty bits at the bottom of the bowl). You will need to beat this quite vigorously, with a good whisk, to get the flour properly dissolved.

Arrange the mussels evenly over the bottom of the tart case and gently pour over the custard. Place it on a baking sheet and put in the oven (same temperature) for about thirty minutes, or until it's cooked. Serve warm or cool, neither fresh from the oven nor chilled from the fridge.

THREE OFFAL OMELETS

There is something essentially winterish about eating offal. I know the Greeks do my favorite sweetbread dish, and the French have those (frankly awful) andouillette sausages, both of which are eaten year round—but I need to feel just a little crispness in the air before venturing too far inside the animal. Chicken livers are exempt from this generalization, because they taste so gorgeous on toast—all year round.

Generally the marriage of offal and eggs is a remarkably good one.

OMELET WITH LAMB'S KIDNEY

This is an absolute favorite of mine. Annie, however, refuses even to be in the kitchen (and, preferably out of the house) when I cook it, on account of the cooking smells created by the juice of the organ.

INGREDIENTS
FOR ONE
- Two eggs
- One lamb's kidney
- Scant half a glass of Madeira
- A sprig of flat leaf parsley

Firstly, turn your attention to the kidney. Assuming that your butcher has already removed the suet and the thin see-through skin on the kidney, cut it in half through its length. The little white-ish vein needs to be removed: with your index finger of your non-knife holding hand, pin the kidney to a chopping board by firmly holding the white membrane bit. Since you are going to chop the kidney into little pieces it doesn't matter at all how many slices you take to part the fleshy bit from that unwanted plumbing. Carefully slice the kidney into little cubes, about 5 mm/¼ inch square.

Now heat a little knob of butter in the omelet pan and, very briefly, fry the kidney pieces; don't over-do them though. Remove them and keep warm. Pour the Madeira into the pan and boil it hard to reduce it to almost nothing. Pour this over the kidneys and also keep warm. Wipe the pan clean.

Make the omelet as usual and, when it's ready, pour the kidney slop over the top, fold, sprinkle with a little chopped parsley and serve.

You may prefer to cook the kidney and omelet at the same time using two different pans. I find this unnecessary since the omelet cooks so quickly.

OMELET WITH BLACK PUDDING

Some Sunday mornings just don't go to plan. For whatever reason, you didn't have breakfast, you're hungry, and it's still a few hours until lunch. You don't feel like doing the full English, and toast and cereal just won't hit the spot. Try this—it's a bit more fancy than just black pudding and fried eggs.

INGREDIENTS
PER PERSON
- Two eggs
- About 2.5–3.75 cm/an inch to an inch and a half of sausage-sized black pudding. If you've got the really big bore type, just one thick slice will do

Dead easy this: Just chop the pudding up, fry it briefly in a little oil or butter and keep warm. Wipe the pan clean and make an omelet. Put the cooked pudding on top, fold it and serve.

CHICKEN LIVER OMELET (WITH MANGO CHUTNEY)

Until you try it, you just won't believe how good chicken livers are when put with some mango chutney. The marriage also works well when you spread a little mango chutney on toast or a bruschetta and top that with the sautéed livers.

Chicken livers are widely available and absurdly inexpensive. Every supermarket and butcher will sell them frozen, normally in little tubs (in which case they must be completely defrosted before cooking). My local Waitrose sells enough livers to feed this to four people for the price of half a dozen decent eggs.

A word of warning about cooking the livers, though. Whilst pretty much everyone knows that they mustn't be overcooked, a liver that is actually raw in the middle is quite the more revolting option. If in any doubt about their doneness, just cut one in half and have a look. Serve them firm, yet ideally a little pink in the middle.

INGREDIENTS
FOR ONE PERSON
- Two eggs
- Three or four chicken livers, depending on your appetite
- A little flour for dusting, seasoned with salt and pepper
- A tablespoon of mango chutney (use your favorite type—I prefer mine hot and smooth, without any mango-ey chunks)
- A couple of knobs of butter
- A splash of brandy (optional)
- A little squeeze of lemon

Get your omelet pan hotter than usual. Whilst that's happening, trim any greenish bits off the livers. Cut them into pieces, big enough to provide a real mouthful. Toss the livers into the flour and pat off all the excess flour—the thinnest possible dusting is all you need. Put the butter in the pan and tilt it around until it's all melted and the pan is coated in sizzling butter. Now add the pieces of liver and fry until just cooked. You should have slightly crunchy, crusty edges on the outside and quivering pink insides. You can test for doneness by pressing them with your finger—they will feel a little firmer when just right, and like rubber if they're overdone. If you're using it, add a splash of brandy and ignite it (tip the pan towards the gas flame or use a match if cooking over electric). Squeeze over a splash of lemon juice, and season with salt and pepper. Tip them out of the pan onto a warm plate.

Wipe the pan clean and make the omelet as usual. When ready, slide the omelet onto a second warm plate. Spread the mango chutney over the omelet and cover with the livers. Fold it if you want to I don't normally bother, on account of the fact that it's quite full! If you do want a folded omelet, I suggest that you dress the omelet on the plate. Like my recipe for omelet Alaska it gets a bit tricky trying to do it all in the pan. It's then simplicity itself to take a fish slice, or your fingers, and flip one side over.

LEEKS VINAIGRETTE

Leeks are one of the best winter vegetables. They are available, fresh from the farm shop, right through until Easter time. But I think they're a bit past it by then—best cooked without mercy in something warming and sloppy. No, the young November leek requires—and deserves—something a little more special.

A simple leeks vinaigrette is a classic. It is timeless understated elegance. It is the distinguished English gentleman actor at some awards ceremony—perfectly dressed in his aging dinner jacket (probably Dougie Hayward), proper dress-shirt (Frank Foster), and simple black bowtie (anywhere on Jermyn Street). Sadly, these days, he is surrounded by young impostors wearing their ill-advised long frock coats, wing-collared shirts, and anything but a proper tie around their necks. It's enough to make anyone raise an eyebrow.

In the middle of winter you should forget about salads. Perhaps the occasional properly bitter leaf one is okay, but certainly not those bags of lollo rosso or icebergs. It just doesn't fit does it: Summer salads and snowflakes? Try this as a separate salad course. It makes a good starter. Have it before or, better still, after a jugged hare or something else very rich that would beat-up a dainty salad, but leaves you wanting something green before a little cheese or pudding.

Annie and I like this as a weekend lunch. But, a generous plateful please—five or more leeks between us, perhaps a poached egg each and as much bread as we care to tear off a crunchy baguette. It can be scaled up or down, genteelly garnished with chopped egg, or mounted by a whole one that's been lovingly poached just-so.

Use little, shortish leeks. The idea is to cut off most of the green tops but to have a little of the graduation to pale green still showing. If your leeks are too long, then they'll end up hanging off the edge of the plate or may have to be cut in two, ruining their presentation.

I always arrange the leeks in the classic manner. Side by side, alternating root to top. This gives you a truly beautiful presentation. Whether you add a little chopped hard-boiled egg, or a poached egg that has been allowed to cool (freshly cooked hot poached egg and cold leeks are a weird combination in the mouth) is entirely up to you. Whatever best serves the occasion.

If you want to serve chopped hard-boiled eggs on top of the leeks, it seems sensible to cook the eggs in with the leeks (put into the boiling water for seven minutes for solid eggs, five or six for eggs with a slightly squishy yolk). Poached eggs will require an altogether higher degree of care.

I'm even more vague than usual here about quantities of ingredients; it all depends on the size of the leeks, how many you want to eat, what the occasion is, and what sort of eggs you're putting on top. I think the absolute minimum is three halves per person—two halves on a plate looks damned weird.

INGREDIENTS
- Some leeks, essentially all about the same size
- Hard-boiled or poached eggs

FOR THE VINAIGRETTE
- Extra virgin olive oil
- Lemon juice (allow about one lemon for two people)
- A clove of garlic, crushed
- Dijon mustard—I personally prefer the sort without grains/
  seeds

Trim the green tops off the leeks and peel off any nasty or coarse outer leaves. Cut off the roots but leave the stump on—it's needed to hold the leek together whilst it cooks. Next cut each leek in half down its length, from top to bottom. Gently pull back the outer leaves just far enough to see if there's any mud or grit hidden in there—rinse them carefully under the cold tap if you suspect there is.

Bring a large pan of lightly salted water to the boil. Add the leeks and cook until tender—they absolutely do not want to be *al dente* or have any significant crunch to them. It depends on how big and old (or, preferably, small and young) they are. Check them after two or three minutes, and every minute or so after that. Even big ones should need no more than five minutes in total.

Have plenty of kitchen paper ready. Lift the leeks carefully out of the water and place them immediately on the kitchen paper. Tipping them into a colander is too violent and may break them up. Once they are all out, pat them dry with more paper. Use plenty of it—it's cheap.

While they are cooling make the vinaigrette. Squeeze the lemon juice into a bowl, add crushed garlic, salt and pepper, and as much or as little Dijon mustard as you like. Emulsify this with a small whisk, then add your best olive oil. Whisk again.

Once cool, arrange the leeks on a plate, side by side, alternating tops next to bottoms. Spoon over plenty of the vinaigrette—be really generous with it. Add a little pile of chopped hard-boiled egg, or the poached egg on top, bang in the middle.

Always serve it with some good bread and a nice crisp white wine. Simply marvelous—I implore you to try this.

CHICKEN WITH PEARS & PARSNIPS

I just kinda threw this together the last time my sister came for dinner. Parsnips are her favorite vegetables and are completely un-obtainable where she lives—with those cheese-eating Frenchies.

I wanted to do a simple roast, along the lines of my Roast Chicken with Fennel, but needed to get some parsnips in there, too. And I hadn't got any fennel.

I first reached for a couple of apples, but they were so bruised they were only fit for the compost heap—my son had been prac-tising his over-arm in the hall with them. Fortunately, I had a couple of firm pears in the fruit-bowl, waiting for that perfect moment of ripeness. They were as hard as bricks. Anyway, because the pears are cooked, their ripeness is of no importance; in fact, being quite firm is probably preferable. So fate intervened. That parsnips and pears are both in season at the exact same time is a big fat bonus.

In the end the pan was so full that I fished the parsnips out and cooked them on a separate tray. Either way seems to work well.

INGREDIENTS

SERVES FOUR HUNGRY PEOPLE

- Two small chickens, about 1.1–1.2 kg each—or one bigger one
- Four large parsnips
- Three firm green pears
- Two onions
- Half a bulb of garlic
- A big, two fingers and one thumb, pinch of dried flaked chili
- A glass of Manzanilla sherry, or dry white wine

Joint each of the chickens into eight pieces, saving the rib cages, wing tips, backbones, and ankles for tomorrow's stockpot. Peel and quarter the parsnips. If the parsnips have particularly long spiky roots, then they can be cut off first to form separate fifth pieces of their own. Cut the pears into quarters and remove the woody cores, not just the pips. No need to peel the pears. Peel the onions and cut into quarters, or smaller if they're particularly large, trying to keep a little segment of the root cluster on each piece. Break the garlic bulb up into separate cloves, leaving them whole and unpeeled.

Put the parsnips, pears, onions and garlic into a large baking tray, season and rub with a little olive oil. Place the chicken pieces (except the breasts) on top, season these and drizzle with a little more olive oil. Sprinkle with the flaked chili.

Roast in the oven, preheated to 200°C/400°F/gas 6, for half an hour, then add the breasts and all the sherry or wine, and roast for a further twenty to twenty-five minutes.

VARIATIONS   I've cooked this with a few sage leaves thrown in and, on one occasion, with a little cinnamon (about one teaspoon) sprinkled over everything along with the chili. Both variations were lovely but, I think, not both at the same time. Pork chops—one per person—instead of the chicken also works well.

STEWED CHICKEN WITH QUINCES   I served this just the other day for some good friends for dinner. I was cooking at their house—always a fraught occasion. There were six of us eating. We started with beef carpaccio and rocket salad, then this dish, followed by a big lump of Roquefort and finally, a little glass of zabaglione. I cooked the chicken and quinces up to the point where they are added together and took it over in a big pot. The evening couldn't have been easier. Cut up the carpaccio, dress the salad; turn the heat on under the chicken, boil some rice; take in the cheese; whip up the zabaglione; let someone else do the coffee. If I'd wanted to make it even easier on myself, I could have made crème brûlée, instead of zabaglione, and saved myself a ten-minute beating in the kitchen.

Once, when put on the spot, I quickly said that a quince tastes like "a really fragrant apple." That's not a bad description, actually, but it undersells its unique perfumed taste, the texture—neither apple nor pear but the best of both—and the scent ... That citrus-y, apple-y scent alone makes having a bowl of them in the kitchen worthwhile.

If you don't have a quince tree growing in your garden, and chances are you haven't, you'll have to buy them. They are in the shops from about October until January, give or take a week or two. They're not too expensive; you'll find them in the area where all the bizarre fruits are kept. (The fruit that looks like the food they eat in Star Trek.) My local Waitrose never has more than half a dozen for sale at any one time and I have been known to clear the shelves!

They are always yellow, slightly paler than a banana. They don't change color as they ripen—in fact they don't really ripen—they remain as hard as rocks. The ones I buy are quite big and have, sadly, virtually no scent. They are about the size of a big baking potato. I'd previously bought some at an autumn-tasting on a fruit nursery near Clacton-on-sea (Ken Muir's Nursery www.kenmuir.co.uk): they were a variety called Meech's Prolific (I've since planted one in my garden). The fruit is smaller than the supermarket fruit—about the size of an apple—and, wow, did they smell good. The boffins at the local fragrance laboratory could do a lot worse than synthesize that smell and make it into air fresheners. I'd hang one round my neck.

Quinces must always be cooked; they are inedible raw. The skins can be tough; some food-writers suggest leaving it on; I always peel them first.

If you can't find any quinces, try making this with apples instead. It will be a poor imitation of the real thing but still worthy of your efforts. Use a firm apple, possibly a russet, definitely *not* a Bramley. Peel and core them before frying, but (obviously) don't poach them first!

I've seen recipes for chicken and quinces in a few books but the clearest incarnation is in *The Book of Jewish Food* by Claudia Roden.

Apparently it is a Moroccan version. I've followed her ingredients, except for having upped the quantity of saucy bits. The logistics are a little different too—we also disagree about peeling the quinces.

- Two onions
- One teaspoon ground cinnamon
- One teaspoon ground ginger
- Four chicken legs, whole or divided into thighs and drumsticks, your choice
- One big quince, or two little ones
- Two lemons
- Two tablespoons of honey

Get a pan of water boiling and squeeze in the juice of one of the lemons. Peel, quarter, and core the quinces (they may need further subdividing, please use your common sense). Add them to the boiling acidulated water. They will need five to twenty minutes— depending on size, variety, and so on. Fish them out when they show the first signs of becoming tender; no later. Do not over- cook them. Place to one side, ideally on a piece of kitchen paper for them to cool off a little.

Warm a big heavy-bottomed pan, with a tight-fitting lid, on a hob. Peel and slice the onions. Pour in a little sunflower oil and add the onions. Cook for a few minutes without coloring. Sprinkle over the cinnamon and ginger. Stir it all together. I find the onions' instant color change, and the smell coming from the pan, immensely satisfying. Lay the chicken pieces on top of the onions. Add a little salt and pepper. Put the lid on, turn the heat down to low and cook, undisturbed, for thirty minutes for leg and wing meat, fifteen for breast—they will get an additional cook- ing time later. The juice in the onions and chicken will provide enough sauce: honestly.

Whilst this is happening, fry the poached quince pieces in a lit- tle more sunflower oil. This gives them a pleasant caramelized taste. When browned, lift them out and put them on more kitchen paper.

When the chicken has had its allotted cooking time, add the quinces, the juice of the second lemon, and the honey. Leave it all to cook, very, very gently, for another thirty minutes with the lid on. Stir occasionally, with great care. It's done when the quinces are soft, yet intact, and the chicken is loose on the bone.

Serve immediately with boiled rice or couscous.

NOTE Pretty much all couscous which you can buy in this country is pre-cooked. It therefore simply needs rehydrating (doesn't sound very appetising does it). So, to prepare couscous: simply pour an ample sufficiency of the stuff (look at the side of the packet for a guide on quantity) into a shallow bowl. Ignore their cooking instructions. Cover with boiling water from the kettle, enough to cover it amply—about the depth of a shallow puddle; stretch some plastic wrap over the top; and leave it alone for fifteen to twenty minutes. Season and fluff it with a fork. I like to add a little chopped mint and lemon juice. Serve immediately.

As you can see, couscous is the Smash of Northern Africa—but nicer.

ZABAGLIONE Given that I always have fresh eggs in the kitchen and a bottle of Marsala wine near the cooker, I can always knock up a quick pudding at a moment's notice.

This is one of those dishes that people think terribly difficult, but it is, actually, simplicity itself. I've read recipes that suggest using sherry instead of Marsala wine. I've tried a few and none of them came close to the dish which you make when using real Marsala. It isn't expensive and when paired with the best eggs you can get ... it might even be good for you!

INGREDIENTS
SERVES 6
- Four best quality egg yolks
- Two tablespoons caster sugar
- 125 ml/4 fl oz dry Marsala

You will need a large mixing bowl (preferably stainless steel, but Pyrex will do), and a pan of water that is on the brink of simmering (when it has a lid on). Use little enough water to ensure that the bottom of the bowl is not in the water. The bowl needs only the heat of the steam. An electric whisk will save you some serious arm ache, but scores very low on style points: *dix points* for technical achievement, *nil points* for artistic integrity.

In the mixing bowl, vigorously whisk the egg yolks and sugar together until they are pale yellow and quite creamy.

Moderate the heat to achieve a "barely there" simmer—with a lid over the pan. An unlidded pan that is set to the right temperature, will quickly reach a rolling boil once you put the bowl on top—that is an important point to remember (and one that I cannot recall any other food writer mentioning—ever)! Take the lid off the pan and replace with the bowl. Add all the Marsala to the creamed eggs, whisking constantly. Soon the mixture will start to form a foam, before swelling up to create a large warm, quivering soft mousse. At most, it is likely to take fifteen minutes on the heat, maybe less. It's ready when it has the exact texture of fluffy, summer's day cumulus nimbus (clouds).

It is best served straight away, spooned into tumblers or wine glasses. I like to serve plenty of those Langue du Chat biscuits to dip into it. Almond thins are also good.

SOMMELIER TIM'S WINE TIP

Eggs, chocolate, and watercress (obviously not all together), are a wine waiter's nightmare—all three are tricky to match wines to. Good Sauternes or, indeed, any other dessert wine, won't taste at its best when served with this. The solution is simple: bring some more Marsala to the table. I like to drink it cool but not chilled.

STEWED APPLES & CUSTARD

Normally the reserve of infants and octogenarians, a bowl of stewed apples and some good custard is a dish everyone can enjoy. Peel and core some of your favorite apples. Bramleys will turn to a mush, so look for some Arthur Turners or other firm cooking apples that retain their shape when cooked. Place them in a saucepan with a little sugar (this entirely depends on the apple and your taste, but—let's say—start with one teaspoon per large apple). Cook until just pulpy—don't reduce to the consistency of apple sauce. Serve warm with custard.

VARIATIONS

Add a cinnamon stick, and/or some dried fruits such as sultanas whilst stewing. Or, for a slightly toffee flavor make the sugar into a light caramel before adding the apple.

Steak and Eggs on Christmas
Morning
Mum's Way with Roast Chicken

DECEMBER

Stuffed Chicken's Neck
Boxing Day Stew
Eggnog
Mince Pies with Custard

December is a minefield for the misguided food writer. Almost without exception they are lured into a ridiculous belief that it is okay to reinvent the Christmas dinner. Well—it isn't! In modern Britain the Christmas meal is turkey, served with all the trimmings. The French prefer to cook a goose, and that's okay by me. In fact, we Brits always did a Chrimble goose for many, many years—then along came those globalizing Americans with their culinary imperialism. They were aided and abetted by a sympathizing tweedy gentleman in Norfolk: and, lo, we all started eating frozen turkey.

I'm actually inclined to agree with the Frenchies on this issue. I start subversively lobbying the cause of the goose in late October—but I'm forever outvoted since ... well, always, actually. Mind you, for the last ten years I've been cooking in my father-in-law's kitchen—this year it's me, in my own kitchen, start to finish. I am in charge. So, I really should have put my foot down this year—I've only myself to blame for my own speedy acquiescence. Next year, next year ...

There are legitimate alternatives to the turkey and goose; if you're cooking for one—a pheasant, and for just a few people—try a really big, slow growing, well-fed cockerel (Basil escaped this fate this year by the skin of his teeth)! In the end, I cooked a teeny-weeny little turkey (9 lb), and four adults and two children only got through one breast! But, what I can't understand is a person choosing to serve beef, or ham, or a flock of little game birds, or nut cutlets (how miserable is Christmas lunch for a veggie?) for the big festive meal.

Nowadays you can't just walk into a supermarket or, probably, most butchers, and expect to buy a nice, big cockerel. This was the sort of bird that would feed a family of six with some leftovers. They're a special order for Christmas. Now you'll need two roasting birds to stretch to that many people. The reason for this is simple economics. The farmers get their birds to market at the perfect point for the birds' weight-gain-to-food-consumed. In the business they call it "feed conversion." More weight—less feed—quick as possible. That's the idea. The average little chicken for sale on a supermarket shelf will be about four to six weeks old and, in its short life, will have eaten no more food than twice its own body weight. I have a friend, who is a classic car dealer and part-time turkey farmer and, just like the chap at the local farm shop who raises cocks for the Christmas market, he buys in the day-old chicks in June/July. Obviously they will have eaten many times their own weight in food as they grow slowly to maturity in time for the Christmas slaughter. Combine that with a decent bit of space for them to move around and you have a well cared for, well fed, bird.

The thing that brings me round to talking turkey is the trimmings. They are almost exactly the same as the way mum used to serve a roast chicken when I was little—roast potatoes, bread sauce, chipolatas, bacon, forcemeat stuffing, gravy (lots of gravy!), and vegetables. Take your seasonal pick from parsnips, sprouts, carrots, and frozen peas. These days you'll probably get cranberry sauce too: That's Delia's fault, remember.

So you can follow my recipes for your Christmas meal. Just remember to cook the turkey for twenty minutes per pound in a medium-hot oven. Avoid filling the cavity with stuffing; put just a little in the neck flap and cook any extra separately. If you shove some butter under the skin on the breasts, then it won't dry out. I promise you. Remember to let the bird rest before carving.

My December recipes aren't exclusively about Christmas day. There are plenty of other meals to be cooked and eaten in December. Leftover turkey works very nearly as well as chicken in some of the "leftovers" recipes. The Persian Chicken Supper should be do-able by now. If you're drying the limes on a radiator they will take a couple of months to become golf-ball hard—they need to have skin like that of a dehydrated toad! Mussels are at their very best in the depths of winter. The lightness and fishy freshness of a mussel quiche comes as a welcome change during that no man's land on the calendar between Christmas and the New Year. Ditto a simple poached egg and bitter leaf salad.

The Boxing Day stew recipe was originally just that. Something I invented in about five-seconds-flat whilst looking in the veg drawer. It works so well that I've since made it with leftover chicken and chicken stock.

For dinner on New Year's Eve I suggest you stay home, put your feet up, open some wine, maybe watch a film, and get an early night. If you've been lumbered with entertaining some people, remember to keep the food simple, but serve an extra course or two. Maybe a simple bit of fish, then a sorbet before going for the main course. If you stick to just the usual three, you'll have finished eating at the usual time 10-10.30 and people will want to go home (understandably) before midnight. Either that, or, they'll get hammered and start navel gazing as they spiral downwards into deep despair at how meaningless and futile their life sometimes seems. I say best avoid all that nonsense in the first place. Nevertheless, Happy New Year—everyone! But, please keep it in perspective: tomorrow is just another day.

DECEMBER'S DIARY

FRIDAY 5 DECEMBER
Just two hens-a-laying (maybe three) —Beatrice and a Welsummer —can't tell which one with the Welsummers. Suspect only one 'cos never yet found two eggs on the same day. They are poor layers. Angelica looks awful — poor thing. In worst stage of moult. Princess Amidala is through hers — but expect both will wait for the warmer weather of spring before laying again.

TUESDAY 9 DECEMBER
Another beautiful day. Giant clear blue skies —dashed with vapor trails, flying westward.

WEDNESDAY 10 DECEMBER
Good weather couldn't last. Raining again. Tried to climb up the earth bank to see the chickens. The path has been torn up to be re-laid properly. Had to turn back on account of the mud.

THURSDAY 11 DECEMBER
Bloke came back to finish off the garden path. Whilst not finished it is once again usable. He has also delivered five

bales of straw for the chicken run. I'll get it turfed in the spring. Straw will do for now —good compost too.

MONDAY 15 DECEMBER

Ordered a turkey for Christmas lunch this morning. I suspect that Basil knows he's off the hook. Was chatting to path-laying bloke who also keeps some chickens. He'd be happy to take Basil (the one remaining cockerel) off our hands. Annie made him promise to give Basil a long and happy life. I wonder if he will.

THURSDAY 25 DECEMBER

Wonderful turkey for lunch. Of course it was far too big; we'll be eating it for days. Can't help wondering what that cockerel would have tasted like.

WEDNESDAY 31 DECEMBER

Have had a lot of fun with my hens this year. The children have really enjoyed seeing the little chicks in the incubator, and then more under Angelica. Whilst it was fun to have more than forty chickens at one point, I started the year with five and I end it with seven. This seems to be about the right number to supply a family of four with all they could want and still have a few eggs left over during the summer. Part of the fun is getting new chickens and planning to have them start laying just as the others will be going seasonally off-lay.

Sure, if I had the space I'd have a lot more chickens —and then I'd eat them. The trick clearly is to have lots of the same breed so that you can't tell one from the other. I'd happily wring one bird's neck, every week or so, for the table. As it is, each of my birds has a name and I can recognize which one laid which egg. I have my favorites.

STEAK & EGGS ON CHRISTMAS MORNING

"My wife called joyously from her cabin: 'Charles, Charles, I feel so well. What do you think I am having for breakfast?' I went to see. She was eating a beef steak."

Evelyn Waugh, *Brideshead Revisited*

This has been our Christmas breakfast of choice for the last several years. We had a hiccup last year (on account of the children) and only had time for some toast. I recommend a cup of tea, or orange juice, and a glass of Champagne to go with it. It is Christmas!

It's of the greatest importance that the steak has been well-hung. Hanging beef allows time for the flavor of the meat to develop, for much the same reason as game birds (such as pheasants) are hung, it adds flavor. Supermarkets and shoddy butchers rarely do this; it ties up money in sides of meat that are hanging in the cold store. The meat also loses weight as the water in it evaporates, so they lose even more money. Expect the meat to lose that fresh reddish-pink that some people (incorrectly) seem to associate with good meat. The truth is that a tasty well-hung piece of meat will become quite dark, "black as a hat" as Gary my previous butcher says. It should be kept ageing for at least three weeks, and will taste even better after five or six weeks. When prodded, the meat will not bounce back but will yield to a finger pushed into it.

For this, ask for a steak from the tail end. A whole fillet tapers, getting narrower, towards one end. If you get a steak from the middle or, worse still, the thick end, then, to be the correct weight, the steak will be far too thin. It needs to be at least 2.5 cm/an inch thick, preferably two, or you won't get the blackened, charred outside and meltingly soft rare bit in the middle. If you don't want your steak, at worst, rare in the middle, cook a cheaper cut. A well-done piece of fillet is a waste of your money. I like mine super rare—done "blue." That's barely even touched by the heat on the inside.

INGREDIENTS

FOR TWO

- Two small fillet steaks, about 125 g/4 oz each cut from the tail
  end
- Two eggs per person as you like them
- A splash of milk, or single cream if scrambling the eggs

To cook the steak, heat a frying pan until it is as hot as you can get it. Now is the time to open some windows and the back door and turn the extractor fan on—full tilt. Season the steaks with some salt and pepper and then (special tip given to me by my friend Paul, in turn given to him by his father) rub both sides with a little dark soy sauce. Sounds a bit weird, but it works brilliantly. Then pour over just a little plain cooking oil (sunflower for preference) and rub that onto the surfaces, too. Don't use extra virgin olive oil; all the little particles in it that make it taste so good will burn and really smoke your house out. Put the steak in the pan and don't touch it. You'll be able to see the edges start to turn color slightly. That is the meat cooking. Once you can see that cooked color come slowly creeping up the side a bit, turn the steak over and, again, leave it alone.

The best way to tell if a steak is done to your liking is to prod it gently with your finger. You'll develop a feel for this as you cook more and more steaks but there is a "rule of thumb" (no pun intended—honestly) for those inexperienced with the feel of steak. Touch your left thumb and forefinger together, assuming that you're right handed (go on, do it now—no-one's watching). You should now be making the internationally recognised hand signal for "it's okay" (except if you are in Greece, in which case you'll get yourself a slap in the face). Push your right forefinger into the fleshy lump at the base of your thumb. The amount of give which you can feel is a pretty good indicator of how a rare steak will feel whilst still in the pan. If you then touch your thumb onto your second finger that will give you the feel of a medium steak and, by touching the third finger, your thumb will feel like a well-done steak.

Once you're happy that the steak is cooked as you like it, take it out of the pan and put it on a plate in a warm place (by this I mean somewhere out of a draft, rather than in a low oven). Leave the steak to rest for a couple of minutes. Conveniently, just long enough to make the eggs.

My preference is for scrambled eggs with a steak. I like just two large eggs. Put a little non-stick pan on a medium heat and melt a reasonable sized knob of butter, just a little more than you'd spread on a piece of toast. I cannot overly recommend using an ordinary, non-stick, pan—trying to clean scrambled eggs from an ordinary pan is a rotten job that will take you ages.

Break the eggs straight into the pan along with a drop of milk or cream—really no more that the splash you put in a cup of tea. Break them down a bit with your favorite wooden spoon. Do not try and beat any air into them. Season them very lightly. Immediately start stirring with a wooden spoon. Don't stir constantly, but keep them moving around until they are done as you like them. But remember that they will continue to cook and firm up a bit, even once on the plate. I like my scrambled eggs a bit sloppy, "loose" I think some people call it. My wife prefers them so well cooked as to have a bit of bounce to them—each to their own.

Put the steak on the warmed plates, spoon the scrambled eggs next to them. Place onto trays with the tea and fizz and go back to bed to eat it.

MUM'S WAY WITH ROAST CHICKEN

This is pretty much how I remember eating roast chicken on a Sunday as a child. It is exactly how my grandmother would roast a chicken. I expect, one day, my children will also learn to cook this. It is also how I cook a turkey on Christmas day (cooking times will vary).

It is easy to see how, given its fowl nature, a Sunday roast chicken and the bits that go with it, are much the same as you would expect to see dished up with the Christmas Day turkey:

Bread sauce, and/or stuffing, little chipolatas, and bacon rolls—all add superbly to the roast potatoes, roast parsnips (my sister's all-time favorite vegetable), carrots, peas, and whatever other vegetables are in season.

Gravy was a big thing in our house. Every week, mum would feign distaste as her three boys picked up their dessert spoons to finish off the gravy on our plates—as if it were soup. In our defense we picked up this dubious habit from dad.

It generally isn't possible to get such big chickens as we used to have (mum recalls them being about six or seven pounds)—I've certainly not seen them in the supermarkets. You would need to go to your local butcher and ask him for a large roasting chicken. He may need to order a really big one for you. It will certainly be a young cockerel—but don't worry—it will have none of the toughness that you might expect. Simply roast it like the great big chicken it is.

Families with four children aren't, it seems, as common as they used to be. I heard recently that the average number of children per family is no longer even two-point-four, but down to one-point-six. I think it's easiest to round up the quantities in this recipe to feed four people. I suppose that it also takes the pressure off finding such a great big chicken.

INGREDIENTS
SERVES A FAMILY OF FOUR, WITH NOT VERY MANY LEFTO-
VERS
- One good chicken, about 2 kg—as big as you'll find at the
  supermarket
- One onion
- A sprig of thyme
- Butter

TO GO WITH THE ABOVE
- Half a dozen chipolatas
- Eight pieces of smoked streaky bacoe
- One large packet of Paxo

- Vast amounts of bread sauce
- Good simple gravy
- Roast potatoes
- Various vegetables of your choice—but there should be at least
  two, preferably three different types
- Perhaps, cranberry sauce (but only, really, if you're stuck with
  having to entertain an American)

First, be sure to take the chicken out of the fridge about an hour
before you start cooking it. You don't want to be putting it in
the oven when it's still fridge cold. Make sure there is no bag of
giblets inside the bird—it is pretty unlikely these days, but you
never know. You need to decide whether to truss the chicken's legs
together—or not. Many say the bird looks neater (not to my mind)
if trussed. I reason that the legs cook more quickly if left all akimbo;
they also aid me in telling when the chicken is done (see below).

Toss a little seasoning inside the chicken. Take the onion and
slice it into onion rings, stuff half of them inside the main cavity
of the bird, keep the other half—you'll have need of them later.
Now take an impossibly large knob of butter and smother the
chicken with it, all over, breast, back, legs, wings, and especially
the parson's nose. Place the bird in your favorite sturdy roasting
pan and add a little seasoning to the outside; be a bit heavy handed
with the salt—it'll help the skin to crisp. Make sure the oven has
reached 200°C/400°F/gas 6.

Put the chicken in the oven.

After twenty minutes, take the chicken out of the oven and
turn it down to 180°C/350°F/gas 4. Baste the chicken with the
butter in the tin, then drain off most of the butter—it's done its
job. Place the unused onion slices in the pan to help later with the
gravy (this onion thing is an addition of mine—mum used Bisto).
Put the chicken back in the oven until it's done (about another
forty-five minutes, maybe an hour).

The chicken is ready when there are no pink juices coming
out of the thickest part of the thigh when pricked with a skewer

(so says everyone). I prefer to feel to see when it is ready. With a bit of practice it is possible to tell when the chicken is done, just by splaying the legs very gently outwards. If it's cooked, the legs will move much more freely—this is a doddle once you have mastered it—but it does take practice. Until you feel confident—keep prodding with a skewer.

Take the chicken out of the oven, remove it to a warm plate, and put a piece of foil over it. Let it rest in a draft-free, warmish place.

The real trick, with a big Sunday meal like this, is timing. Plan on having the chicken come out of the oven at least fifteen to twenty minutes before you want to eat. It needs this time to rest and for the juices to settle back into the meat— or else, when you carve it, all the juices will just pour out and go all over the carving board. Result: one very dry chicken. If the other bits and pieces are ready a bit too soon, then five to ten minutes resting will do (just). Similarly, the bird will still be hot enough if left untouched for thirty minutes before carving.

Carve it as you like. Unlike dad, who used to stand at the head of the table, and always did a brilliant job of carving the Sunday joint, whatever it was (there was always much dramatic swishing of blade on steel before he began), I prefer to do it all in the kitchen. Just remove the breasts whole and slice them diagonally into three or four pieces, take the legs off, dividing them at the knee, and serve the wings—each cut into two joints, minus the tips. People can then help themselves to their favorite bits.

Take it to the table with all the trimmings and vegetables in appropriate separate dishes.

THE TRIMMINGS

GRAVY To make the gravy, you must start with all the gooey onions and other burnt bits in the bottom of the roasting pan. If there is a little too much buttery fat floating on top, gently tip all the juice into one corner and skim some fat off with a spoon. Put the roasting tin on top of the cooker and bring it

quickly up to a sizzle, scrape the black sticky bits off the bottom and generally smush the (by now very well cooked) onions in the pan to help dislodge the blackened bits. Pour in a glass, or so, of white wine or dry vermouth. This needs to have the alcohol burned off, which should only take a minute or so at high heat. The wine helps to dislodge all the bits in the pan. Chances are that you won't think this enough—eminent Swiss psychologists have recently identified your particular phobia as "zee gravee anxi-etee"—so add just a little of the veggie boiling water; then a teaspoon, or two, of that instant chicken gravy powder. Chicken stock is a better bet, but who makes chicken stock on Sunday morning? Let it cook at a gentle simmer, taste it and see if it needs anything. It may need salt, pepper, a small squeeze of lemon to taste and perhaps half a teaspoon of redcurrant jelly.

SAUSAGES Take the chipolatas and gently twist them in the middle to make double the number of sausages of half the length. Cut them into those halves, and then either grill them or bake them in a separate dish in the oven with the chicken.

BACON Unless you have managed to get hold of some really thinly-sliced streaky bacon, you will want to stretch it (quite literally) a little further.

Lay two pieces of plastic wrap—with the bacon in the middle—flat on a work surface or large chopping board. Use a meat hammer, a rolling pin, or the side of your largest knife to beat and smooth the bacon, to make it as long and wide as possible. Remove the bacon from its plastic wrap sandwich and cut each piece in two, then roll each up like a little sleeping bag. Some people like to wrap the bacon around the tiny sausages. I find it just stops the sausage from browning properly. If you can't resist the urge to wrap something up, try using prunes (creating the classic devils on horseback), dried apricots, or even just an almond. All work well but do detract from the quintessentially English theme. If you feel an urge to do this (and I sometimes do) they could be appropriately served as a prelunch nibble with a nice glass of Champagne or some good chilled sherry.

Sommelier Tim says: Sherry is a very much underrated drink. I really can't think why. I generally keep three or four bottles of different sherry in the bottom of the fridge door (I've just got up and had a look and, I have: a fino, a manzanilla, a moscatel, and, my current favorite—Lustau's Old East India). These are a long way away from the average "cream" sherries that you'll remember from granny's sideboard. You'll have to search for a good sherry at a decent wine merchant—but it is worth it—they make an excellent aperitif and, for what they are, they are an absolute bargain.

And of course, you can't make trifle without it!

STUFFING Take a packet of plain Paxo. Follow the instructions on the side. That's it.

Don't be tempted to stuff the bird with it; it will slow down the cooking and make the gravy taste like Paxo. Cook it in a separate buttered dish in the oven.

BREAD SAUCE I remember reading Michael Winner, in his *Sunday Times* column, going on about how, when having Sunday lunch in some impossibly grand and ludicrously expensive hotel, one of his previous girlfriends had asked for both stuffing and bread sauce with her roast chicken. The maitre d' had been appalled and said something along the lines of "oh, no mademoiselle—not both, never both together." Mr. Winner of course told the pompous arse to shut-up and get her both as requested. Quite right he was too.

One Christmas—I must have been a young teenager—a toasted-sandwich maker arrived (a very practical Christmas present for someone). This was about the time that they were first made so it was, in fact, quite a novelty. It was the sort that sealed the contents of the sandwich by crimping the sides of the bread and giving it a, sort of, scalloped shell surface at the same time—not at all like the George Forman Lean Mean Grilling Machine or the Starbucks' panini toaster that are more commonplace today. The best sandwiches which we made during those couple of days after Boxing Day were cold sliced stuffing (at Christmas, mum abandoned the Paxo and made it from scratch. When cold, it would slice quite readily), bread sauce and Heinz salad cream. Just try and imagine that.

In the very unlikely event of there being any bread sauce left over, just feed it to your chickens—they'll think it's Christmas.

INGREDIENTS
MAKES BARELY ENOUGH FOR FOUR
- 600 ml/one pint full fat milk
- 125 g/4 oz butter
- One medium onion, skin removed, roughly sliced
- Six cloves
- A pinch of nutmeg, freshly grated for preference
- A bay leaf and/or a sprig of thyme
- Splash of double cream
- About 150 g/6 oz of fresh white breadcrumbs

The milky infusion can be (and is actually best) made at least the day before. Place all the ingredients, except the cream and breadcrumbs, into a saucepan and bring to the merest simmer. Allow this to bubble very gently for ten to fifteen minutes and then take it off the heat. Let it cool down, then pour the whole lot, unstrained, into a suitable jug or bowl, and stick it back in the fridge until the chicken is cooking in the oven.

Once you are ready to make the sauce, strain the milk through a fine sieve into a clean pan. Add most of the breadcrumbs; you will need to use your skill and judgement as to how many of the breadcrumbs you should add to achieve the consistency you like. Stir it a little and then allow the crumbs to soak up the milk, adding a few more crumbs if you feel it needs it. Keep warm but do not let it bubble.

Every year, until now, I've cooked Christmas lunch at my father-in-law's cottage. Bread sauce is always a part of the traditional meal.

I make up the milk infusion a couple of days in advance and on Christmas Eve, after it has been infusing in the fridge for twenty-four hours, I strain it through a fine sieve, then pour it back into the empty plastic milk carton—it is, obviously, the ideal container for transport. It keeps quite happily in the fridge overnight, or until you need it. But be sure to write something to identify it on the label (or, even better, put a piece of Sellotape right over the top) to prevent accidentally using it when making a cup of tea.

STUFFED CHICKEN'S SKIN

If you ask your butcher nicely, chances are he'll happily save you a load of chicken skins (and I had to get through quite a lot of them in order to get these recipes right).

Whatever your source of skins, making a little stuffing sausage makes carving the stuffing, and hence the bird, a lot easier. It can also be a meal in itself. What you choose to stuff it with is entirely up to you.

SOME SUGGESTIONS FOR THE STUFFING

Rather than giving you just one definitive recipe, what I have here are a few guidelines, some ideas, my jotted down ramblings. The idea of making a stuffing is to use up the bits that you have to hand, to stretch the meal a little further. The quantities of ingredients in these recipes are thus of little importance. Near redundant.

I'm not so keen on the light-as-a-feather chicken mousse filling. I like it all a bit more robust—think fancy Paxo rather than savoury Angel Delight. Remember to adhere to the basic principles of having a main flavor, typically meat, something for a little bulk—like bread or flour—an egg to set the mixture, some herbs and seasoning and you won't be disappointed. Try it with some booze in the mix too. Brandy is especially complementary. If you don't have any breadcrumbs, try smashing up some plain ordinary water crackers. They work remarkably well and have helped me out on several occasions.

A MEATY FILLING If you have a chicken with its innards you will probably have a liver and heart, so this seems to be a sensible starting point.

I finely chop all these ingredients; the liver and heart, a little bacon, and some other raw poultry meat, chicken, duck, pheasant, even pigeon. All these can be bought, quite easily, (even at a supermarket) denuded and butchered to breast fillets. Mix them all together, add some seasoning, herbs—thyme, parsley—then stir in an egg and add breadcrumbs until you have the sort of consistency you like. Instead of egg and breadcrumbs try using a favorite sausage of yours.

To stuff the leg, or indeed other skin, sew up everything—all except for one hole. Spoon, or by other means persuade, the stuffing into the sock-like skin. The stuffing will expand, and the skin will contract, while cooking—so keep it fairly loosely packed. Sew up the remaining hole.

Poach the stuffed skin, in slightly salty water, for twenty or thirty minutes, until it is quite firm when gently squeezed. It helps to squeeze it while still raw so that you have something to compare its later feel to. Remove it from the pan and slip it into the oven to catch a little color—ten minutes, next to the roast potatoes, should be plenty.

SIMPLER STUFFINGS At its simplest, it can be just fried onions and garlic (cooked until they are translucent, no more), seasoned and bound together with flour and an egg. Try adding a little "va-va-voom" by mixing in some ginger, mace, or pimenton.

Also worthy of recommendation is simple mashed potato stuffing. I got this idea from Simon Hopkinson's Gammon & Spinach (Macmillan 1998) recipe for Roast Goose Stuffed with Mashed Potato. Boil and coarsely mash a few potatoes, fry a roughly chopped onion in goose fat or butter. Mix them together with half a clove, or so, of finely chopped garlic, some chopped sage leaves, and a little grated lemon rind. Salt and pepper, obviously. Stuff all this into a neck, you'll have plenty left over, poach it briefly (the potato is cooked—you just need to firm up the skin) then brown it in the oven.

If all that seems like a lot of effort, thin down some good sausage-meat with breadcrumbs and an egg, add a few little favored extra spices, and poach and roast.

BOXING DAY STEW

Actually I came up with this on the 27th—but "27th of December Stew" just ain't such a snappy title. It was originally conceived with some turkey, but leftover chicken is every bit as good.

Surely everyone knows turkey stew? It's the grey bits of turkey, onions, carrots, potatoes, maybe some dumplings, and an argument over whether or not ketchup is allowed; the kids all want some—the parents say no. I wanted to cook something much lighter, fresher tasting, yet still undeniably winterish. It had to warm and comfort the way only properly *big soups* can.

The starting point, as always, is the carcass. Strip all the meat off that, then break it up a bit, add some stock vegetables (carrot, celery, onion, sprig of thyme, bay leaf, and parsley stalks if you have them) and simmer it slowly for an hour or two. I never worry about over-reducing stock—you can always add more water, if needs be, at a later stage. What I do make sure of is that no skin gets in. That would make the stock, because of the browned bits, somewhat too dark.

I made the switch from normal suet and flour dumplings to these poached meatballs simply because I prefer them in something like this, and I had a little bit of ground beef in the fridge— and no suet.

When you've finished, what you will have in front of you is a bowlful of off-white, very light soup, with yellow and white roots, some vivid green from the cabbage and parsley. Its meaty goodness comes in the form of little chicken shreds and dense yet fragrant meatballs that are as small as a child's marbles. It is the light and refreshing stew that's needed to soothe and calm the bloated soul at this time of year.

INGREDIENTS
MAKES ENOUGH FOR A GENEROUS SUPPER FOR TWO
- One normal onion
- Two sticks of celery
- 900 ml/1½ pints of light chicken stock
- Two medium turnips
- A thick slice of swede (to provide about the same amount as the two turnips)
- Some beef dumplings (use the recipe from Persian Chicken Supper)
- Two or three dark green leaves from the outside of a Savoy cabbage
- A handful of chicken leftovers
- Juice of one lemon
- A little chopped fresh parsley

Put a large heavy-bottomed pan on to a medium-high heat. Put a little knob of butter and a tiny splash of sunflower oil in the pan. Peel and finely chop the onion, add that to the pan. Stir it occasionally while you prepare the other vegetables. Don't let it catch and go brown. Next peel the celery, removing the stringy ribs. You can either finely chop the celery or cut it into batons— it depends whether you prefer celery as a background flavor or as a separate vegetable. If finely chopped, add it now; if you've gone with batons hold them to one side. Now peel the turnips and cut them into quarters or sixths depending on their size; keep them to one side. Cut the skin off your appropriately sized piece of swede (you'd never find one small enough), and cut into cubes about two-thirds the size of your turnip pieces. Put these to one side with those turnips. By now the onions, and perhaps the celery, should have become soft and translucent. If not, cook them a little longer.

Pour in the stock, or possibly spoon it in if it has become really jellified. Bring it up to a gentle simmer, no more. Add the turnips and swedes. If you like the cabbage and celery quite soft, add them now—I prefer them with a little crunch so I leave them for another ten minutes. Once this has returned to a simmer, add the meatballs.

As the meatballs start to firm up after about ten minutes, just fish one out with a slotted spoon and squeeze it gently between finger and thumb to check that they've become firm. Add the chicken pieces, cabbage, and celery (if you didn't earlier) and leave to simmer for another five to ten minutes. During that time, check the seasoning adding salt and pepper as necessary. Add the lemon juice at the very end, this helps to keep its flavor very fresh.

Ladle the stew into large soup plates and sprinkle with a little chopped parsley (a little grated lemon zest would also work well). Serve immediately.

VARIATIONS

If you have a very pale stock perhaps add a little double cream at the end to make a virginal white soup base. I wouldn't recommend it if the stock is a bit brown though—beige soup doesn't appeal, does it?

EGGNOG

There are more recipes for eggnogs in my various bartending and cocktail shaking books than there are for Collinses (although virtually everyone seems to have a Collins named after them, there are, surprisingly, none for Joan or Jackie).

Eggnogs are all rather like flavorsome, alcoholic milk shakes. The one that I liked the most seems to capture the essence of Bing Crosby crooning around the Christmas tree, big new sweaters, mistletoe above the door, and snow on the ground. It tastes as Christmassy as that bloated sleepy feeling you have whilst watching the Queen's speech or whistling along to *The Great Escape*.

It includes a few drops of sugar syrup. You can buy this from some places (it may be labelled *sirop de gomme)*, but it's a cinch to make. Heat two parts granulated sugar and one part cold water until it boils. Skim the surface, let it cool and pour it into a very clean bottle. Unsurprisingly, it keeps rather well in a cool, dark kitchen cupboard. A 2 oz measure is the standard large size cup/lid on top of a cocktail shaker. I think it's okay to assume a splash of cream and a splash of syrup.

INGREDIENTS
PER GLASS
- One egg yolk
- ¼ oz double cream
- ¼ oz sugar syrup
- 2 oz dark cream sherry
- Milk, preferably full fat
- Freshly grated nutmeg

Put the egg yolk, cream, sugar syrup, and sherry into a cocktail shaker. Add plenty of ice cubes. Shake well. Pour into a tall glass. Fill to the top with milk and sprinkle with the nutmeg.

VARIATIONS The more drinkable eggnogs
(I found one made with Chianti that I *cannot* recommend) are all largely the same—the exception being the white rum version that uses the egg white rather than yolk. Try replacing the sherry with dark rum, brandy (with perhaps a splash of port), or whisky.

Generally I prefer my creamy cocktails a bit less milky—more cream and alcohol. Brandy Alexanders, that type of thing. A mix of equal parts brandy and bourbon, and no milk—but a big splash of cream, poured in a martini glass will produce a Brigitte Bardot (hopefully the younger sort).

MINCE PIES WITH CUSTARD
Mince pies are the thing to eat at this time of year. No one will ever invite you into their home and offer you just a cup

of tea and a biscuit in December. I make them in industrial quantities from the beginning of the month until the end.

All you need is a packet of dessert pastry, a rolling pin, a couple of pastry cutters, some butter, a jar of best quality mincemeat (seriously, don't bother making it), a little fresh minced beef, and some egg-wash.

Butter a tray with little dents in it—you know the sort—a dozen little holes for baking jam tarts in, I also use mine for Yorkshire puddings. Roll out the pastry—as thinly as you dare—and cut out circles that are large enough to curl up the sides to form little baskets. Now mix the proprietary mincemeat with the minced beef at a ratio of about 2:1 respectively (by volume), no need to measure it. Using a teaspoon put little amounts of this in the bottom of the tarts. Brush some egg-wash around and then add smaller thinly rolled pastry rounds on top. Pinch the pastry edges with your fingers to seal. Brush on more egg-wash, pierce the top plumb-centre with the tip of a knife and twist it round a quarter-turn; this just opens the top to allow any steam to escape. Sprinkle the top of each with a generous pinch of caster sugar.

Slide these into a hot oven until they are a pale golden brown and are smelling just wonderful. Let them cool a little in the tin before removing them with a wire rack. If the mincemeat has bubbled out and is causing a big sticky mess just use less next time.

These will be thin, crisp tasty morsels not at all like those big deep-pan versions you get from supermarkets. I like mince pies and I want to eat two or three at a sitting, that can't be done with the big versions.

This year after the children's carol service in our little Parish church where we were married, I was offering around a couple of plates of these to the congregation. One lady said, "What fabulously thin pastry with just the meanest little scraping of mincemeat inside." I must have looked taken aback, because she immediately added "they're marvelous, may I have another." I realized it was a compliment.

But when to serve them with custard? After Christmas lunch; just warm them through in the oven, with a little warm custard poured over the top. Give yourselves half an hour after eating, retire to a comfy chair with two or three of these on a dessert plate and, armed with a spoon, eat them slowly whilst you watch the children play.